AT BELLEAU WOOD
WITH RIFLE AND
SKETCHPAD

AT BELLEAU WOOD WITH RIFLE AND SKETCHPAD

Memoir of a United States Marine in World War I

Louis C. Linn

Edited by LAURA JANE LINN WRIGHT *and* B. J. OMANSON

McFarland & Company, Inc., Publishers
Jefferson, North Carolina, and London

Library of Congress Cataloguing-in-Publication Data

Linn, Louis C., 1895–1949.
  At Belleau Wood with rifle and sketchpad : memoir of a
United States Marine in World War I / Louis C. Linn ; edited by
Laura Jane Linn Wright and B.J. Omanson.
    p.   cm.
  Includes bibliographical references and index.

  ISBN 978-0-7864-4904-0
  softcover : acid free paper ∞

  1. Linn, Louis C., 1895–1949. 2. World War, 1914–
1918 — Personal narratives, American. 3. United States.
Marine Corps. Marine Brigade, 4th. 4. World War, 1914–
1918 — Campaigns — Western Front. 5. Belleau Wood,
Battle of, France, 1918. 6. United States. Marine Corps —
Biography. 7. Marines — United States — Biography.
I. Wright, Laura Jane Linn, 1941–, editor. II. Omanson,
B.J. (Bradley J.), editor. III. Title.
  D570.9.L49 2012   940.4'34 — dc23   [B]   2011050068

British Library cataloguing data are available

Front cover: "We were in desperate straits for tobacco" woodcut.
Back cover: "The trench had been torn open from end to end" woodcut.

Manufactured in the United States of America

McFarland & Company, Inc., Publishers
  Box 611, Jefferson, North Carolina 28640
    www.mcfarlandpub.com

To the men and women of the armed services —
past, present and future

Table of Contents

Acknowledgments

Thanks to Maria D. Blanco for typing the original manuscript.

To Richard G. Latture who published Chapter 7 in the Fall 2003 *Military History Quarterly*. He pointed out that this Fourth Brigade Marine unit served in an Army division — the Second. This explains the Indian that my father painted on his helmet.

To Joan C. Thomas, art curator for the new National Museum of the Marine Corps in Quantico, Virginia, who said, "His [art] work is an excellent portrayal of the experiences of Marines in World War I."

And to Bradley J. Omanson, B.J., whose definitive research gives us interesting information about where the troops were and what was happening with the war and when. He found old postcards of the small supply train, the Tunnel of Tavennes and other places my father mentions in his memoir. B.J.'s grandfather, Corporal Alpheus R. Appenheimer, a muleskinner with the Headquarters Division. He, too, was part of the Sixth Machine Gun Battalion. He, too, was awarded the Croix de Guerre. He inspired, in his grandson, a twenty-year study of the battalion. B.J. has a website, www.scuttlebuttsmall chow.com, and is working on a book of his own. Another interesting fact: both men (my father and B.J.'s grandfather) enlisted at the same time and were discharged from service the same day, June 9, 1919, at the same place.

Laura Linn Wright

* * *

I have attempted to acknowledge the assistance of individuals on particular questions and topics in the footnotes. My research into the history of the Sixth Machine Gun Battalion precedes my work on the Linn manuscript by several decades. However, it would never have progressed at all without the assistance and encouragement of a handful of individuals who generously offered explanations, access to unpublished sources, contacts and guidance as needed.

My sincere gratitude to George B. Clark, Michael B. Hubler, Gilles Lagin, Benis M. Frank, Col. Wendell Neville Vest, USMC (Ret.), Kenneth L. Smith-Christmas, Mark Henry and Tom Gudmestad.

There are others as well, from years past, whose names I cannot now recall, who assisted me in obtaining documents from the Library of Congress, the National Archives, St. Louis and elsewhere. My apologies for no longer being able to acknowledge you by name.

Also invaluable in collecting stories about the Sixth Machine Battalion over the years were Clay Appenheimer, Dorothy Schmidt, Edie Ericson, Glenna Omanson, Mitchell B. Young, Ernest Robson and Don Schmidt.

Finally, I would like to acknowledge the generous gift of authors Bradley E. Gernand and Michelle A. Krowl of their splendid history *Quantico: Semper Progredi, Always Forward.* I used it as a primary source in annotating Chapter 1.

B. J. Omanson

Preface

Louis C. Linn always carried a sketchbook and a stub of a pencil in his pocket. He carried them all through the war. He drew, whenever he could, to try to maintain his sanity in a terrible situation. Drawing gave him a measure of mental peace. He was tormented by nightmares. He wrote his memoir several years after the war, partly as a catharsis, using his sketches as illustrations. Or perhaps the sketches brought back his experiences. He made woodcuts from some of the sketches to more vividly convey the bleakness and horror of the war. The purpose of this book is not only to share his ordeal but to display his artwork. The original sketch and the woodcut are both included. His art is impressionistic as is his writing. As Richard G. Latture said, "He puts the reader in a Devil Dog's muddy boots."

Research revealed that he changed names, no doubt to protect

Pvt. Linn in the trench.

1

himself and those he was writing about. But co-editor B.J. Omanson was able to identify many of them.

In the Coda, he tells of an event that never happened. The war had brought home to him how easy it is to step across the line between life and death and between honor and dishonor.

He was crushed when the Second World War broke out. He had thought that they were fighting the war to end war; all their suffering and death had been in vain. He died in 1949.

Introduction

Louis C. Linn was a member of 77th Company, Sixth Machine Gun Battalion, Fourth Brigade of Marines, Second Division (Regular), AEF. Of all the American divisions participating in the Great War, the Second Division suffered the most casualties, captured the second most territory, captured the most enemy prisoners and equipment, and won the most decorations for valor.

The Second Division was the only Army division in the history of the United States to contain a brigade of Marines, and the only Army division ever to be commanded by a Marine. It was due to the participation of this single Marine brigade that the Marine Corps, in six months time, went from being a minor expeditionary fighting force attached to the Navy to being considered a first-rate force of shock troops by the German army. It was this single Marine brigade which made the Marine Corps a participant on the world stage, and prepared it for playing a major role in the next world war. It was this brigade that provided the crucial core of experienced field officers for that war.

Of three major battles, all of which were devastating for the Marine brigade, Linn participated in two, Belleau Wood and Soissons, and in those two he was in the very worst of the fighting. He came through Belleau Wood unscathed, was badly wounded at Soissons, and then, at Saint-Mihiel, was wounded again. In an attack in which only seven Marines were wounded by a concealed grenade, Linn was one of the seven. He was wounded badly enough that he remained in a hospital until after the Armistice. For his service to France he was awarded two *Croix de Guerre*.

Louis Carlisle Linn was born in Laurel, Maryland, on March 19, 1895, to William Edgar Linn, a former member of the Maryland House of Delegates, and Agnes Maud Watkins. He was the youngest of three. When he was five, both his mother and his 8-year-old sister Edna became deathly ill with typhoid. When his mother recovered, his sister was dead and buried.

As a boy, Louis was uprooted several times, moving from Laurel, Maryland, to his grandfather's farm in Howard County, Maryland, to a farm in Langley, Virginia, and finally to a house at the end of the street car line in McLean, Virginia. Louis attended McKinley High School and evening art classes at the Corcoran in Washington, riding in with his bicycle on the street car. He also worked as a page in Congress.

After high school Linn headed west for a couple of years, working on the last of the Geodetic Survey of the Rocky Mountains. In mid–April 1917, Linn, like countless other young men across the country, made the decision to go to war. He enlisted in the Marine Corps in Washington, D.C., on the 5th of June and was sworn in three days later as a member of Company "D" at the recruit depot, Marine Barracks, Norfolk, Virginia, where he would undergo eight weeks of basic training. And it is while he is at Norfolk as a raw recruit that his memoir begins.

The editors' interpolations appear in italics throughout, providing context and additional information regarding Linn's wartime experiences.

Linn in 1917, age 22.

1

In Training —
Norfolk and Quantico

Reveille

Temporarily, just after the outbreak of war, recruit depots were opened at Navy yards in Philadelphia and Norfolk, until Parris[1] Island and Mare Island could be brought to full capacity.[2] The recruit depot at Norfolk could handle 500 recruits at a time. The following took place at the recruit depot at Norfolk. It was here, from June 7 to July 29, that Louis C. Linn received his basic training, consisting primarily of severely disciplined drill and what was perhaps the finest marksmanship training in the world at that time.

Oh! How the memory of morning waking haunts my mind. Those early days when a drummer and bugler played reveille at daybreak on each gallery of the barracks. To be jerked from the freedom of sleep to the realization of our inseparable imprisonment in the trap of military service. Oh! the horror.

Caught in the glamour of uniforms, barracks full of lounging men, the tinkle of guitars and mandolins, stuffed with canteen sweets and canteen pop one lay down to the sad, sweetly plaintive notes of "Taps" and went to sleep with the thought that it was fine to be a soldier. Then, the hard, bitter awakening. In the cold gray dawn you sat up on the side of your bunk and looked on life. About you, some hundred men were doing the same thing; amid groans, coughing, nose blowing, sneezing and spitting. Your lackluster gaze meets that of your comrade of the night before and he smiles and says, "Good morning."

Good, hell: you feel the only satisfactory return to this would be to smash him one in the jaw and you wonder what in the world you found of interest in him the previous evening. Good morning indeed. Under such circumstances the words are an insult.

Imagine two condemned prisoners saying "Good morning" to each other the day they are to hang.

"Oh, damn your eyes," I answer. I have hurt his feelings but I feel better and begin to drag on my socks.

"What heats, what heats," groaned Pete the Greek, my next bunk neighbor.

It was hot. Hot even in the high ceilinged brick barracks where we lived. The stifling humidity made all movement a torture and the thought of the sun drenched parade ground an anguish. Drill call for the afternoon had just sounded.

"Show a little life, will you?" exhorted Sergeant Slater.[3] "We are going up state next month to mobilize. It will be cooler there. Shake it up, fellows."

We "fell in" for drill in the roadway before the barracks. On the wide stone balustrades of the gallery porches lounged lucky guys who did not have to drill, in imminent danger of going to sleep and plunging to their deaths in the roadway below. These watched our movements with a detached and happy indifference.

We marched away, then back and forth across the blazing parade ground. We were shown a new evolution, then made to repeat it an endless number of times. "Right front into line," "On right into line." Our cooking brains mixed the orders, the sergeants swore and we sweated until our clothes were saturated.

I was at this time number three on the rear rank. The only thing lower would have been a small yellow dog, as I was told by those higher up and I presumed better informed. Directly before my eyes was the thick neck of a man named Sloan.

He hailed from Chicago and claimed to

"**It was the culminating moment of our weary months of drill.**"

be a "pug." He had a broken nose and a truculent disposition and since he spoke knowingly of all fighters and fights of importance we had taken this man at his word. For the most part he ignored us as one destined for higher things and only bestowed his conversation upon corporals and sergeants and that small ring of toadies who cling about such persons.

He was not popular or liked but still we respected him for the fights he claimed to have been in. He was continually rowing with his neighbors on either hand for "crowding" him. He made a great show of knowing all the maneuvers for the Non-coms' benefit. In reality, it was this same "crowding" that saved him from detection for what he was, a blockhead.

I had never had any trouble with this man as I had taken pains never to run into him or tread on his heels, no matter what he did. This afternoon he persisted in crowding in before me in a flank turn, when his proper place was behind me.

Twice he disrupted the line by dragging me forcibly back while he jumped in front of me, without catching the drill sergeant's notice. The third time he tried it, I gave him a shove with my shoulder. He dropped his rifle and sprang at me and the blow I got sent a shower of sparks dancing before my eyes. The haphazard blow I struck back took him square in the mouth splitting his lips and setting him down on the drill field.

Before he could get on his feet we were both grabbed by the Non-coms. "What's the trouble here?"

A full explanation followed and Private Sloan was told he was in the wrong.

"I don't care about that," he declared. "I'll show this bird whether he can hit me in the puss and get away with it."

"You can't fight here. I will put you both under arrest. If you got a grudge against each other you can fight it out with the gloves after recall."

"That suits me," declared Sloan. "Are you on?"

I had a lively picture of this guy making mincemeat of me in the boxing ring.

"I haven't got any quarrel with you as long as you keep your mitts off me," I answered. "As for boxing you, I'd be a damn fool to do that. If you wanta fight, you can have it right here now."

"Gone yellow, huh? You know I'm up for Non-com and can't afford to get arrested."

"If you are afraid of being arrested, you're too damn scary to be Non-com."

"That's enough hot air out of you two," declared the sergeant. "Now 'fall in' and watch what you're about."

What a miserable drill I put in. I loathed myself. I had been challenged to a fight and was afraid. A fine soldier I was going to make. Up and down the drill field I went cussing and spitting like a tom cat with a clothes pin on his tail. Finally I tried to provoke Sloan into a fight. I ran into him, got in his way and walked on his heels whenever opportunity offered. He only moaned and directed suffering glances at the sergeant.

The sergeant told me that if I didn't snap to it he would put me in the awkward squad. Recall sounding saved me from that calamity.

This happened the first part of July. On the Fourth we were to have a field meet with the sailors from a nearby Navy yard.

The events in which I took part were in the morning. In the afternoon there was to be wrestling and boxing, with Sloan billed for a star part. I had no inclination to watch him, so I went for a walk.

The road was hot and dusty and the pine woods threw no cooling shade. There was no great pleasure in walking, still I kept on. Then the road wound around a hill and came to a little river.

Along its course were maples and willows so I left the road and walked along in the shade until I came to a fairly deep pool. Being a small boy inside, I slipped out of my clothes and had a swim.

Cooled off and dressed again I stretched out on the shady bank to think this thing out. I had made a mistake. It didn't matter much if I was licked or not, but my spirit did: I had let my friends down.

What a life! Anyway that was settled. This wasn't the most pleasant decision in the world, but the mental peace it gave me was worth it. In the cool shade beside the little gurgling river I fell asleep.

Corporal Cullen, sitting cross-legged on his cot dealing dummy poker hands, was the first person I saw as I entered the barracks late that afternoon. He looked at me for a moment then burst out laughing. He howled with mirth while I stood regarding him. Sergeant Slater, across the aisle, was laughing also with the greatest enjoyment.

"What's so funny?" I asked.

"Oh boy! You are lucky you didn't take that prize fighter on." Cullen could hardly talk. "You might have laughed yourself to death."

Then I noticed Sloan. He was sitting all alone on his cot not looking very happy. "What's up?" I asked. "Couldn't Sloan fight?" "Fight?" snorted Slater.[3] "That sailor made such a fool of him the old man [Captain] had him taken out after the first round and little Davis finished the fight for him. Those Navy officers were laughing their heads off at the old man. Said it was lucky we weren't going over to box with the Germans if that was the best we had in the company."

As I came up the room I stopped at Sloan's cot and stood looking at him. He seemed to have shrunken physically since I had seen him.

"Well?" he said, looking up.

"Maybe the sailor licked you, Sloan, but you sure had me scared to death," I said and went on to my cot. The whole room shouted with laughter. I was unmercifully banged about, sure proof that I was back in my company's good opinion.

The Review

The following account takes place at the newly-constructed Marine Corps training base at Quantico, Virginia. Linn, along with others from Norfolk, arrives here at the end of July 1917 and will remain for the next four months. This military base is so new that when Linn arrives, it is barely ready to receive recruits at all; basic facilities such as water supply and sewage disposal are makeshift and completely inadequate. Yet before Linn leaves, the number of Marines in training at Quantico will swell from just under 5000 to over 10,000.[4] It is here that the First (later designated the Sixth) Machine Gun Battalion is formed on August 17. It is composed of a Headquarters Detachment and two companies, the Seventy-seventh and the Eighty-first (two additional companies would join the battalion in France).

Linn is assigned to the Seventy-seventh Company. Training is intensive and technical. The battalion is equipped with 16 Lewis machine guns and 33 machine gun carts. "The battalion was put through a course of intensive training, being instructed in the nomenclature of the Lewis machine gun; machine gun drill in close and extended order; the tactical use of machine guns; digging machine gun emplacements in conjunction with infantry; building concrete pillboxes at night for machine gun defense of a trench system; organization of direction of fire; target practice; signals, flags flash and sound, and telephones; transmission of orders and messages; reconnaissance; reports and sketches; liaison agents (runners); and terrain exercises."[5]

The day was hot and still. It had rained in the morning but now the sky was blue and a fall saddened sun shone warmly down on the brown and gold earth. The day was timeless; it waited on events, and we waited also. We were freshly shaved, dressed in our best, rifles and equipment perfect. They better be. This was our final review before sailing for France. It was the culminating moment of our weary months of drill. We were all a little keyed up under the nervous strain, as we lounged on our bunks, awaiting the order to move.

Above the crunch of gravel under foot we heard the music faintly, an occasional metallic blare and the soul stirring boom of the drum. With quickening pulses we came down the lane to the parade grounds, our full company and all our officers.

Part of a panoramic photograph of Seventy-seventh Company, 1st Machine Gun Battalion, with Lewis guns, taken at Quantico, October 29, 1917. Pvt. Linn is the Marine standing third from the left.

Other companies marched before us, and faintly we could hear the orders given to those coming on behind.

Then we passed the barrier of the last line of barracks, and the full thunder of the band met us like a great intoxicating wave.

Before us a great level plain, even lines of marching men, little fluttering bright colored guidons, the formally arranged reviewing officers and, back of them, the massed line of civilian spectators, a solid wall daubed with splotches of bright color.

We caught the rhythm of the march music, felt ourselves merged into one unit of moving matter, and swung forward to the joy of movement, timed to sound. Our blood sang down every vein, and every nerve vibrated to the thunder roll of marching music.

We were coming up the field in squad columns. The company before us executed squads left and in the full glory of company front, swung down the field before the reviewing officers. The band thundered its bravest. A minute behind it, we arrived on the same spot and executed the like maneuver. The turning squads coming into the new alignment, swung off for our parade drill down the field.

At this critical moment, Lieutenant Mellor, short and fat, lieutenant of our platoon, must whirl about, marching backwards, to face us and see that we came into exact alignment. He marched backwards into a depression that had held the morning's rain and since then had been ground into a pool of slithery mud, by many marching feet. For a moment he teetered, then with a mighty splash, came down, full on his back, his hands and feet in the air.

Unavoidably we swept down upon him. The first line did have the grace not to step directly on him, but the second and beyond were not so charitable, they walked him under.

I had one glimpse of him, flat in the mud, waving his legs and arms, like and overturned tumble bug, before we swept by. Afterward I had several hours of agony trying to keep my face straight through a lot of serious formalities, when I wanted to lie down and howl with laughter.

Guard Duty

The following account takes place at the newly-constructed Marine Corps training base at Quantico, Virginia.

I remember a lot of guard duties, but only a few stand out in sharp relief. First the old haunting glory of formal guard mount when I was a boot and taken in by all the pomp and circumstance.

The parades, the music, the even files of men drawn up in the setting sun, the exchange of the wretched looking prisoners from the old guard to the new. Then the sharp order, the playing band and the slowly sinking "colors." It was over and we were marching back in silence save for the crunch of gravel underfoot and the irregular slap and click of equipment. At such times I felt like an actor and thrilled to the little obscure part I played. I felt I belonged.

At twelve o'clock one night I went on post in an alley behind "Officers Row" under general orders. This includes halting all persons after dark.

At some time subsequent, as I made the tour of that alley in the pitch dark, I nearly collided with a

U.S. Soldier

fugitive gentleman. With our noses separated only by inches, I stormed out, "Halt," and brought him up teetering on his toes. I was certainly lucky to escape being brained that night. I guess the surprise saved me.

"Who goes there?" I demanded.

"L-L-Lieu-tenant B-Brown," came jerkily back. The lieutenant was so upset, and as we were not four inches apart, I left out the part "Advance to be recognized," and merely said, "Pass, Lieutenant," and presented arms.

Could anything have been more ridiculous, I ask you? This man was in a scrape, uncertain for the moment to what extent, and thrown clear off his service routine, and I going through my little catechism before him.

Soldier looking back.

He entirely forgot to salute and started on, then turned back.

"Sentry," he asked, "is any report made of your watch? I was just leaving Major Stone's — I didn't know there was a patrol here."

He also didn't know that I knew Major Stone had just arrived back in camp suddenly in a car as I came on guard.

"Oh, no, sir," I answered, "this alley is open."

"Ah, thank you, Sentry. Good-night."

"Good night, sir."

As he turned away this time, I noticed against the sky that he didn't wear a hat and I wondered how the major's wife would explain that, if it was still hanging on her hall rack.

Off for France at Last

The following account opens at the Marine Corps training base at Quantico, Virginia, on the snowy morning of December 8, 1917, and ends in the harbor of Saint-Nazaire, France, on New Year's Eve.

The fires were out in the two big coal stoves in the barracks. The place was cold and had a smell of dust. Although it was past midnight, the lights were still on and everyone was up, dressed and excited. There was an abandoned look about the place. The bare mattresses were thrown at the heads of the cots. The floor was littered with the trash of a departing company. On every cot were the arms and equipment of its occupant. We were "off for France" at last.

We filled in that weary "waiting" never separate from military life as best we could. Little groups carried on desultory conversation, or stared unseeing at the opposite walls. Everyone was too engrossed in his own feelings to do much talking. Some few were still writing letters. Those monomaniacs of every company, who, halted for ten minutes, would get out paper and start in to write letters. How the censor must have cursed them.

Kranski,[6] sitting all alone on his bed, was extracting heartbreakingly mournful chords from his mandolin, that mixed well with the disagreeable smell of dust in the cold building. It was not that he was sad. That was the only way he could play. It just seemed sadder tonight. It was a consolation he didn't sing anyway.

Through the sleeping camp and falling snow, we marched to the station. Lines of barracks, on both sides of the way identically alike, in rank and file like an army of houses. All dark now and full of sleeping men and the snow falling, softly falling.

Occasionally we ran upon sleepy sentinels patrolling the streets, coming

The crap game. The barracks at Quantico are in the background Woodcut.

clumsily to salute with their numb fingers, and looking at us with vague wondering eyes, as we go by them.

Then the crunch of our marching feet echoing hollowly out over the "Bridge of Sighs,"[7] and we have left the camp behind.

Several trains were banked at the station with locomotives attached, their steam pipes thrumming steadily and long black oblongs that were companies of waiting soldiers. Still the snow fell; great white flakes sliding softly down; falling over the silent waiting men and the bustling officers who got in each other's way, in each other's cars, in each other's equipment.

The Non-coms came to their aid and we were loaded,[8] and the cars were sliding away. Away through the snow, picking up speed until all the various noises settled down to a steady hum; with the hoot of the great whistle coming back to us, muffled by the falling snow, and the song of our speed.

"Wonder if I'll ever see that old hole again," said my seatmate.

"You can't be lucky all your life," I consoled him, grinning. "You got one wish, we are on our way."

Holstead, round of face, gentle of eye, wandering about the aisle, stopped and said to me, "Would you mind pressing the button? I think I will get off at the next corner."

"That will be Portsmouth, Virginia," I told him. "You had better sit down, it's a long block."

"But I don't want to go to war."

The whole car took up the refrain and began to chant, "I don't want to go to war."

To keep from having your eardrums burst, it was necessary to chant too.

After this relief, they settled down for the night. The brakeman dimmed the light. I could not sleep but sank in my seat, with closed eyes, I gave myself up to the sensation of crashing speed and absolutely relaxed inactivity. After months of hiking, this was joy.

On, on, on, the coach rocking softly on its great springs. Lines of packs and equipment swinging gently, from the racks. Soldier hats and rifles, bayonets and canteens, a whole car full, roared on through the night and falling snow.

The next afternoon[9] in a cold rain we marched along the wharf at Newport News and out upon a pier beneath coaling chutes to where a ship[10] lay. We were marched past a wide stairway rigged against the side of the ship to where a sagging timber with cleats nailed on it bridged the gap and told to climb aboard.

Seeing the almost impossibility of the feat loaded down as we were in overcoats, packs and rifles, someone asked if we couldn't go up the stairs. The someone was promptly told we could not. The stairs were for officers only.

We all managed to climb aboard somehow. I only saw one rifle go into the sea. But I had lost my first fine enthusiasm for this boat.

On board we were taken down into a large bare compartment and told to get out of our coats and equipment. We were going to help load the ship. When we started over to our timber the sergeant in charge said that we were now free to use the stairway.

All that evening we rolled boxes and bales into huge cargo nets that steam derricks lifted on board. At midnight we were given sandwiches and coffee. From then on we worked in two hour shifts, the two hours of relief spent in a futile search for food or warmth. The rain had stopped and it had come on to blow a bitter cold gale out of the north.

Twenty-four hours later[11] I was sitting on a kind of iron box on the windswept deck eating a meal. I had missed so many lately that I was not sure which this was.

Before me two sailors were leaning their elbows on the ship's rail hav-

"We were marched to a sagging timber ... and told to climb aboard ... loaded down as we were in overcoats, packs and rifle..."

ing a conversation. A soldier came out on deck with a dust pan full of dirt. Going to the rail this soldier undertook to throw the dirt over side. The wind caught it up and whirled it right back on board. The two sailors disappeared in a miniature dust storm. When they reappeared they had turned about and were energetically coughing and spitting and rubbing their eyes. When they could talk again one remarked in a politely conversational tone, "The sea is sorta dusty this morning."

Then they turned on the cause of the disturbance.

"You God damn idiot. Don't you know better than try to throw stuff over to windward?"

The soldier stood looking shamefacedly at them, his own amazement at the result mitigating powerfully in his favor.

"When you want to throw something over, go to the leeward side, toss it out and away it goes on the wind," continued the sailor in a more mollified tone accompanying his words with appropriate gestures. "Now look at that deck. If an officer happens along somebody will catch it."

"How do you tell which is the leeward side?" inquired the soldier.

"Listen, pal." The second sailor took up the conversation. "This is the best way. And you will never go wrong if you follow it. See? You walk to the side of the ship and you spit over side. See?" This sailor also went through the pantomime. "Well, if it slaps you right back in the face, that's the windward side. You want the other. See?" whereupon both sailors turned their backs and resumed their conversation. Well, they did what they could to make life intolerable for us. Although it was midwinter we were not allowed in the ship except to sleep on the floor with not even a mattress to soften it. We jogged by the hour on those iron decks to keep from freezing and ate our meals in the lee of anything that offered some protection from the icy blasts.

"Two sailors leaning on the ship's rail having a conversation."

Then we hit the Gulf Stream[12] and all our troubles were forgotten. We went about comfortably in our shirt sleeves. We were given a little water and took baths and shaved. Full of the comfort of being clean again, we drowsed away the long sunny hours lulled by the gentle roll and sway of the ship.

One glorious night we all lay about on top of the

hatches. A full moon shone and the water reflected a path of its light. On deck we were not allowed to smoke or have any kind of light.

Then there was a blast on the ship's siren, cutting the quiet like a knife slash. We nearly jumped out of our skins.

Gun crews sprang to their cannon. We scrambled to stations by our life rafts. The siren was the signal of a submarine attack.

The next minute recall sounded and our anxiety broke like a bubble. Showers of little signal lights twinkled all around us as a fleet of tiny ships took position to defend us against submarines.

For the next few days they offered a new subject of interest. Dwarfed by the immensity of the ocean, they looked no larger than motor launches. We watched them wallow and plough through the rough seas.

"When the war is over I am going to buy me one of those little boats," declared Renet.[13]

"They will probably sell them cheap. I'll just live on it and go around the world."

We all thought this a great idea until one of them came alongside to get a soldier who had developed acute appendicitis to take him to a battleship where he could be operated on. Then we discovered that our tiny craft were a hundred or more feet long with crews of forty or fifty men.

That night a sailor pointed out a little spark of light far across the ocean as we were eating supper and said, "That's Ireland."

The next day[14] at noon came the sudden ear-splitting crash of the ship's cannon intermingled with the siren blasts.

Our ship almost turned on its keel and the torpedo fired at us went harmlessly down our side a few feet off from the ship. The submarine was nearly under our stem and so close that only the forward guns could be depressed enough to shoot at it.

The little "chasers" came flying in to our rescue firing as they came. The submarine submerged. The chasers ran over the spot dropping depth charges.[15] A few hours later we anchored in the lee of Bell Island for safety.

The next morning[16] we banked the rail for our first sight of France. The country lay under a great pall of snow. We watched it saying nothing. The channel narrowed down. The country closing in about us. We realized that another stage was done in our journey to the guns.

We stayed on the ship for some days, then late one night we marched across the city and were entrained in a freight yard.[17]

Although it was past midnight a number of shabby scarecrows were furtively hanging about offering for sale in a secretive manner the most startling merchandise. Small filthy boys in rags would sidle up to us with dubious looking bottles in their shirt fronts. We could do some business with these lads.

2

A Village in the Vosges —
Germainvilliers

Boxcar Pullmans

The following account describes a journey across France lasting two days and three nights, from the evening of December 31, 1917, to the morning of January 3, 1918.[1] As the account opens, the men of the battalion, having disembarked from the USS DeKalb, load onto a French train traveling eastward across the French countryside, finally finding themselves among bleak, snow-covered fields in a strange country. They will not arrive at their destination in the foothills of the Vosges Mountains for another two days and two nights. Their accommodations are spartan. While officers ride in the comfort of standard passenger cars, most of the enlisted men are crowded into small boxcars, with scarcely enough room to lie down. The car in which Linn and his comrades find themselves seems to be a step up from the usual boxcar, with a bench along each wall, and with windows, but it was still a far cry from the comfortable passenger cars of the officers. Not that any of them are all that comfortable, as all the cars are unheated and the temperature, according to the diary entry of one muleskinner enduring the rigors of that never-ending boxcar ride, is minus seventeen degrees Fahrenheit.[2]

Morning was breaking. In the coach it was bitter cold. Wrapped up in our overcoats and blankets, red nosed and bleary eyed, we twisted our cramped limbs and looked about us. There was a change here. We were in France now. This was a French train.[3]

Queer little coaches, made up in compartments, with two hard board seats, facing each other, in each. No heat, no water, no toilet.[4] The whole pulled along by a queer little brassy locomotive, like the outdated ones in our museums, with a wooden coat and a whistle vaguely reminiscent of a peanut roaster, back home.

All through the long night, of cold and discomfort, its peet-peet-peet, had come back to us and we were sick of it. We were one and all, ready to get out. We did not want to ride anymore.

"So this is Paris," remarked Zeke, blinking great red eyes at us, but we were not in a mood to be appreciative. We poured canteen water on our fingers, and wiped out our eyes and announced we were ready for breakfast.

"You've a swell chance of getting any," Zeke was pessimistic because we had not laughed about his Paris joke.

"It won't be long now, fellows," Holstead stood up and spoke down the line of openings above the seats, to the whole coach.

"If any guy in this coach makes another wisecrack between now and when I eat, and I ain't got the least notion when that will be, I'll kill him, and I ain't kidding none," declared Moler.[5]

He was a long guy with a hard face, and he did not grin. Whether he spoke in jest or not, there were no more remarks.

A sack containing canned beef, canned beans and boxes of hardtack was presently thrown in the coach. That was breakfast, also dinner and supper, washed down with canteen water. We kicked our numb feet against the opposite seats, to encourage circulation, while we devoured icy beef and beans with our gloves on.

"Peet-peet-peet," on we went. A snow-banked landscape, not vastly unlike home, sliding, not very rapidly, by the windows.

"I ain't seen a board house yet," observed Moler, who was watching out the window.

"Oh, I guess they got them," defended Zeke, "or where would folks board?"

A hastily built up barrier of feet and legs saved Zeke's life.

"I better not hear anything more out of you until pay-day," was Moler's subsiding threat.

At the opposite end of the compartment Zeke grinned between his overcoat collar flaps, but offered no further witticism. With sleeping and eating, the day wore away. The sun setting painted with old gold the stone buildings and red-tiled roofs of the passing villages, making fields of gold of the illuminated sides of the hills and all shades of blue and violet of the shadowed ones. Then the sun slipped below the horizon and the glory of color was gone.

At dark we stopped in a large station but before we could find a restroom, our train started off again and we had to chase it down the platform to spring aboard. Then away again, over the fields. We bundled ourselves up in groups of twos, but the cold was something terrific. We shivered in that little ice cream freezer, with a chill our clothes and blankets could not combat. And again that miserable peet-peet-peet of the locomotive became odious in our ears, mixing into our broken dreams through another night of cold and wretchedness.

With the return of the sun the next morning our situation seemed a little better. The bitter cold of the night abated somewhat, still no one unwrapped and most of us overlooked the formality of any toilet whatever.

Our train, which up until now seemed on an inspection tour of all the sidings of France, seemed to have finally made up its mind to go somewhere, and hour after hour dug steadily along. One thing that had impressed us from the first was the amazing amount of conversation requisite to get this train to go at all. At any and all times were general and special conferences of the crew, and such chattering one never heard. After the taciturnity of American trainmen, these chattering, gesticulating Frogs[6] were a revelation. Sometimes they got so full of bottled-up talk, they would stop the train out in the middle of some open plain and all of them would rush into a knot and begin to talk all at once, with no one to listen except us and we couldn't understand a word. Engineer, fireman, conductor, brakeman, oiler and whoever else went into a crew, howling and squealing and gesticulating at one another.

The first few times we looked on, hopeful they would soon begin to fight. No group of American men could talk with one another like that without a fight. These Frogs, however, never did, so disillusioned we would yell at them, "Pipe down." Let's go from here.

Now, this day wearing away, what had been a crying need before became a desperate necessity. We had been eating steadily for two days and nights and there was not a toilet on that train. What were we expected to do, explode? We asked to have the car stopped, for a short time somewhere out in the country, but the car couldn't be stopped; it had to be off those tracks at a certain time, it seemed. When we had not cared, it would not do anything but stop, but now, when we wanted a stop, nothing short of shooting the engineer could halt it, and our condition was getting desperate enough to do that — only the coal car was in the way. Hour by hour, the time went, everything else was forgotten, in this universal need. This concentrated thinking, however, only made us suffer the more. In sheer desperation, two of us made a successful trip to the couplings between two coaches. A general exodus was threatened, but after a look, Sergeant Slater refused to allow anyone else to follow our lead.

The afternoon wore slowly away, and so did the men's endurance. At about four o'clock the train finally stopped, in the station of a large city, full of people, who came to see real American soldiers. The real American soldiers did not see them. What they saw was relief at last, and they took it the instant their feet hit the platform, with a disregard of convention and their spectators that was heroic.

The French took the surprise well, silently shaking with laughter. They turned their backs until their visitors might be in better condition for viewing.

Back in the coaches afterward, the men were willing to grin shamefacedly out of the windows, but they were sore at such a spoiled reception.

Now on that platform was an old codger, with a great white beard, combed out to perfection. He had gold lace and uniform enough for a rear admiral, and dignity and conceit enough for a second lieutenant. In his gyrations he came opposite the window in which Moler was leaning, as full of pent-up ill humor as a boil.

As the train began to move Moler leaned out and, taking this venerable personage by his beard, wagged his head comically up and down, saying, "Yah! Yah! Yah!" full in his face. He dragged the old fellow some steps down the platform, finally releasing him, to bring a happy and untroubled countenance into the car, as he drew up the window.

From the roar of laughter and applause that arose from the Frogs, this seemed as well appreciated as anything else that had gone before. This was one on them too.

In Billets

The following three pieces, "In Billets," "At Half-Past Three in the Morning," and "A Ghost among the French," all take place in the small rural village of Germainvilliers in the foothills of the Vosges Mountains of northeastern France. It is here, in several villages a few kilometers north of Damblain, that the Marine brigade will be billeted through January, February and half of March 1918.

The winter of 1917-1918 is the coldest in living memory and accommodations for the enlisted men of the Second Division are far from adequate. The stables, barns and chicken coops where most of them are billeted are only minimally heated with tiny stoves, and wood is tightly rationed. It is illegal to cut firewood in the surrounding woodlands, except under close supervision, and in any case fires are only allowed for a few hours each afternoon.

Bad as this might be in itself, the situation of the men is made all the worse by the fact that at least half of their time is spent outdoors, frequently in freezing rain or snow, on forced marches of ten to twenty miles, spending the nights in open trenches — often standing in icy water — and undergoing intensive training in open field maneuvers, mortar and machine gun firing, grenade throwing and

"We went to live in a little manure pile town." Woodcut.

digging emplacements. When finally they are permitted to return to their billets for a rest, it is often so cold, and the fire so meager, that they are unable to get dry. Not surprisingly, widespread illness is a problem, and this winter in the Bourmont Training Region will became known as the "Valley Forge of the AEF." Yet little of this hardship makes its way into Pvt. Linn's account.

We went to live in a little manure pile town in the Marne province,[7] while we received our final instructions in human destruction.

The houses were half and half. Everything on one side of the ridgepole was barn, on the other dwelling house. The stable cleanings were piled under the parlor windows, in the front yard. The size of this pile was an index to the financial and social standing of the inmate.[8] For the most part, the people lived on the first floor, sleeping in queer little cupboards, with sliding doors, one bunk above the other as on shipboard. They were very friendly and kind but we were at such a disadvantage in not being able to talk to them.

One old Frog used to come into our billets every night and sit absolutely silent, looking from one of us to another as we talked. Finally he would say, "*Amérique beaucoup distant.*" We could never understand what that meant, and he would sadly shake his head, so we would sadly shake our heads to keep him company. After that he would go home.

One night Zeke took a chew of tobacco, and, seeing the old fellow eye his plug, offered it to him. That old Frog put the whole thing in his mouth, much to Zeke's chagrin, for there was more than a chew in the piece.

Now that old Frenchie had made a mistake. He had probably never seen chewing tobacco and thought what Zeke gave him was something to eat. He must have thought something like that, for he proceeded, before our startled eyes, to chew up and swallow that chunk of tobacco. Subsequently, he got right sick and had to go home, after a lengthy session at the manure pile before his door. His wife was convinced we had poisoned him, and would never let him return.

Now ever so often there would show up in the town a queer little old Frog, in a kind of uniform, with a drum. As soon as he had gone some way in among the houses, he would unsling his drum, and proceed to beat out a lively tattoo, ending off with several rolls and lots of slow loud beats. On hearing this drumming, the French people would come out of their houses, and gather around the player, who, having completed his drumming, would take a paper from his pocket and proceed to read in a loud declamatory voice for some time. Then, putting up his paper, he would re-sling his drum and start off down town. The people would turn and go back into their houses, as if nothing had happened.[9]

One day a little group of us discerned his figure coming down the road; his drum identified him at some distance.

"That old Frog," declared Renet, "walks clear over here all the time and reads how we are licking the Heinies, and those people just turn and go back into their houses without a word, never give the old boy a hand or anything."

"Is that what he reads about, the war?" asked Porky.

"Well, I can't think of anything else he would be spouting about," declared Renet. "He is a soldier, ain't he?"

After some discussion we decided to be an appreciative part of his next audience, and gathering up all our lounging buddies, we trailed him in to his first stand. No sooner than he had run through his repertoire and put up his paper, preparing to go, we burst into wildest applause. Hurled our hats in the air and shouted, "Hurrah," 'til we were hoarse. The startled Frogs turned back to stare at us in astonishment.

Now that old drummer, instead of being elated, blackened his face even more than a lack of soap and water already had, with a scowl, and muttering something about "*Les Amériques cassé idiot,*" to himself, marched away leaving us to pick up our hats, highly amused nevertheless.

Our interpreter had been a surprised witness to the whole affair and now came over to inquire in stilted English why we had applauded. Our explanations were not a great success. He went away still puzzled, but he told us what the drummer had read. It was a notice of some farm leases falling out and requiring renewal.

Just a quaint old custom of France, but we had started something. No matter where he beat his drum, after that, we would be there and applaud until our lungs hurt. He was a taciturn old codger and I bet he came to hate us during our stay. He certainly used to give us plenty of black looks, not all dirt, either.

One night Cob[10] and Hern[11] came in somewhat the better or worse for wine. They had been to the village cafe and Cob had a lovely black and blue eye, with pink edging. Cob was next to me in squad; a good looking but stupid lad, who was almost wordless, he was so quiet. He was always sewing something sitting on his bunk.

"Well, Jesus Christ, Cob, I never expected you to get in a fight," declared Corporal Cullen.

"I ain't been in a fight; I never seen the guy that hit me," denied Cob.

"He sure saw you well enough," mused Renet, and he regarded Cob's eye with amusement.

"I could lick him or any darn guy in this billet," declared Cob, bringing his good eye to bear menacingly on Renet.

"Ah! You are full of hop, go beat up the guy who soaked you before starting in on us." Renet was baiting him because he saw that he was in liquor.

Cob still sat on his bed but his wine was beginning to warm him up and he was getting mad at so much teasing. Everybody in billets came over to view his eye and pass amusing comment thereon.

"Why in hell didn't you do something?" we demanded of Hern, a great gangling Irishman, with watering little blue eyes. No one ever expected to hear of his doing anything, he was so servile; still it got our goats that Hern had stood by while some man had knocked out his buddy, and not done anything to retaliate.

"I tell you he wasn't fighting Cob," declared Hern. "This fellow out of the Forty-second, I know his name but I cannot recall it, he hit another fellow he was quarreling with, and missed him and hit Cob in the eye, that's how it was. A accident. The Forty-seconds got the guard tonight and they came and put us out."

The room shouted with laughter. A guy takes a slam at a friend in an animated discussion and misses him and wallops Cob in the eye. "Ho! Ho! Well, why in hell didn't you take a blind swing at the door post, miss it, and knock his damn jaw off? Was anybody holding you?"

"The guard came in," declared Hern.

"Guard, hell, you was afraid that guy would take a wallop at you and not miss."

Now Cob out of all this teasing had got the idea into his wine-befuddled brain that his honor in the company demanded that he go and hit this man who had walloped him. Up to the time of our teasing no thought of retaliation, for an accident, had entered his head.

Cob was on his feet again now demanding of Hern. "You know the guy what hit me, don'cha? You know the guy what hit me, don'cha? That's all I ask."

"Yes, I know him." Hern was mad too now. He volunteered to lick the whole Forty-second single handed, with the guard thrown in, but Cob only wanted him to identify the man who had hit him.

Cullen said, "Don't let them fools go back there, they will just get in trouble and the guard will pinch them. You two get in your beds, you're drunk," he ordered them.

There was, however, no dissuading them; they were just drunk enough to be unmanageable.

"Let them go," Renet said to Cullen, which in fact they already had. "Half a mile through the snow will probably cool their tempers; they will probably forget all about it before they get there."

"Cob was on his feet again, 'You know the guy what hit me...'"

Most of us leaned to this opinion also, and we went back to our interrupted occupations of the night.

We did not see this interesting pair until the next morning at drill-call and, wonder of wonders, Cob then had two black eyes. He gave us to understand that any comment meant war, but there was none to make. We were amazed that he had had the nerve to go back and fight. However, the sequel came out. After he and Hern had wandered around awhile, they had been assailed by a great thirst, and had paid the town pump a call. In the snow, Cob slipped and banged his good eye against the pump wheel. Then he had a pair.

At Half-Past Three in the Morning

This brief impressionistic sketch of insomnia and misery takes place in the village of Germainvilliers sometime in January, February or early March 1918.

The guardroom was full of a bitter, acrid smoke. A miserable fire of wet green sticks smoldered in an open fireplace. The hiss of these sticks, the howling of the wind outside and Corporal Cullen's sniffle made up the only sounds heard in the room. A little group of supernumeraries, held on account of the violence of the weather, hunched miserable and forlorn over this smudge, in voiceless apathy.

I stared at the bare cracked wall, the empty cupboard, the little group at the fire, and at Corporal Cullen, a great overgrown kid, endlessly running over a pack of cards on his bed. He had a cold in his head, but was too lazy to use his handkerchief. He merely jerked each third breath up his nose with a noisy revolting sound. The whole place exuded dampness and a smell of mold.

At half past three the next morning, we were awakened to go on the new relief. We sat up, stiff, sticky and miserable with a numbing cold in all our joints and that miserable uncomfortable feeling that comes of sleeping all night in your clothes.

Men were moving about the room, and their shadows, cast by a lighted lantern sitting on the floor, ran fantastically back and forth over the ceiling and walls. The fire was out now, added to which some maniac kept going in and out the door, letting in, in the process, draughts of a still icier air, and little flurries of snow that lay unmelting on the dirt floor.

No one spoke a word. In a corner behind the plastering, a rat was gnawing steadily and Corporal Cullen, heavy-eyed and stupid, sitting on his bed in his overcoat, still sniffled regularly. God, how I envied that rat. It was free.

I remember dimly those next two hours of blackness and driving snow, and a cold that seared your face like a hot iron, but I give you my word I suffered more in those first minutes of waking as I contemplated existence.

A Ghost Among the French

The following also takes place in the village of Germainvilliers sometime during January, February or early March 1918. It is an account of a peculiar sort of haunting, in which Linn so strikes a group of strangers by his uncanny resemblance to one of their own recently killed that it is as though he is their dead comrade or brother or son come back to haunt them. This strange occurrence will happen to Linn three times during the war. This is the first.

The day I paid my first visit to the store, in the little manure pile town in which we were quartered,[12] started something for me. We had only arrived the day before and I had been wandering about with various companions, viewing the points of interest. Happening to see the store, I went in. A young woman, rather pretty, pink-cheeked, blond and plump, was waiting on the counter. She wore two shawls, one over her head, the other on her shoulders, and fingerless knitted gloves, for the store was entirely unheated. She smiled and chatted vivaciously with her customers, but the smile was rather marred by two badly decayed front teeth.

Everyone having been waited upon and it being my turn, the young woman turned to me with a smile.

"*Comme ça—*" She stopped talking and stopped smiling and suddenly stared at me with round, startled eyes. I took a quick survey of myself, looked all about me, then back at her in some puzzlement. I couldn't find anything startling. My clothes were quite all right. But she was fleeing for the back of the store, leaving me to stare at a pile of perfectly square cubes of soap, with ornate medallions of some emperor impressed thereon.

From the room behind the store there now came an explosion of French conversation, in various voices, none of which I could understand, and I was seriously contemplating loading up on what was in sight and departing, when a sudden exodus from the back lined the counter with a staring French family. They stared at me, steadily talking all the while to each other. I stared back until I began to feel uncomfortable, lit a cigarette, and finally to put an end to the situation, asked to have my canteen filled with Vin Rouge. The young woman took the canteen, and went away, leaving a young girl and a middle-aged couple to go on with the visual inventory of my person. The girl was not at all hard to look at herself. She was slimmer than her sister, and prettier. Had nice even teeth, red lips like a rosebud, and her bright eyes, unbelievably heavily lashed, were slightly slanted like an Oriental's. So if she stared at me, I certainly returned her compliment with interest. Still the thing was puzzling.

When my filled canteen was returned, I got another jolt; they refused to take any pay for it. We played checkers a while with my silver franc, pushing it back and forth over the counter, until I gave up, and departed with the wine and money. I left them still staring at my back and very much wondering in my own mind what it was all about.

Several days later, I went in the store with a chum who had some frankies[13] to spend. Garden,[14] who came from New Orleans, was leaning on the counter talking to the proprietress in French, which he understood. After we came in, they looked at me continually, and it was evident that I had been the subject of their conversation. Presently Garden called my name and beckoned me to come over. The young woman was giving me a radiant smile, only marred by her two bad teeth; and as this offered a chance at the solution of this family's weird behavior, I went.

Garden offered something in the way of an introduction, but as it was in French, it meant nothing to me. The lady offered no word, only smiled and took off her mitten to give me her hand. I released it as quickly as possible, almost as if I had been burned, it was so soft and warm.

Garden explained the enigma. They had a brother who looked very like me, even acted like me, so the lady had assured Garden. He had been killed in the first year of the war and my sudden appearance had frightened them. They thought I was the brother reappearing to go on with the war for France. It had taken all Garden's assurances that I had come from America and didn't understand twenty words of French to in any way shake their conviction. I am certain they never completely lost that first idea.

While Garden was telling me this, the lady had gone to the back of the store and returned with a

"They had a brother who looked very like me..."

photograph of her brother, which she gave to me to see. Well! We certainly were alike. The picture might have been one of my own. I had a job ridding myself of the idea that it wasn't.

Everyone in the store crowded around me to see it. They would stare at the picture and then at me, and I'll be darned if they didn't begin to look at me as if I were already beginning to push up daisies on my own account.

I walked out of the store in a variegated frame of mind and left my chum to drink wine and eat *bisques* alone.

At six o'clock one evening, I was relieved guard, and came sloshing through the mud and snow of Rue Grande, fagged out physically and mentally. I wanted to cry, I was so tired and sick of it all. Sick of the senseless work, of the filthy billets, of the filthier talk; sick of the enforced companionship of men who revolted me, the smells of their unwashed bodies, their vile habits. I did not even wish to see one of them again, and yet I felt lonely.

At the bridge I stopped, and, leaning on the stone parapet, stared off down the stream lost in some fanciful day-dream. I must have stayed there for some time before the sound of approaching footsteps roused me, for when I looked around it was black night.

The faint glimmer of the lighted store window fixed my attention and I decided to go in and get a bottle of rum. That was the only period to put to the mental condition I was in. I wouldn't know or care after that what conditions life offered. All this ran through my mind staring at the pale square of light in the blackness. No other house showed any lights. It was dangerous. I went in.

The store was empty and as no one came, I sat down, dejected, on a box, my rifle still slung on my shoulder, to wait. I heard nothing, but someone touched me and I looked up. It was the plump lady of the store, Mademoiselle Marie, and she was smiling as per always. We looked at each other. I was puzzled. I never could get just how I should act with her. Any other girl smiling at me like that would have gotten a good hearty hug and kiss, despite her bad teeth, but with her I was lost.

Apparently deciding something in her own mind, she slipped her hand under my arm and nodded for me to come along, which I did, with some reluctance. She led me around the counter, up some steps and into the rear room. The heart of the family, just finishing supper. They all made noises, apparently of welcome, for they were smiling, so I bowed. Mademoiselle Marie gave me a chair at the table and departed, leaving me lost and uncomfortable. The others watched me steadily.

I was presently given a saucer of jelly, but no bread to put it on, and a cup of cocoa. I dispatched these delicacies in as business-like a manner as I could, slightly nauseated by the raw jelly. All was attended by a dead quiet that made my mastication sound like a riot in my own ears.

Then I looked up into the small round eyes of my host, who, after a second's silence said, *"Amérique beaucoup distant."*

Ha-ha, I knew it now. "You said it," I agreed. *"Oui, oui."* America was certainly a long way from this room.

He smiled with satisfaction, pulled his drooping mustache, and looked at his wife, tossing her the ball.

She said, *"Quelle âge avez-vous, mon petit?"*

This was easy enough. I answered, *"Dix et dix et une."*

At this she launched into voluble French and I was lost instantly. The young girl, she of the long-lashed eyes, Mademoiselle Felicia, seeing that I had not understood, simplified matters.

"Mon frère qui est mort et vous avez même chose âge."

I said, *"Oh, je comprend."*

Then the old lady got a velvet-lined box and inside was the medal of the *Croix de Guerre*, awarded to her son for bravery under fire.

I held the medal in my hand and thought of this French lad, that I was so identically like. He had probably sat in this same chair and held this same medal as I was doing. I wondered what thoughts has been in his head, that was now gone. It gave me a kind of a turn at that, and all the time these Frogs watched me in the queerest way. They just couldn't separate us.

I played checkers with Felicia until eleven o'clock and took my departure. I must have been in an improved state of mind, however, for as I went through the store, I remember telling Mademoiselle Marie to have her teeth fixed.

She said, *"Oui, oui,"* but of course she did not understand. I had spoken in English.

As I was leaving the door, Felicia, from the steps, called out to me, *"Revenir demain et après-main et tout-le-jour. Bon Nuit Zhim."*[15]

It must have been pretty near that often that I went. I certainly seemed welcome. So through long winter evenings, I lounged by the side of Felicia, knitting beside the fire.

She was certainly exotic and different from any other girl I had ever known. Memories of glances, from her long-lashed eyes, stayed with me through the miserable hours of drill, in rain and snow, and made the day brighter; mannerisms of hers would keep me company through the weary watches of midnight guard. I guess I was falling in love.

She asked me endless questions of America, my home, what I intended doing. *"Après la guerre."* What I had done before. I think her first question was *"Avez vous une marié, Monsieur Zhim?"*

"Non." Here I received one of those glances mentioned above. What would I do after the war? Why, come back and marry her, and sail for America.

Now for some reason I could never understand, this always got a laugh from her. She would tilt back her head, reducing her eyes to two sparkling lines, and laugh in the most thorough enjoyment. I loved to hear anyone who could laugh in those days and I certainly loved to hear her girlish racket but I did not appreciate her choice of material to laugh at.

We were not always very decorous either. She knew well enough how to tease, and was almost as elusive as a shadow to catch after mischief. The old folks must have held their breath for the furniture, but they only laughed at our games, no matter how boisterous.

Ah, yes, I was still playing the brother. Felicia had been her brother's pet. Penned up and caught after some prank, she would bury herself in my arms and turn up her cheek to be kissed, and because of that French boy, it was her cheek I kissed and not her lips. She was never embarrassed with me; if she had ever been for a moment I would have known that at last I was a separate individual and not a ghost.

I was a ghost for them all. The old man would give me glasses of brandy on the sly, pat my shoulder and say, "*Bon homme du soldat,*" but he meant his boy was a good soldier. "*La mère*" gave me things to eat and smiled as she watched me eat them. In her own mind she was seeing me as a tot devour those same goodies. For Mademoiselle Marie, I was younger brother, consulted, asked for help, and last, for Felicia, I was playmate, to be climbed over, hugged, beaten, kissed, teased, and played with, and the ghost of this dead boy stood ever by, holding me rigidly to take no advantage of my position for opportunity had not been lacking.

Something like this was traveling through my mind that night, as I devoured my supper in the cold draughty mess hall. I know I was making faces to myself as I ate.

Why be so big a fool? When the gods offered me a prize, I suddenly turned angel. The French boy? I would probably be dead myself before green grass came again. Would he meet me with condemnation on the other side? Oh what did I care anyway? A ghost indeed! I was no ghost, not yet, I was very much alive, no one was stopping me, then why should I stop? I made the ghost for myself. Oh, hell! Damn all this useless reasoning, I would go on...

I became conscious of Corporal Burk's[16] voice from the head of the squad table.

"Hit him with something, he's asleep," then seeing that he had caught my attention, he leaned down to the table and said, "Steal us a candle for billets, Jim."

"Steal your own candle, I'm always stealing them," I said.

"I know but you always get away with it. Will you?"

We had no lights in our quarters. Stealing candles from the mess hall was one popular way of securing light, not popular however with Hoburna,[17] the mess sergeant.

"All right," I agreed, "but you come along and fog me."

We started down the aisle against the wall. The candles were there and not many of them either. The whole building was dark. Hoburna was walking up and down the center aisle to be sure no one did what we had in mind. He must have been suspicious for he kept paralleling our course.

"Push me against this one," I warned Burk.

When we were opposite, Burk gave a laugh and me a playful shove. I reeled against the candle and down it went. Hoburna came over toward us. I stooped and set it back in its place. Hoburna turned away and we passed out.

"No luck," said Burk disappointedly.

"Here's your candle." I gave it to him.

He stared at me in amazement. "But you set it back," he said.

"I set back a half an inch of the top, enough to burn until we got out. I snipped off the top as I picked it up from the floor."

"Say! You are right smart, I'll get you a commission as private for that," he promised.

As we sloshed our mess gear about in a pail of water, already cold from sitting in the snow, with a skim of grease and plate scraps half an inch thick on top, by way of washing them, Burk recounted my stratagem to Sergeant Sike,[18] also washing his mess gear.

"By God, I bet he could go back and get another right now, " averred Burk.

"A canteen of wine if you do, and give me the candle," promised Sike.

My success went to my head. I said, "You're on, Pop," and went back to the mess hall.

When I came out at the galley end it was eleven o'clock, and I straightened my back with a groan of weariness. I left behind me a neat row of carefully scoured boilers and I did not have any candles.

As I got carefully into bed that night, for I wanted no notoriety to be given my return, I mused that there was surely something wrong with the saying "The devil takes care of his own." He had certainly flopped for me.

And that was all of that. The next morning I was beaten into life with the glad tidings that we were off to the front. In a long line of motor trucks, we left that village forever behind. The plump lady, the old couple and the girl with the beautiful eyes, only the ghost of the dead boy took place with me and was not left behind.

3

The Trenches — Verdun Front

In mid–March 1918, the entire Second Division moves from the Bourmont Train-ing Area north to a "quiet sector" of trenches, the "Troyon-Toulon Sector," east of Verdun. Here the as-yet-untried Americans, under French tutelage, will begin their initiation into trench warfare, occupying trenches within a 14-kilometer stretch of rugged woodland along the east bank of the Meuse, across which lay the plain of the Woevre, and the German army.

Shortly after their arrival, on March 21, General Ludendorff launches the first of five great offensives on the Western Front, designed to crush the British and French armies and win the war before sufficient numbers of fresh American troops can enter the fighting and tip the balance of power in favor of the Allies.

The initial blow falls on the Somme front, on the British Fifth Army, recently weakened by the fighting at Passchendaele. Within a week the Germans advance forty miles along a fifty-mile front and by April 5 they have taken Bapaume, Albert, Péronne, Montdidier and Noyon, coming within a few miles, and easy artillery range, of the crucial railway hub of Amiens. The specter of a breakthrough to the sea, with the capture of the channel ports and separation of the British and French armies, looms ominously.

On March 26, at Doullens, near Amiens, at an emergency meeting of the Allied high command, General Foch is appointed commander of the combined Allied armies. He vows to "fight in front of Amiens ... and not retire a single inch." Amiens survives, though only as a ghost city subject to continual artillery fire, while the German storm continues. By April 5, they have captured 1,200 square miles of territory, 90,000 British prisoners, 975 big guns, inflicted 164,000 casualties on the British and 70,000 on the French. All this, however, has come at substantial cost to German strength, which begins to show signs of faltering.

On April 9, Ludendorff sets loose a second offensive against the British, cap-turing Armentières, but stopping just short of Ypres and Bethune. The British line wavers but does not give way, and by late April Ludendorff has accepted that he cannot achieve his breakthrough in the north.[1]

During all these events, meanwhile, the Second Division remains amid the relative quietude of the Verdun trenches, gaining crucial experience before they, too, will be thrown against Ludendorff's divisions.

A Ghost Among the Russians

This is the second of three instances where Linn appears to a group of strangers — in this case Russian soldiers — as the ghost of one of their recently killed comrades. The encounter takes place on the evening of 17 March 1918. Seventy-seventh Company, aboard train #24, has been enroute from Breuvannes since about 1:30 in the afternoon.[2] It is now about 6:30 in the evening, dark and cold, and the train has stopped for an hour at a French military depot where the north-south line splits into a wide "Y," with one branch turning east-northeast, and the other heading northwest toward Bar-le-Duc. According to orders[3] issued the previous week, the Marines are to be issued a hot meal by French authorities, however the meal they receive is meager and cold. But Linn describes this stop not for the food, but for the company: a group of soldiers also traveling toward an unknown fate on this cold winter night, who receive the Marine private with unexpected hospitality.

The train moved slowly and jerkily through a snow-blanketed landscape, and the bitter cold of after dark had invaded our heated coach. Sunken in the collars of our great coats, with gloved hands driven up into our cuffs, we sat in a dumb apathy of cold. Two lines of facing men, swaying evenly to the lurching of the car. Then it stopped and we were ordered off.

Sounds of frosty snow, crunching underfoot, and the bitter but invigorating air of outdoors after the stale cold of the car. We were lined up on the embankment, wondering what in the world we were to do in such a place.

Miles of snow-covered country stretched away on every side, not a farm, not a light, only the coldly snapping stars. We were just dumped out on the side of the road, nowhere. Then the train rolled away and we saw the depot. We went down a stairway from the embankment into what appeared to be a summer resort, overtaken by winter.

It didn't look very hopeful. Everything was open air and that air was too fresh. We were cold and sleepy and there was no fire and only tables and benches in the snow to sleep on. At open counters we bought cheese, beer, bread and sardines. That was all they had. This was a French military depot,[4] and at the snow-bound tables we sat down to eat and rest while a January wind licked up little eddies of snow about us, and swayed the electric lights that fairly crackled in the cold.

We ate in little huddled groups, the food so cold it was tasteless. The beer was like a draught of the wind down your throat, and brought no warmth. After they had eaten, the groups solidified and there was no movement or sound.

I couldn't sleep in that cold, so I drifted down to where a group of Russians[5] in wooly shakos were listening to a wheezing accordion.

They were very friendly and polite. They made room for me on one of the benches and gave me some straw to put about my feet; they had nothing else. I in return gave them American cigarettes, and we all lit up, smiling at one another. We tried to bridge that gap of conversation, but we could only make gestures of good will. It was criminal, they looked like a group taken from *With Fire and Sword*.[6]

The accordion player sat cross-legged on a table and had curly black hair, which escaped from under his shako, set rakishly on one side. His black eyes sparkled in his swarthy face as he inhaled his cigarette with gusto.

I felt better just looking at them, so lively-eyed and unconscious of the cold. The lad next to me, who knew as little French as I did, undertook with me a conversation in that language, but we failed utterly to exchange any ideas.

Two of the Russians began a dance, and we stopped talking to pat and shout encouragement. They danced the usual wild Russian dance, whirling with one hand above their heads, reversing, and with the other hand above their heads, then down on their heels, kicking out before them, then in flying hop with whirling arms.

I applauded madly and envied them. Their exercise was making them warm. At that pace they would soon be sweating, and I longed to join them, and drive some life into my numb body. Then the two men dancing beckoned for me to join them.

I would not have gone, thinking the invitation mere politeness, but the rest urged me with gestures that seemed to imply, "It doesn't matter how badly you do it, it's all in fun," and the boy pulled off my helmet, substituting his shako and thrust me from the bench. I slipped off my overcoat and joined the two.

The accordion player shouted and played more loudly. The time grew faster and I was laughing, but dancing madly. I tried to guess their changes, and blundered through somehow. They laughed at my mistakes, but encouraged me with gestures and shouts. My stiffness wore off and though half the time I danced one thing and they another, still I flew as madly as they did, and at least I did not fall down.

The blood began to whiz through my veins; there was a wild exhilaration in this flying motion, in the frigid night. The accordion player was outdoing himself, and all the rest were patting loudly, and letting out little high-pitched, piercing yelps. I was having a grand time, warm and happy.

We were skipping in a line, arms about each other's waists. I was in the center. High kick, drop on heel and quick skip, the line turning on me as on an axis. We came around to face the player under the flooding light of an electric bulb.

He glanced up at us smiling, but the smile froze. He missed the note, fumbled wrong ones, and stopped with a jerk. We also stopped. He was staring round-eyed into my face. My two partners, following the direction of his gaze with their eyes, were also overcome with astonishment.

The player leaped from his table, and leveling his finger at me, shouted some words which I did not know. I shook my head and raised my hands in a gesture of incomprehension.

All the Russians were on their feet now, all talking and gesticulating, and pointing to my face. The player sprung upon me like a wolf. He grabbed my shoulders, his face close to mine, and working convulsively, his eyebrows meeting above his blazing eyes. He kept shaking me and shouting that unknown word in my face, as if he were trying to wake me up. Hands grabbed me everywhere and in the struggle we wavered this way and that. The lad I had sat next to came to my rescue. Everyone shouted, but he out shouted the rest, with continual recurrence in his shouting of a word I knew was "America." We finally came to a panting stop.

In that minute of silence our bugle suddenly blew assembly. It brought me back to earth and where I was. I was an American soldier, not a wild Cossack. I pushed aside the men who ringed me in, caught up my overcoat and started up the yard.

The young Russian kept pace beside me. He thought I felt insulted and was trying to explain. His French was now inspired, or my understanding was. The name shouted at me was the name of one of their comrades. In the shako we were identical. He was dead. He had won the *Croix de Querre*, and they had loved him greatly.

My company was already filing through the gate as I slipped into my pack. I took off the shako, worn until then, and traded it back for my helmet. This lad had been kind to me and I held out my hand, for a parting clasp. I got a surprise: he gave me a solemn hug, and I felt his lips brush my cheek.

My company was loading on the train as I ran up the steps. At the top I turned to wave adieu and then sprang on the already moving train.

In Billets Again

Seventy-seventh Company arrives at the town of Lemmes at 4 A.M. on March 18, detrains, and marches eastward through Ancemont to the town of Rupt-on-Woevre, just outside of which they are shelled.[7] A kilometer or so north of town is what appears on a trench map from 1916 as a wood, named "Nivolette." According to the battalion history, it is in Camp Nivolette that they are billeted,[8] and it is in this camp (which Linn refers to as "Flatfoot") that the following, "In Billets Again" and "Movie Night at the Y," are situated. Seventy-seventh Company will remain in Camp Nivolette until the night of March 27. This first account involves the house of a disgruntled French woman—apparently a farmhouse situated within or close to the camp.

We were assigned to a one-story stone house of three rooms. The whole place was filthy dirty and the flagstone floors made it as cold as a vault.

All the time we were moving in and putting up our cots and storing our equipment, an elderly French woman kept ranging through the rooms. She had a sharp hooked nose, little black red-rimmed eyes and a mouth puckered and sunken from the loss of teeth.

She got in everyone's way and was a most through nuisance. We wondered who on earth she was and why she kept hanging around where she was so evidently not wanted.

In the front room there was a tiny fireplace where a bit of fire had been started, with such scraps of wood as we could find. The sergeants had first place on each side. The rest of us grouped about as near as we could to the dancing blaze, which brightened if it did not warm the room. Outside the snow fell in great white flakes.

"She brought our captain and liaison officer..."

Presently from the rear there burst out such an uproar that we all rushed out to discover the cause. We found the French woman in a tussle with Private Thorpe, releasing torrents of noise one pitch above a scream.

"What have you done to her?" we asked.

"I haven't done anything, but I bet I break her God damn neck if she doesn't let go of me."

"Let go of me!" he yelled into her face. He was obeying the common idea that if English couldn't be understood when spoken, it might when yelled.

"What started it?" asked Slater.

"I don't know. When I came out in the yard this old crow jumped on me. I think she has gone crazy. I haven't done a thing to her."

"Let go of me!" he roared in her face. "Pull this old bitch off me, Slater, will you? I'm gonna get mad in a minute and lam her one."

At this moment she noticed us and leaving Thorpe she rushed on us squealing and howling and waving her arms. We retreated laughing but there was no shutting her up. She followed us back to the front room never letting up for a minute. Her uproar was beginning to be unbearable.

"Shut her up someway, can't you, Jim?" said Cullen.

For answer I caught this bell-dame by the scruff of the neck and conducted her struggling and squealing to the front door and sent her flying head first into a convenient snow bank. I slammed the door and fastened the latch.

Inside an eager crowd was watching her further maneuvers through the dirty window pane and passing amusing comment.

"Takes more than a snow bank to cool that beauty," observed Moler.

"So this is Paris," quoted Thorpe.

She spent about five minutes squealing and howling outside, then went away down the street.

"This is one crazy God dammed country if I ever saw one," declared Moler.

Half an hour later she was back and she brought our captain[9] and liaison officer[10] with her. The minute they got into the house, she turned on the uproar.

The captain looked slowly about as if surprised to find any of the house standing. Then he noticed us at attention and said, "At ease, men."

"I don't see anything wrong here. It looks just like it did when I inspected it," he continued, addressing the French officer. Then he turned to Slater.

"Sergeant, this is the woman who owns this house. She came to the office with a claim for five hundred francs. What damage have the men done?"

"We haven't done anything but move in, sir."

"She say they burn up her furniture in fire," said the liaison officer pointing to our miserable blaze.

"She say they tear down her back fence and burn it, also crack window panes," he continued.

"There wasn't any furniture here, sir, and all the cracks in the window panes are so old they are black with dirt. No one has done any damage here."

Slater spoke to our captain, but the French officer looked haughtily about him and shrugged his shoulders, "She say so."

The captain stood for some seconds thoughtfully tapping his boot with his cane. "Tell her we will give her fifty francs."

After some squealing this was pronounced acceptable and they all departed.

The whole billet broke into vituperation of the French, but Sergeant Moore said, "Wait a minute. One knavish old woman is not all of France. How about that Virginia store keeper who made us pay a quarter a pack for cigarettes, when he found he had the only ones we could get. That tribe of blood suckers is international."

Movie Night at the "Y"

There is nothing unusual about finding a YMCA in a French camp occupied by Americans. The "Y" follows American units around, and makes do with whatever shelter can be had. In another of the military camps near Verdun, Camp Massa, an impromptu Y is set up in a cowshed.[11] Despite this willingness to share in the rough conditions of the soldiers, Linn's jaundiced view of the YMCA is widely shared. On the whole they much prefer the Red Cross which, unlike the Y, does not charge for their services and refreshments, and is not overtly religious.

The "Y" at Flatfoot[12] was a great big uncongenial frame building. Its floors were always carpeted with several inches of mud, in various stages of drying, and there were a lot of hard board benches about a stove that never had any fire in it. On one side was the counter and at the other end was a blank wall, on which movies were thrown. At regular intervals on its arid, dusty walls, were pairs of tiny cheap flags, American and French, crossed. That, far from decorating, made the place look mean and parsimonious.

Two very superior "Misses," of about the vintage of General Grant, officiated here and they were as deficient in attractions as their place of business. One searches their faces, figures, gestures and speech in a vain effort to find a faint little echo of feminine charm. Believe me, though, they hooked our frankies. Those two old rain crows could peck a coin out of your hands before you had finished naming what you wanted.

They made a little go a long way at that "Y." A faint tincture of cocoa in cups of warm water, sold for half a franc; two hard-tacks with bully-beef brought the same. The only reason I can assign for our buying it was the American's necessity of always spending money, if he had it, and there was no place else to spend it.

When the movies were to start, all the benches were put in rows and we sat on them. They were all the same height and as the screen was low, on account of the roof, you had only a partial view of the picture between the ears of the two men before you.

One night, at these movies, I had a funny thing happen to me. There was a rule, rigidly self-enforced, that you could sit only on the benches. On this night, the two soldiers in front of me folded their overcoats into cushions, securing in this way some five or six inches in elevation. Their own view was then perfect, but I could hardly see the top of the screen. I spent most of the picture trying to figure out some revenge proportionate to their selfishness, but I finally got interested in the picture and forgot my revenge, and my burning cigarette in the desperate affairs of the actors. I was watching the screen through the hole between the elbow and side of the man in front of me, which necessitated my stooping forward instead of sitting up straight, as I normally would have.

After some time, in spite of my abstraction, a danger of suffocation forced me to look about me to see where the rag-smoke in my nose came from. I found it in a smoking red crater in the cushioned overcoat of the men before me. In leaning forward to see this picture, I had brought my cigarette in contact with his overcoat. My first impulse was to tell this man his coat was afire. My next was not to tell him. He was a lot bigger man than I was. Instead I started spitting desperately into that hissing crater as fast as I could collect moisture to spit. The rattle of the projector and everyone's absorption in the picture saved me from detection.

I, personally, didn't see any more of the picture, but I got the fire out just before it ended and the lights came on. I debated a scramble for the door, but realized that would be a dead giveaway, so did not move. The two before me picked up their coats and, moving out toward the door, began to get into them. I leaned against a timber and watched. My victim got his coat on. He and his friend were talking animatedly, probably about the picture they had enjoyed so much. When he started to button the coat, his hand came in contact with a button-hole as big as a saucer. He looked down in surprise. His coat had developed two series of port-holes, one down the front and the other down the back. His face was a study. I got to laughing until I thought I would have hysterics. The whole "Y" was laughing at him by then, even the two old girls at the counter. He and his friend sneaked out like a couple of whipped curs and I often wondered if they ever used their overcoats for cushions again.

The Lilliputian Train

On the night of Wednesday, March 27, Seventy-seventh Company leaves Camp Nivolette, marches through the Tranchée de Calonne to Fort Rozellier and proceeds northward to Camp Joffre, in the Moulainville Sector.[13] "The Lilliputian Train" and "No Man's Land" take place in the general area of this camp which is somewhere close to Eix and the front line trenches.

In a rest camp just behind the lines[14] we were living in a most ideal way. We didn't do any work and we got three meals a day, just the same. There was, however, as there usually is, a fly in the ointment. We didn't have any money.

Now there had been an order passed that soldiers at the front could get credit at the "Y," so we tried to get our tobacco and chocolate on tick. We got turned down. We appealed to our officers and they, having nothing else to do, took up our case. That "Y" secretary, on the flimsy grounds that he was not regularly attached to us, turned our officers down too.

That secretary was a character. I think his ideal state of bliss would have been running a pawn brokerage, if society had given him one; I'll bet he would have made them a fortune. He had a face like a hatchet, a pursed up mouth, and a pair of little ratty black eyes, and they were pursed up too.

What he told our officers was nonsense. The real reason was that this was a French officers' training camp, and these officers bought for cash everything they could get, this purchasing being done through his own runners, who of course were Americans. On top of all that our company had to feed that old goat and his runners.

There was running through that valley a narrow gauge railway,[15] on which the supplies were brought in daily. Our supplies and the "Y" man's supplies, along with all those for the front. The train that ran on this railway was the answer to any small boy's dreams. A little steam locomotive, not over six feet long, nor more than four high, yet built identically like a standard one. The engineer sat on a miniature coal car, with his hands and feet in the caboose, and fired the engine between his knees. This miniature engine pulled a whole line of little four wheel flats, on which the supplies were piled, and a train crew of three or four merry Frogs.

A lot of us were still small boy enough to delight in this Lilliputian train and we attended its daily arrival with delight. Its crew as proud as punch of their efficient little toy were tickled to death with us for making so much over it. We soon got to know them well and would welcome and congratulate them on each safe arrival, as their trip in was not without its danger.

The Heinies could see the little ribbon of smoke, left by the engine, from their sausage balloons and would shell, by indirect fire, the path it had to fol-

An example of the French Decauville 60 cm light railway train, Linn's "Lilliputian train."

low. Sometimes they knocked cars off the tracks or delayed it by blowing up the rails. Not the safest job in the world to do every day, by a long sea mile.

We would be given notification of their coming by a shrill whistle down the tracks. The next minute we would see them round the hill, going like a bat out of hell, with the crew hanging on for dear life and that little old engine wide open and roaring.

Once around the hill and up in our valley, they were in a sort of haven of safety. Their faces would relax as they climbed off the cars and they would be all smiles and grins when we rushed down to bang them on the back and yell, "*Trays beans.*"

One day the car brought in a new stock for the "Y" man. We stood about eyeing those boxes of tobacco and goodies with a speculative and angry mien.

The "Y" man's runners soon showed up to cart off the stuff. They were a taciturn crew, who would have nothing to do with us. We knew their game, however, and were quite ready to start trouble, if provocation were offered.

One of them picked up a sack and started for the "Y" hut. I was directly in his path. I had been cutting something and had my penknife open in my hand. I did not notice this man or I would have stepped out of his way, for the sack was heavy. Instead of going around me or yelling "Gangway," he ran into me with the sack. Caught off guard I had to catch myself with my hands to keep from sticking my nose in the dirt. That was too much. Regaining my equilibrium, I put my whole weight on the back of that sack, in a hard shove, and he not being able to travel at that speed went down in a pile with the sack on his neck. He scrambled up pretty lively, as if he meant business, but I was waiting for him. He spat the dirt out of his mouth and said, "Gettin' smart, huh?"

"Who in the hell you knocking about, with your damn old Y. M. Secure stuff anyway?" I returned.

He changed his mind about the fight and picking up his sack started off. Then we noticed that out of a hole in the sack, probably cut by my knife when I gave him the shove, was pouring a stream of almonds. Everyone began to scramble for them, even the Frog train crew, and the bird with the sack never even looked around, probably he thought it was I cutting up behind him.

I was still in the same place when the next runner came up. This accident had given me an idea and I still had my knife in my hand.

"Don't you cut this sack," he said, stopping before me.

"Oh, shove off," I replied, and stepping quickly behind him, I slit his sack. This time it was English walnuts that rained down. He shifted the sack to hold both openings, so I cut another slit for him. There was no help for him. He may have had a peck of nuts left when he got to the "Y." The next runner had a big paper carton on his shoulder. He thought he was safe and passed me grinning. As he did I inserted my knife just behind his hand, and cut down the side, and across the bottom. Immediately there poured down his back a cascade of little packs of cookies. I had hoped for tobacco but took what came. The runner hugged what was left to his breast and started to run, but another knife reached under his arms and again the cookies poured down.

The whole camp was in an uproar by this time. The whole track to the "Y" was lined with grabbing soldiers and literally nothing got through. Every package the runners picked up was slashed open, and its contents became public property. That "Y" secretary was in hysterics, jumping up and down and yelling for the guard as if the German army were invading us.

Hastily catching up all we could carry we fled to our holes and feasted high on the "Y's" unintentional Christianity, well pleased with ourselves, at the trick we had put on him.

No Man's Land

The following episode begins at Camp Joffre on March 31, the day before Seventy-seventh Company leaves for the front line trenches at Eix.[16]

That afternoon Rats and I went down to enjoy the arrival, for the last time, of this little train and to say good-bye to the train crew. We were leaving the next morning to take over a section somewhere on the front.

Walking up and down the platform was Lieutenant Roper. He was out of our company but not our platoon lieutenant at the time. We didn't care much for him. He was a big raw-boned man who always wore an anxious, puzzled look as if he were not quite sure of himself. He put an embarrassing necessity on us to look out for him if he were in charge of anything.

He returned our salutes and continued walking anxiously up and down. We sat on the bank and rolled cigarettes. We had already heard the faint far-away whistle of the little train approaching.

Presently the company clerk showed up and gave him some message. The two stood talking for a while. The lieutenant looked still more worried and upset. Then his eyes lit on us and coming over he said, "I want you two men to come along with me. I'll need your help."

"Shall we go for our arms?" I asked.

"No, you won't need them." And with a worried glance up the tracks, he added, "You wouldn't have time to get them."

So! We were going for a ride on the little train! What a lark! We exchanged delighted glances.

We seated ourselves in the little car behind Roper. The train crew grinned at us and away we went down our valley and around the spur of the hill.

The danger of shelling seemed slight for the train traveled up a wooded ravine and into a large forest. The train crew sat smoking, no longer anxious. Finally we arrived at a big French battery on top of a wooded hill. That was the end of the line or at least as far as the engine went. The cars that went on from that point were pulled by horses.

Here we found a Headquarters sergeant and private. The private was holding a harnessed horse. Roper and the sergeant walked up and down talking. Roper couldn't stand still. He waved his arms and snorted and looked more exasperated and worried than ever. The sergeant walked back and forth with him but remained undisturbed.

Finally Roper walked off and the sergeant, looking after him with a grin of pity, shrugged his shoulders and came over to us.

We were to have taken over the section in front of this battery and some carloads of our equipment had been sent in two nights before in anticipation of our arrival. Now the orders were changed and we were taking over a front somewhere else. So our equipment would have to be retrieved. The rub was that the French would not let us go in for it until after dark.

This sergeant was a small man with a face as round as an apple, criss-crossed in every direction with wrinkles and burned as brown as leather. He had an athletic figure and bright sparkling blue eyes. He spoke in short staccato sentences that radiated competence. We were disappointed to find that the sergeant was not going to be a member of our undertaking.

While we waited for dark he went over to one of the cars and sliced off a number of steaks. Presently we all had supper with the French Non-coms of the battery, our sergeant supplying the steaks, they the bread, potatoes and wine. We all made a hearty meal.

We went in a bunch down the railroad track, several groups of loaded cars and little groups of overcoated Poilus with their long bayoneted rifles. They were all talking animatedly as we moved off into the twilight. The animation of the men only seemed to emphasize the desolate loneliness of the bare gashed hills in the fast-closing day.

After about an hour of steady walking, everything stopped and the Poilus sat down. We sat down too. Only the man from headquarters stood holding his horse.

We were on the brow of a low hill. At its base were some dark irregular mounds of rock, the remains of some shell-wrecked village. All around stretched bare desolate country and a cold wind rattled the dead weeds. The Poilus were mostly silent now only exchanging occasional remarks in undertones.

Roper bent over and whispered, "They call that 'Death Angle,'" pointing to where the railroad having reached the village made a right angle turn.

"The Germans have got the exact range and can always hit that spot. They make you wait here until some shells come in, then they hurry you around before another batch arrives."

"Have you been here before?"

"Yes, I brought our equipment in. That's why they are sending me to get it out."

Two flashes of fire and crashing detonations shattered the stillness. Then we all got up and hurried forward to get around that unhealthy turn as fast as possible.

Soon after that our party began to disperse as groups left us to go to their stations. Half an hour later the last group of cars pulled off on a siding. As we moved past them the single Poilus seemed surprised and taking a step after us called, "*Allo.*"

I had stopped but as he only stood looking anxiously at me and Roper continued marching ahead, I hurried after the others.

Walking on we passed several places where the track had been entirely blown away by shells, further on we came to a trench. Two French soldiers with bayoneted rifles sprang up out of it before us and barred our way. Roper ignored whatever it was that they were trying to whisper to him and insisted we must pass. He didn't know any French, only gestures.

We passed through the trench and then waited while two Frogs took out sections of barbed wire. These, I noticed, they very carefully replaced after us. Again we were marching forward.

I didn't feel a bit confident. The railroad had completely disappeared as a railroad. Sections of it were laying in any direction or sticking straight up in the air. Finally we got into a gully. The horse made a slight rattling as he slid into it and from directly before us came the rat-tat-tat of a machine gun. Then a star shell shot up into the air exploding almost above us. We crouched in the gully. The horse stood as still as a statue.

When the light had burned out Roper whispered, "I believe I have gotten lost. There shouldn't be any trench there."

"Crawl over and find out where we are. If we all go they might take us for Germans and fire on us."

We certainly had gotten turned around. The first thing I ran into was the barbed wire again. I squirmed and wriggled through it and crawled up the embankment of the trench and peered in.

I think it took me a minute to comprehend what I saw. I was looking at a trench full of German soldiers. Some were lounging at the firing step talking, others were busily filling sacks with earth that still others were digging with nothing but a pen knife. I stared, too scared to move.

Outside the French wire we all met up again. We stood a fine chance now of being shot by the French before they could recognize us.

Roper decided to go in himself and get some directions. We had found another gully and gotten into it. The cold wind still blew mournfully. Drifting masses of clouds blotted out the stars.

Both lines were quiet. Occasionally a star shell would shoot up into the sky, burn for a while and fall back to earth.

We waited and waited and still Roper did not return. Had the fool forgotten us? We knew positively that this was the French line. You could trace both lines from here when the star shells were up. There had been no shot so we knew that he had not been killed. Why didn't he come back or send someone for us?

Finally Rats and I decided to look for him before we froze. Rats said, "If that fool doesn't get us shot tonight it'll be pure miracle."

The man from headquarters did not say anything, neither did his horse. We promised to come back and get him as soon as we found the lieutenant. This private's conversation seemed entirely reserved for the horse, whose mistakes he had meticulously pointed out along with directions for future improvement. To our proposal he merely nodded.

Going through the wire some tangled strands squeaked and the machine gun response was instantaneous. We went up the face of the trench on our hands and knees and dived into it. In seconds we were face down in the mud with our hands tied behind us.

I had been prepared for some such reception. I was laughing at Rats and the job we made of getting on our feet.

We were taken along the trench then through a canvas-covered door into a cave in the hill. A small electric light was burning. There were tables and benches and bunks against the wall. Some French Non-coms gathered about us.

"*Allemand?*" they asked.

"Non, Amérique."

"Oui! Amérique!"

It must be explained that this occurred early in the American participation and few French soldiers had seen an American soldier.

Their faces began to relax and our hands were untied. We were invited to sit down. It was explained that an officer would come and decide what was to be done.

I explained that we had left one *comrade* and one *cheval* just outside the wire.

It was difficult to guess what they thought we were. A regular storm of conversation was being carried on around us. They treated us with courtesy but they weren't taking any chances.

We were presently conducted into a tunnel running right into the hill.[17] Narrow gauge railroad tracks ran along this tunnel. It was lit by little electric lights in the roof.

A short walk brought us into a much larger tunnel running at right angles,

A postcard of the *Tunnel de Tavannes.*

well lit and bustling with life, then into a quite large room with an arched ceiling of something like corrugated iron. At a rough board table two or three French officers were seated looking at papers. They looked up at our entrance. One of them smiled and said, *"Bon soir, Messieurs."*

"Bon soir, Monsieur."

"You are Americans?" he continued in French.

I assured him we were.

"Then why do you come from the German side?"

In the best French I could muster I told them all about our evening's wanderings. At its conclusion they fairly shouted with laughter and the officer I had been addressing got up to shake hands with me.

I turned to meet him as he came around the table and saw Roper seated on a chair against the wall.

"I'm a prisoner," Roper informed me.

The French officer caught the word prisoner and said, *"Non prisonnier. Non."*

I introduced Roper to this officer. The officer introduced himself. Everybody shook hands and we were all presently seated at the table drinking tea royal and smoking cigarettes.

Roper said I should inform this officer that Ratting and I were only privates. Probably he was right but I was enjoying this moment. Instead I asked when we should set about finding our stuff and getting back to our company.

The French officer told me that he had sent a guide with our horseman to get the cars and as soon as they were fetched we could start back.

There were a good deal of interruptions at this time and officer after officer was called away. Finally the captain, after a short talk on the telephone, struggled into a trench coat and bolted after wishing us luck.

There was no one in the room now except the man at the telephone, a black-eyed boy who smoked cigarette after cigarette and smiled at us when not busy with his phone.

"Help yourself and pass the rum please, Mr. Roper," said Rats. At that moment a French private at the door beckoned to us to come and we all hurried out after him. He kept saying, *"Viet viet"* and urging us to come quickly but that was impossible for the tunnels were now full of soldiers moving out to the front and we were trying to go in the opposite direction.

Finally we turned down a side tunnel almost empty of men and pushed aside the heavy canvas curtain and stepped into an inferno. It was all we could do not to jump back.

"What the devil is it?" gasped Roper.

"Must be an attack."

The man from headquarters still led his horse only now it had a line of little cars to pull. In the shadow of his helmet his eyes looked as big as saucers. Rats and the lieutenant disappeared. I yelled and waved at him to get going and threw my weight against the last car to get them rolling.

The railroad paralleled the front for a mile or more before turning back into the country. We went as fast as a man and horse could run. Shells screamed and burst about us. Up hills I pushed, on the downgrades I crouched on the car with my foot on the brake.

Then came a tremendous explosion directly in front of us. We all went into a tangle. The terrified horse spun round, knocking down its driver and tangling in its traces it fell. All the cars were derailed and upset.

The horse struggled to its feet while I was dragging the driver out of the mess. He had not been hurt badly. He caught the horse's bridle and stopped its floundering.

What to do now? I looked around for someone but there was only the roar and crash of the firing. Above us a shell had started a fire which was moving downhill toward the tracks. I wanted to junk the whole thing but at the same time I was feeling a wild exhilaration.

That headquarters man was a brick. He was just as scared as I was for his hands shook so he could hardly hold the traces. He had gotten his horse straightened out, the cars uncoupled and was trying to tilt the first one back up on its wheels. We dragged it over to where the tracks began again. The horse pulled them around one at a time and we lifted them back on the rails by main strength. Under the circumstances, I think we could have lifted a locomotive. We got them all back on the rails and coupled up beyond the break and started out again.

We got past the fire before it reached the tracks. Finally we reached the turn and started back into the country. There were still plenty of shells and screaming iron about us but they got fewer as we put distance behind us.

I persuaded the driver to ride his horse. His leg had been hurt in the crash and lifting and straining at the cars had not helped it. He was not keeping up with his horse.

When we reached the top of a hill I would unhook the singletree and hand it to him on the horse. Then I would jump on the last car and ride. The faster they went the better I liked it. Their momentum would carry them halfway up the next hill where I would jam on the brake and wait for the horse to catch up.

I came flying down a steep hill and piled up all the cars on my own account. The tracks had made a right angle turn and the cars were going too fast to make it. While I rubbed various bruised parts of my anatomy and swore, I looked about and identified my whereabouts. I was back at Roper's "death turn." It was so quiet and peaceful here compared to what we had come from.

A little while later we pulled into the battery station and stopped beside the loading platform. A group of officers were on the platform. Their angry voices had reached us above the noise of our approach. Now in the quiet we heard Roper speaking in a propitiatory tone, "I should have known better than to depend on them. All they had to do was hook the horse to the cars. But instead they walked right by them. Got the French to let them through the front line. Got lost out between the lines. I had to get the French to lend me a patrol to find them. Took nearly half the night."

So that was my big night's work. How I had planned to spread myself telling my buddies all about it. What really hurt was the disappointment in Sergeant Slater's voice, "Hell, Jim, I thought you had some savvy."

The companies had been asleep by the road. They were presently roused up and the regiment got under way. Next to me Grantham nudged my arm and said, "Got some bad news for you, Jim."

"Now what?"

"They got the train crew this afternoon."

"Got the train crew," I repeated stupidly. I was suddenly too weary to understand. "Who got them?"

"Who? the Krauts, that's who! They hit the engine with a four-hundred-and-ten[18] as the train was going back empty this afternoon. Killed the crew to a man. We ran down and pulled them out of the wreckage but they were all dead. They all rode up by the engine. I guess they thought the front was the safest."

He went on with his account of the tragedy but I was no longer listening. I was seeing again those bright merry faces, feeling the hearty handshake and hearing the cheery voices of that little band. It could not be. I could not understand.

It had begun to rain. The drops drummed on our helmets and rain coats. I was more weary than I ever expect to be and angry and sad. I wondered how my legs could go on.

Roper got a step from that night. I don't know what other lies he told but subsequently he put on a bar and became First Lieutenant Roper.

Horseradish

On Sunday, April 1, Easter morning, Seventy-seventh Company leaves Camp Joffre before sunrise and arrives in the front-line trenches at Eix, relieving a French unit at 5 A.M. They will be in support of Third Battalion, Fifth Marines, and will occupy these trenches until the night of May 12–13.[19]

I remember our first front was at Verdun, or rather to the side, at a little place named Aix.[20] It was early spring. I think it was Easter Sunday, we went in. It must have been, for it was Sunday, and a holiday. We had doughnuts for supper, by way of celebration. Each man received two.

Later, on a work detail, loading the galley equipment, we found a whole can of these confections that were left over. When the cooks were not looking, we stole the whole can, and, taking them aside, ate them all. How many did we each have? Why, about a peck, I should judge. There was easily a bushel in the can.

With everything loaded and ready, we lay down at the side of the road, to wait for black night. It was bitter cold. An empty desolate landscape, fast darkening into obscurity, stretched away before us. Behind rose some low hills, pitted with shell craters, and crowned with the blasted remains of a grove.

Bits of hay and lines of burlap strung on wires above the road danced a noiseless eccentric dance in the cold wind. A further camouflage of wattle twigs ran along the road, behind which we crouched for warmth.[21]

Far away the roll of a heavy barrage filled the air with its steady menace and the knowledge that at any minute we might be in for the same thing made our nerves tingle. Nothing happened, however; that threatening quiet remained unbroken.

The order came at last, and we began to move. In the darkness our way seemed weird and fantastical. Queer and unaccountable engines of war would loom up suddenly before us, prophetic and unnerving. We advanced in as near a silence as could be maintained, yet in the hush about us a very earthquake of racket seemed to travel with us. Partly over the brow of a hill we came to a halt and remained waiting. In whispers, the news obtained from some unknown source, we learned that we were at "death turn." After a time six or eight shells screamed in and exploded just before us and immediately after that we were hurried forward to pass this turn before the next group of shells should arrive. Not long after this we began to pick up the occasional flare of the rockets and a little later reached Aix (Eix).

We had stopped in a village street, fantastic with dancing camouflage of hay and burlap, strung between the shell-wrecked houses. Everything was black and silent. All conversations were carried on in a hurried anxious whisper. The same aching quiet was here; the same thunder roll of the big barrage far away; just a steady ominous mutter. Occasionally a star shell shot sizzling into the sky, and exploding, hung there like a great arc light, throwing a weird theatrically unreal light over us all. For the time it burned everything stopped dead still and did not move again until it had expired.

In little groups we were taken away to our respective stations, and the carts and the French, whom we had relieved, retired before the coming day.

We, I mean now the little group, of which I was one, took up our residence in one of the stone vaulted cellars of the town chateau. There was six inches of water on the floor, with rafts of duck boards for runways. A framework of boards about three feet apart had been built against one wall and chicken wire nailed over all. The wire sagged between each pair of boards, and each one of these sags was a bed. It was inky black in this place, day or night, but since it had the wreckage of a stone chateau on top of it, it was practically bomb-proof.

We worked only at night. Daytime, when we were not napping, we would prowl about the wrecked town, or hunt rats.

In the debris of the wrecked church, Blanche[22] found a little hand-carved virgin, somewhat the worse for shell fire, and bringing her back to our hole, he tied the little statue to our door post with a piece of barbed wire.

"God damn you, Mary," he admonished the little effigy, "you better take care of us."

Those old trenches just teemed with rats, so did our cellar. The French would not kill them. They had some idea they could tell when there was gas, by the action of the rats. That did not go with us, however. We felt any time we had to wait for rats to notify us of gas, it would be too late for the news to be of interest. Besides, they had such a miserable trick of crawling over your face, just when you were trying to go to sleep.

We amused ourselves by gassing them. We would pull the bullets from about a peck of shells and, taking out the powder, pour it in some populous-looking rat hole and, after lighting it, put a stone and dirt over the mouth of the hole and all the other holes nearby, since they were all intercommunicating. This burning powder engendered a poisonous gas that would permeate all through the runways and when we kicked off the stones out would come the rats, pretty sick and partly blinded. Then the fun began.

"The order came at last, and we began to move."

Now there was one poor chap in our cellar who never took any part in our amusements. He lived in mortal terror all the time and spent most of it in pitch darkness, seated on the edge of his bunk, with his gas-mask on. We had nicknamed him Horseradish.[23]

One night, when we were all sitting quietly talking, while we waited for the supply train to come in, this yap jumps into the middle of the floor with a mighty splash and yelps out, "I smell — I smell — horseradish." He then submerged in his gas-mask. That was how he had gotten the nickname.

We used to line up for chow along a high wall, over which at varying intervals of time, shells passed, exploding in an open field some hundred yards below. This place, known to be a headquarters, received a steady shelling day and night, but as comparatively few casualties resulted we paid little attention to them; in fact, they added a sort of zest to living. You soon learned to judge pretty well the landing spot of isolated shells as they came singing down through the sky. A quick jump would put a wall between you and the explosion. When the fragments stopped screeching you went on your way with a "Not that time, Fritzie boy."

Well this Horseradish lad would crouch against that wall as if it needed a prop and tremble so violently the lock on his canteen cup would jingle like a cow-bell. As soon as he got his food, he would dive back in his hole, like one of the rats, and eat it sitting on his bed with his gas-mask out and ready.

On this particular day we were lined up so, and right behind Horseradish was Blanche, a French Canadian lumberjack, and a great joker. As a particularly low shell came screaming down across the sky, Blanche raised his canteen cup, and just as the shell went over our heads, he brought the cup down with a bang on Horseradish's tin derby.

We all jumped, and Blanche burst into a roar of laughter. Then he stopped. Horseradish was weaving around in the queerest way, his face a sickly green. Then he plunged down on the ground and frothing at the mouth he began to beat his head

There was one poor chap in our cellar who spent most of his time with his gas mask on, Horseradish.

upon the ground, his body giving spasmodic lurches. I tell you it was a sickening sight. We stood looking at him, too astonished to go to his aid. He was behaving, for all the world, as if he were mortally wounded.

Well, a bucket of cold water first, then a cup of black coffee brought him around, and he was assisted over to the cellar and put to bed.

We discussed him awhile. Everyone agreed it was cruelty to keep him here. He was really no coward. He stuck, but his terror was beyond his control.

"And all those fine big heroes in Tours sorting mail," said Burke, "writing their girls back home how wild they are to get up on the line and fight."

Just behind the chateau, in the lawn, were buried some fifty or more French soldiers, and a few Heinies. A rat had gone in at the head of one of these graves and brought up a flaky white matter, the stench of which passes all imagination.

Humfers,[24] a stupid lout, for a joke, got some on a stick, and would thrust it beneath the nose of anyone he could catch off guard. Trying to thrust it under my nose, he daubed it full in my mouth. I had a strong stomach, but when I got through vomiting I crawled weakly down into the cellar and got into my bed.

Humfers and Norton[25] decided to go ratting that afternoon. Blanche and Simmes[26] had gone off somewhere, so being shorthanded, to expedite the work, this interesting pair began knocking out the bullets, instead of pulling them.

The shot awakened me, so I came out to see what new deviltry was afoot. Horseradish sat up in bed and put his gas-mask on. At the stone coping of the stairway, where they had been working, Norton was standing, holding one of his hands tightly in the other, and looking pretty yellow about the gills. From between his fingers streams of blood were beginning to run and drop in bright crimson streams.

"What have you done?" I asked.

"A shell went off in my hand," he explained.

"Good Lord, come on over to the dressing station."

"No, I can't go there, I would be court-martialed. See if you can get the hospital apprentice to come over here and dress it."

The apprentice came over, and finding the hand only cut, and no fracture, bound it up. Each one of Norton's fingers had been laid open.

"If that hand begins to give you any trouble, I will have to put you on the books and report it, and don't you say I dressed it, either," said this functionary. At the top of the stairs, he turned back to say, "You are a fine bunch of soldiers. Some of you scared to death, some sick, and the rest of you shooting yourselves, playing with your arms. God help us if the Germans do come."

"Oh, go take a dose of Brown's Mixture,"[27] we told him. Brown's Mixture was supposed to be full of hops. That evening, lounging in the chateau yard, feeling a lot better, an idea of the past night recurred to me, and I proceeded to put it into execution.

An infernal rat had for the past three nights taken up his stand beneath my head and there coughed by the hour, gassed a little, probably, but there he would be, cach-cach, cach, hour after hour. It wasn't loud but it was only a few inches from my ears and drove me frantic.

Beating on the wire had no effect, or yelling at him. He would not go away and the wire was so close meshed, I could not get anything to go through it to poke him.

In an outhouse of the chateau I had noticed a discarded French bayonet. It had occurred to me the night before that this was the thing for that rat. The French bayonets were not little swords like ours, but triangular pieces of steel, tapering to a point, and half again as long. A perfect instrument for this work.

Securing the bayonet, I carried it to the cellar and put it at the head of my bunk, ready to hand, for the night.

At about ten o'clock we were all sitting about an old tin drum in which we would build a little fire — the nights were still bitter cold — while we waited for the supply train.

"You know," said Simmes, "I haven't heard a shell since supper."

The rest of us, casting back in our minds, discovered we hadn't either.

"Bertha sprained her wrist slinging stuff this morning," suggested Norton.

After a time Simmes spoke again, "You know, boys, this place is getting so quiet, I am getting fidgety," he said. Simmes always said "You know" especially if telling you something he knew perfectly well you didn't.

"Wait until we get our own artillery in here. It will be lively enough then."

"We were down to that Frog battery, down the valley below us this afternoon."

"No, we didn't get any vin rouge, you can just as well lay back down."

Simmes' last remark was addressed to Humfers, who, at the mention of the French camp, had popped up from his bunk.

"Well," went on Simmes, "we asked them why they didn't shell that big chateau over behind the lines, that is so full of Heinies, and this artilleryman said, 'If we shoot the Bosch, he will shoot back at us.'"

"That looks like damn poor logic to me," I averred, "seeing all the shells that go over us in search of that battery."

"Yes, but that's just it," Blanche now spoke, "the Germans can't locate those guns and the French won't fire much because then they would, and would blow them all out, if they wanted to come over here."

"Is this an endurance contest or a war?" we wanted to know. The French may believe in hiding their guns; the Squareheads believe in shooting theirs.

"No vin rouge, though?" we asked.

Not a drop; waiting for it to come in tonight.

I went out to the head of the stairs, to see if I could hear our supply train coming. They were easy to hear. They would come at a wild gallop, disregarding everything. The drivers used to get half drunk every night for this run. The Germans knew at what time we received our supplies and used to shell the road. The wagons would come up as close as they could, then try and rush through, in one of the intervals between fire.[28]

It was a wild business. One night a new driver missed the turn into our courtyard and drove our supplies over to the Germans. The next day we had to live on our emergency rations.

Hearing nothing of the train, I had just come back in, and sat down, when about ten shells exploded simultaneously about the chateau.

"Mother of God, what's that?" inquired Blanche.

"Hoburna[29] must have broken wind," suggested someone. Hoburna was mess sergeant and enormously fat. All loud noises were attributed to him.

That first ten was a sort of notification. A perfect avalanche of shells was beginning to roar around us now. They came screaming, whining, and roaring down across the sky, to explode in detonations that kept the earth quivering. Screaming fragments struck the walls and thudded down into our doorway. Occasionally a concussion primer would bury itself in the debris above our heads, and at the explosion our ears would rattle, and lines of dirt would run

"The French won't fire much because then the Germans would locate their guns." Sketch.

The woodcut made from the sketch. Linn chose this art form because the heavy dark lines better convey the feelings of fear and foreboding that accompany war. Notice how much more ominous the cannon looks when you can't see the end of the barrels.

between the stones. Still they didn't send anything big enough to drag us out. The din was appalling.

"What's that funny noise in here?" Humfers demanded suddenly.

We all became aware of a queer rattling sound in the cellar. Our keyed-up nerves gave a jump. Had a shell come in? Was it escaping gas?

We tried to locate the sound and finally did. It was Horseradish's teeth chattering. We stood about him laughing nervously, Blanche illuminating him with our candle. He was shaking from head to foot, in a spasm of terror; his teeth keeping up a ceaseless rattle.

"It would be a mercy to him to knock him unconscious 'til this is over," declared Blanche grimly. We wrapped him up in all available blankets.

The war of exploding shells always seeming to have arrived at a pinnacle beyond which it must fall off, continued to increase. Continuous streams of dirt were now being shaken down through the rocks overhead, and it was necessary to yell to each other to be understood.

"Christ, but they are catching it out front. Why doesn't our artillery open up? Damn those Frogs, are they asleep or dead? They are shooting up signals for the artillery all along the line." Blanche sprang in from a moment's peep over the door parapet.

Still no sound came from our rear; our batteries were as silent as the grave. Everything continued to come to us.

We sat about our boiler, there was nothing else to do, and drew mental pictures of what it must be like a hundred yards ahead, in the front line. Talking was too much of an effort, besides, we had nothing to say. Occasionally we would shout to one another, "Why don't that damn artillery shoot?" Still that iron hail broke about us, and still from our guns came not a sound.

Almost unnoticed by us there came a change. From being one moment in the center of an inferno of exploding shells, we came to be a little island of quiet; ringed around on the front by the crashing German cannons, and behind by the exploding shells. The curtain of fire had been moved back to cut us off from any support. Everything now went clear over us.

Almost on the instant our machine guns broke into frantic action. The whole line crackled with rifle fire and exploding hand grenades. Star shell trailed star shell, sizzling into the sky and still the frantic signals for artillery support remained unanswered.

"Here come the Heinies," cried Blanche, his eyes aglitter.

"You needn't make a fuss, they will never come here," I said.

"You don't know. There may be lots of them. We haven't many men out front."

This was true, so I shut up and looked over my automatic.

The rattle of machine guns played on. Still the German cannon flashed and still the crash of shells continued behind. It was impossible to go out. The air screamed with flying metal. Our front line was not a hundred yards away, but what was going on there we could not know.

Blanche came back from the door and said, "You fellows get your guns ready. Our fire is slacking and there is too much hand grenading. The Square-heads[30] may be through."

Armed, we banked at the door. Our fire had dwindled to next to nothing, only occasional bursts with intermittent pops from hand grenades. The German artillery fire began to slacken too.

Then from behind there burst a roar that made us jump in surprise. The French had opened up at last and the roar of their cannon took up the sinking song of the Germans. They fired with a will.

We listened in pleased surprise to the speed of their delivery. While we listened, an ear-splitting bang from behind nearly knocked us down. We whirled as quickly as we could catch our balance, fully expecting to see the rear of the cellar full of Huns. There was Horseradish, his rifle shaking in his hands.

"Brain that fool," cried Norton.

"Take that rifle from him," said Blanche.

While this was being accomplished, there came a rattle at the door, and something landed head-first on our cellar floor.

Again we whirled to cover our rear, but it was one of our men, a runner.

"Put out that candle," he directed, scrambling to his feet. "'At's right, on your toes, boys. Who's in charge here?"

"I am," said Blanche.

"Put a sentry at the stair head; challenge everyone who comes in the yard. Some of the Heines are through and they are in behind us. The line is closed again, but they may drop in on you."

He was already scrambling up the stairs in the dark.

"Anybody hurt?" we screamed after him.

"Got a few," he answered, and, watching his chance, shot away into the night.

Blanche took over the first watch. He had a faint hope he might get a shot at some enemy. There was no sense to standing there in the pitch dark and I was fed up on excitement for one night. I began to feel faint too and decided to go to bed. I wasn't expecting any trouble from those Germans. Their own situation appeared too desperate to make them very dangerous.

I stretched wearily out. It had been a big day and I turned my mind to something for relief; some pretty girl whose kiss I could remember; anything away from this inferno.

Then I froze. From right behind my head came that miserable cach-cach-cach. In spite of the racket that night, my rat was coughing as usual. For a minute I saw red. I was more infuriated at that rat than at the whole German army.

I reached my bayonet and softly rolled back my blankets. Then for a long time I remained with the bayonet poised, moving its point from hole to hole until I should be sure I was directly over that rat. Then I drove with fury.

On the instant there issued from beneath my bed a scream of anguish, then squeal on squeal. I was startled myself and would have jerked the bayonet free, only it was embedded in some timber so far I could not release it. Then I realized what had happened. I had stuck the rat through a foot or some fold of skin, hurting but not killing him. Loosening the point very carefully, I tried to make another jab before he got away, but I missed and he was gone.

In the silence, I became aware of a commotion at the end of the cellar. I heard Norton say, "Throw a hand grenade."

"Don't throw any grenades here." I yelled, "I was killing a rat."

"Good God! What next?" I heard Blanche exclaim.

"We thought that was your screaming."

"What ran out that door?" demanded Humfers. "You saw that, didn't you, Blanche?"

"Yes, something did run out that door, as sure as hell," admitted Blanche.

Again we were all in an excited knot at the door.

"Norton, get up on that step. Sentry, get a blanket over the door and let's have a light in here," directed Blanche.

Two of us held the blanket and a light was struck. Only the familiar interior of the cellar and our own persons were disclosed.

Blanche scratched the back of his neck in puzzlement, glancing from one of us to the other. Then he was struck by an idea.

"Where's Horseradish?" he demanded.

Where was Horseradish? Gone forever as far as we were concerned, for we never saw him again.

Devil Rum

The following takes place in March 1918, in the front-line trenches at Eix, where Seventy-seventh Company is in support of Third Battalion, Fifth Marines.[31]

The guardhouse was a tent and Sergeant Moffet, of the guard, was a kindly man. Off post, we sat about a red hot Sibley stove[32] and drank red wine spiked with raw rum. It was early spring, sometime in March. The weather was raw and wet. Everything was muddy. We lived in it, we ate it, our clothes were plastered with it and our hair was gritty with it. The bottle from which we poured the drinks was daubed with it, and we all drank to alleviate it.

Each new relief, as it went on post, its personnel hanging on to one another's coats to keep from falling down or getting lost in the dark, was in a complete state of intoxication. By the time they were again relieved they had either relieved themselves by vomiting, or slept off the effects in the rain and snow, and were ready to start in drinking again.

Moffet was paying, and he knew no better use in the world for money than buying liquor. He had drunk steadily since he had taken the guard, yet he was not drunk. It was he who kept track of the changing reliefs.

You think me lying or stretching it a little? Well, I am not. All this was nothing notable. I remember not one but dozens of guards worse than I have described this one. Where were our officers? I don't know, drunk too, I suppose. We did not see any of them.

Drawing of two Marines in a trench, on the back of a letter to Linn's parents, written April. One Marine is dozing on duckboards; the other is peering over wattle reinforcements with a periscope.

At midnight perfect bedlam reigned in that tent. The men fussed, cursed, dealt infuriated drunken blows at one another, made up, hugged and danced and wept. Some, who had made the mistake of going to bed, were dragged out naked on the cold mud, fought over and wallowed about. While they struggled to get into their clothes, icy canteen water was poured down their backs and soft mud daubed on sensitive parts of their bodies.

Through all this uproar, Moffet, lean and brown, with gray hair and an intelligent face, sat serene and happy before the stove door, which he threw open from time to time to replenish the fire. To the snatches of words hurled at him from various quarters, he turned a smiling, untroubled face.

To me, sitting beside him, he said, "I like to see the boys drink and have a good time, but I would like to see them carry their liquor better; they couldn't drink with my old maid aunt."

Standing behind me, with a grimy hand twisted in my hair for support, was Sheep Burns. He heard the remark that only tinkled into my head and out again and immediately took offense.

"You hear that?" he cried, in his anger wagging my head. "Moffet said we drink like kids."

"He did. I'll show him some drinking, I will. Just watch."

Pouring his canteen cup full from the rum bottle and shouting to attract general attention, he put it to his lips and drained the liquor without a stop. Then he fell in a pile on the floor. The tent shouted with laughter.

"Some drinker, Sheep; try lemonade next time."

Moffet was straightening him out and was trying to rouse him. Finally he looked up with a serious face and said, "I believe he's dead, or at least dying. For God's sake, get a pill roller quick!"

Ten yards from that tent in the pouring rain and slithering mud, every sense deserted me. I had been perfectly sober in the tent, conscious of everything happening about me. Now I was unconscious — drunk. I knew in a vague way I was sent for something in a hurry, but I knew nothing more. I did not know who I was, or where. I went floundering through the mud and rain, falling down, getting up, in a mad hurry to get somewhere; where, I did not know.

In one clearing moment of sanity I screamed for the guard, and a sentry, sobering up, came to my call. He finally understood my errand and sped upon it for me, but it was useless.

The surgeon said the boy was probably dead when he hit the floor. That was all of that, except doing slow time to Sheep's funeral.

The Cat

This takes place sometime in April or early May 1918, in the front-line trenches at Eix.

In the long bright twilight of a spring evening, a patrol was gathering in the shell-shattered main street of Aix and looking itself over. By mutual consent they had gathered in the one spot in town where their concentration would be sure to bring the most abject terror. The spot was a mutilated wall opposite the ruins in which the YMCA was located.

I was not on that patrol, at least not then. I merely joined the group for sociable reasons, and to add my bulk to the possible attraction to German shells. It was still light and the Heinies sausage balloons were still up. We were in full view and of some numeric importance.

Did we want to be shelled? Oh, well, we were indifferent. We got shelled anyway, but if we could get Bertha to lay a few "G. I." cans on, or near, the "YMCA cure," life would indeed be fairer and sweeter. For many reasons we did not like that "Y," nor its operator. It very nearly took a shell to open it up anyway.

For two and one-half hours a day it was open for business. The rest of the time it was closed tighter than a Scotsman's purse. The devilish inconsistency of the thing was, the hours it was open were at night when we were always at work or on duty.

This fool man's mania about his own safety gave us a pain. The whole town teemed with life, but his house must appear untenanted and deserted, and no one must come near it in daylight.

If after a snow we approached his door, from different angles, so that lines of tracks converged there, he would go perfectly rabid, lecture us savagely, refuse all purchases, sometimes even close up the "Y," and leave for days, or until the snow melted, and, mind you, there would be convergences of tracks all over that town at those times.

Yes, he even appealed to the officers for assistance, but I don't think it got him any help. Strange, I didn't seem to remember much about any officers on that front, but I guess they were there.

I remember that evening, though. Lying in a shell breach in the wall, I stared up at the sky, which seemed a million miles away; sun warmed blue with a faint drift of pink fish scale clouds. The whole vast dome seemed absolutely still-stopped.

Behind us, in the shattered remains of an orchard, a single bird was whistling the sweetest little catch-note and the evening was mild and pleasant. In imagination, maybe inspired by the little singer, you smelled the odor of bursting blossoms and the fresh earthy smell of new broken ground.

At this luckless moment, a stray cat still alive in the ravaged town took it upon itself to walk sedately across the road, in the direction of the singing bird.

Now that cat had a history, and a slight knowledge of it may shed some light on our behavior. The mystery began with the way he continued to live, even given his due allowance of lives; true, food was plentiful. Those old trenches teemed with rats, but whereas the rats took to their holes to escape fire, this cat went wandering around during some of our heaviest bombardments. Now in each of these barrages, we would be sure to get one or two layers, seasoned with mustard. So while it was possible that a cat might be so lucky as never to be hit, still a cat that could remain alive in a town regularly dosed with gas was a pure phenomenon.

So much for his staying alive; the use he principally put that existence, it seemed, was scaring the life out of a lot of poor American soldiers by suddenly popping up beside our heads at a midnight listening post, where we lay watching the star shells blossom in the inky sky, or sliding down the parapet behind us on to the echoing duckboards. On these occasions, something located in your feet would fly up into your throat and completely put your breathing out of commission.

His coups were endless, and the amount of ammunition already expended in futile attempts to shoot him would have been enough to have wiped out the whole German army, if shot with any degree of accuracy. He had one wise precept, never to appear in daylight, that he had rigidly adhered to. Now at the zero hour, with the men, the time and the place, he walked calmly across the street. Surely the hand of fate guided that cat. Poor cat.

The response was instantaneous, but having an automatic instead of a rifle, I led with the first shot. Fate must have had something to do with that too. One rifle shot at that range would have ended that cat, whereas my automatic merely cut away one hind leg from the poor animal and sent it down the street in a series of erratic forward pitches and side falls.

"Kill it. Don't let it get away to suffer now that you have hit it." Some fifteen men stood up and fired at that animated ball of fur, and all missed. The ground was torn away over, under and around that cat, as if by magic, yet never a shot touched it.

Corporal O'Day ended the run. He fired one shot in a lull in the volleying like a punctuation mark to a sentence. It popped out clear and alone. The cat, with sharp lurch at the impact, rolled over and made no further move.

The sudden silence that followed came like a shock. O'Day looked suddenly worried and then the thin nasal cachinnation of the "Y" man broke, in an impassioned tirade, unnoticed on our ears.

My automatic was locked open. Mute testimony that I had stuck eight futile bullets in the path that cat had run. I remember abstractedly taking out the clip and freeing the mechanism. I was beginning to feel through my pockets for fresh shells, when, like a magnified echo, a sudden roll of sound came back to us from the enemy line. For a second we listened, immutable to that ever increasing sound.

"Duck," and we melted into flowing animation.

Later, in the cellar under the chateau, Sergeant Mathews laced us proper, in a little sheepish bunch. I lost my dog robbing job,[33] and was ordered to report to O'Day for duty on that patrol.

After a prolonged artillery bombardment from both sides and with both lines awake and fretful, we were ordered over on our miserable patrol. We spent several hours exploring the bottoms of shell holes, with our noses, under the flaming star shells. Then we ran into a German patrol and got scattered and lost all over "No Man's Land." The rest of the night we spent crawling back. Just before daylight we crawled into our own trenches. In spite of all the machine guns, rifles and grenade fire, we had not suffered a single casualty from this heroic undertaking. I doubt if the Germans did either. That poor cat was the only mortality of the day.

The "Y" man left, however. That final bombardment we brought down on his head was too much for him and he left firmly convinced it was all done out of spite to him.

4

Toward an Unknown Front—
Ancemont, Heippes, Hargeville,
Venault-le-Châtel

The following three accounts all occur just before or during the interrupted journey in mid–May 1918 from the Verdun Sector to the Montjavoult Training Area around Chaumont-en-Vexin, northwest of Paris. On the night of May 12–13, Seventy-seventh Company, including Linn, is relieved by the French in the Eix-Moulainville Sector and marched to Camp Savoyard. Early the following day all the companies of the battalion rendezvous at Ancemont and begin the long march southwest and away from Verdun.[1]

That Girl

This takes place sometime before the rest of the company was relieved by the French on May 12.

I remember once being attached as an escort, with my bunkie, to the supply train. Each company of the battalion had to supply men for this purpose. At first we did not like it. We were leaving our first front, hiking back through the country, and we wanted to drill along with our heroic companions; not trail along at the side of mule carts.

However, the thing had its compensations. The rest of the escorts proved to be dandy fellows, amusing talkers, good thieves, and generous to a fault. The headquarters' officers were friendly and democratic. They even gave us their horses to ride at times, while they stretched their legs in a bit of a hike.

The drivers of the wagons would weary of sitting all day and change off with us. If the major hove in sight one of the lieutenants would ride down the column and yell, "Hop on your seats, drivers; get in formation escort. Here comes the major."

We carried nothing but our automatics and wandered up and down the column at will. As long as there was one or two of us at the end to see, nothing was lost, we were never checked. We foraged both sides of the road, and visited all possible wine shops. With our many lifts we were as fresh at night as when we started in the morning, and we enjoyed our trip immensely.

Strange as it may seem, the companies always ran away from us on the road. From early in the morning, we seldom saw them, until sometime in the evening. We would pull into some small town and find the streets overrun with our men and the brooks lined with feet washers, solicitously inspecting blisters.

For a whole week we trailed across some lovely corner of France. The month was May and the weather beautiful. The people we passed seemed beautiful too, and always turned smiling faces to us, especially the young girls, that is, except one. People toiling in the green fields, or on barges on the rivers, waved to us. From gateway and window came smiles and greetings. So we wound our serpentine way along the tree shaded river banks, where another train in reverse marched below us, in the water; over antique bridges and through old wall guarded towns. We drank beer and wine in a hundred different cafes and each day the thing began anew, with a new set of scenes and events; only the people always smiled the same, except that girl.

The thing was nothing, yet it sticks in my mind. I even remember that town, its houses, streets and turns, as if I had but marched through it yesterday. And it is funny, for I have forgotten the looks of a hundred towns, in which I was quartered for days.

We saw it first, quite a way off, that town, its gray stone houses gleaming starkly in the sunlight across an upland plane. At somewhere about noon we were passing through its bare unshaded streets. It was not large. A pedestrian could easily traverse its greatest distance in fifteen minutes, but it was distinctive. All the houses were large, two or three storied, of gray stone, with ornamental doors and window frames. There were a good many stone porticoes, walled yards, and ornamental iron fences. The street was very wide. It was nearly, if not quite, three times the usual width, but there were no sidewalks and no shade trees. Despite its fine houses and ornamental stone work, the place seemed bare and dreary lying so on that open plain.

All the people we saw were well dressed, in keeping with the town, and no one seemed to be working. No one showed a very lively interest in our passing, nor returned our greeting with any great enthusiasm. And then there was that girl.

My canteen was empty and I was very thirsty. I had looked forward with certainty to getting it filled here, but there proved to be no fountain in those bare streets, and no open pump. We had marched nearly across the town, an abrupt turn in the street bringing the country again into view, on the far side, and my canteen was still dry on the inside. I would have to ask some resident for water.

Just after we made the turn, I saw two girls standing in a doorway watching the passing column and walked over to them. One was grown, the other was a little girl in short skirts. They both were dressed in city fashion and both were lovely girls, or maybe all girls looked lovely to me at that time.

The little girl watched my approach, but the older one looked steadily over my head at the passing column. Directly before her I stopped and said, "*D'eau, mademoiselle, s'il vous plaît?*"

She brought her eyes down to look me steadily in the face for a second, then once more returned them to the passing train, with a slight elevation of her chin.

I hate to be snubbed as badly as anyone, and she certainly took the wind out of my sails. A refusal of water to a thirsty soldier was something

Top: "And then there was that girl..." Sketch. It seems like a happy encounter.
Above: This is the woodcut that Linn made from the sketch. Notice that the soldier's uniform is much more prominent and the lady's outfit and the dark sky are more severe.

quite new to my experience of France. To add to my discomfort, Lieutenant Hollis, riding down the column, had taken in the whole scene and since I had not taken my canteen from its sheath, I knew his impression was that I had tried to flirt and got turned down. He gave me a wide grin of amusement. If I had had the canteen out, I would have sent it flying at his head for that grin.

The lieutenant passed, and I looked back at the girls. The older still watched with fixed gaze the passing train, but the little one was watching me shyly from behind the other.

"*D'eau*," I said, puzzled and shook my canteen to indicate its emptiness. "*D'eau*," she repeated. "*Oh! Oui, monsieur*," and she held out her hand for my canteen.

She returned almost directly with the filled canteen and stood smiling and making little bows as I thanked her.

I wanted to give her some little thing to show that other girl that favors done me were not unappreciated, but I had nothing to give. Then I remembered the French children were amazingly fond of our hardtack. The wagon carrying my pack was just passing. I ran across to it, slipped a box of hardtack out of my emergency ration and came back. I held out the box to the little girl and said, "*Biscuit*."

"*Pour moi?*" she asked, her face shining with delight as she took the box. Now the older girl came suddenly to life. She seemed suddenly to become conscious of what was happening.

"*Biscuit? Oh non, non!*" She snatched the box from the child and thrust it back into my hand.

"*Non, non, vous et...,*" and a whole lot more French that I did not understand. Her face however seemed to have softened. The large gray eyes looking squarely into mine were kind and sad, no longer haughty.

She had snubbed me, however unnecessarily, I thought, and I was still smarting inside. I waited until she was through talking, then said, "*Ce petite mademoiselle donnez-moi de l'eau. Je donnez sa biscuit a souvenir*," and I again gave the box to the little girl. I was turning away, but she caught me by the shoulder saying, "*Une minute.*"

She had taken the box from the child for the second time, and I guess my look was pretty black, for her tone was almost pleading as she said, "*Attendez-vous ici une minute?*"

I nodded assent, wondering what now, and she went quickly into the house.

The little girl and I stood watching the train. The wagons rattled slowly by, the drivers giving us curious glances. They had lost interest in our endless exploits. Hollis, at the end of the column, had turned about and was riding back, far over on the side, to come close by us. I could see by his face he had some smart crack to make in passing.

He came slowly on. He had me hypnotized. I could not look away or pretend that I did not see him to save me. I could see him just opening his jaws to speak, when a hand touched my shoulder and I turned to find the girl offering me a great glass of cold milk. As he passed I drank his health and gave him such an insulting wink, he ordered me to fall in the column, but he rode on without waiting to see if I obeyed.

I returned the empty glass, made my thanks to the unsmiling lady, and joined the column. I turned back once to wave. I watched to see if I got a response. Both girls waved, but only the little girl smiled.

Subsequently at inspection, I heard the captain say, "Where is your other box of hardtack?"

"Rats ate it, sir."

"Where are the pieces? They didn't eat the box too, did they?"

A Ghost Among the Tommies

The following takes place either in Heippes, after the first day's march (May 14), or in Hargeville, at the end of the second day (May 15).[2]

A British Tommy.

I drifted into the English canteen, a neat and delightful place, with a big coal stove burning brightly, English girls behind the counter and shelves piled with delicacies. Everything a soldier's heart could desire, and I had money. I just lounged, taking them all in. It was too good to buy, and so spoil my appetite.

I walked through a latticed door, decorated with crossed English flags, and came into the bar. Another coal stove burned here, and the place was full of kegs and barrels. Two heavily mustached Tommys were the presiding geniuses.

On benches at one of the tables was a group of English soldiers. One of them called out, "Hi, Sammy,[3] come over and have a bit to drink." They were drinking ale from a tin bucket. It was pushed over to me on my arrival, then recommenced its rounds. Each man drank in turn from the bucket.

Conversation started. Where was my outfit from? What service had we seen? Why were we here? Enlightened on these points, they gave me their own histories. After that the conversation became more general. We talked on all things from modern equipment to the Allies' war policy and laid out the campaign we would prosecute.

The tin of ale, in the meantime, went round and round, and as soon as it was emptied one of the men would take it up to the bar and have it filled again.

Our conversation had given way to individual chats and arguments. One man was idly turning the pages of a "Graphic."[4] I was explaining "Black Jack" to a little rat-faced, but war-humanized Cockney who had seen it played but did not understand it. Another lad, of about my own social level, that I wanted to talk to, leaned on his elbow listening to the explanations, and nodding from time to time as I caught his eye.

The man looking at the Graphic suddenly interrupted my explanation by shoving the opened magazine to me and saying with a crooked smile, "'Ere's your picture, matey."

Everyone stopped talking and looked at us for a second. As I took the magazine I had that queer sensation of familiarity with this event, of having been with these same men through this same moment.

On the open page of the magazine was a photograph and from it a face looked at me, with the same face with which I regarded it. We were so identical that the ego that was mine slipped into the picture and from its flat surface looked back at me, the living soldier. I was becoming hypnotized. Who were the living, who the dead? Or were we all dead and only dreaming we were alive?

To break the spell, I reached for the bucket to go and have it filled, but the Cockney caught it from my hand, shoving me back on the bench.

"Hear! You're a blooming guest, 'ands orf," and he took the can to be filled himself.

This was the episode of the French boy over again. I took back the magazine again and looked. The picture was in memoriam. He had been awarded the Victoria Cross, but he was dead and his ghost seemed standing at my elbow.

I wanted to get away now, and as if to hold me, these soldiers tried to give me everything they had. I emptied my own pockets of all the American insignia I had and fled. The ale had made me sick and the canteen goodies remained untasted.

An Assassination

The men of the Marine Brigade leave Hargeville at 8 A.M., and arrive in a severely exhausted state at Venault-le-Châtel that evening at 9:30, having covered 40 kilometers.[5] Here, in an area of small towns a few kilometers east of Vitry-le-François, the brigade will encamp from May 16 to the 18th, to rest and refit. The men will see to their personal effects and equipment, tend to their blisters, and undergo a light schedule of training.[6] It is thought that divisional maneuvers in open warfare could be conducted here, but the area will soon be deemed unsuitable and the Second Division will receive orders to move further to the west.[7] The following dark episode occurs during the day of May 16 and the subsequent night.

Our company led the battalion in that forced march and Old Wappejaw, [Captain Culper], mounted, set a fierce pace. Up to about eleven o'clock we kept pretty close to a four mile an hour clip, and for troops that means damn near running. Hardened by months of service, lean as greyhounds, we swung into that hike, with singing muscles and an actual joy in movement. At eleven o'clock we at the head, or what was left of us, reached the top of a five mile climb, completely shot: all in, burned up, with a quarter of our company lying senseless in the ditches behind.

Major Colin[8] and two officers of staff finally captured the head of the column, their horses white with lather, their faces red as fire. Major Colin ran his horse across the shoulder of our noble captain's horse, blocking his road. Everything stopped.

"You God damn fool, what are you trying to do?" His voice was so choked with fury that it was only a hissing whisper. "Kill the battalion?" His eyes flashed lances of fire into Old Wappejaw, stammering loose-jawed on his horse.

This happened at a fork in the road, and in the triangle was a wayside cavalry. I was not interested further in the conversation of that little knot of men, so I staggered over and dropped at the foot of the cross, claiming its thin ribbon of shadow. The rest dropped where they stood, in the ditch, in the dust of the road. A few had energy to climb the bank and escape the furious heat of the reflecting macadam.

The officers, infuriated, still talked. The sun picked them out in lines of fire, and beneath them their sweating horses lurched to each racking breath, with flaring nostrils and rigid necks. They wavered in the heat; everything wavered. The road seemed to have melted and begun to flow, and there was not a bit of shade on that high plateau.

Then the march began again, and on through that burning afternoon. We moved at a snail's pace now, with many rests. Like a maimed animal we dragged along, all order and formation lost. We moved any place we chose,

"Major Colin and two officers of staff finally captured the head of the column..."
Woodcut.

but we kept moving, and the sun seemed to be just above our heads, and burning us all to cinders.

I was dizzy and half-blinded; my head seemed to have no connection with the awkward jerking thing that was my body. It seemed to be floating along in space, sometimes before me, sometimes to the right of me, sometimes behind me. It took a willed effort to bring the two together. Only the persistent intention to go forward, while consciousness lasted, stayed steady in my head.

Someone hit my shoulder.

"Quit that."

"Quit what?"

"That infernal jabbering."

"I wasn't jabbering."

"You are a liar, or I'm crazy, and I don't care which."

That afternoon lasted an eternity. It had been so long since I had drunk I couldn't remember it, and there was no water on that plateau. I was not only thirsty, I was dried up, burned up.

Finally we began to descend and motion was easier. The sun seemed also to be getting farther away. In that strange unreal quiet that sometimes follows a day of stupendous heat, we dragged into the "Rue Grande" of Flurett[9] and were appointed billets. The whole battalion was in the town and we being the lead company had the guard.

We seemed to have brought a wave of exhaustion into the place, or else our exhaustion reacted on the natives, for they seemed as lifeless as we were. They moved with slow lethargic steps and seemed to be hardly conscious of our presence.

Evening came on, then night. A night of fantastically unreal quiet; not a breath of air; not a sound. The tree leaves hung wilted and still.

I was patrolling the "Rue Grande." The road beneath my feet loomed gray, the trees were black masses. There were no lights. At the end of my patrol was an old Gothic church with a squat bell tower and flying buttresses, some of them broken away. The thing looked like some partly decomposed monster, prophetic and terrifying. I began to dislike that end of my post.

At ten o'clock, Burk[10] and I made the rounds. We merely walked into each billet and put out the lights. That was the order for the night and we executed it. There was some verbal protest, as some of the men were drinking, but it went no further. As we left each billet, Burk said, "Don't light 'em again, yuh hear?"

I paid the Gothic church another visit, and returning found Burk lounging against the fountain, watching a faint light in one of the billets and there was the sound of men laughing and swearing. After we had watched for some time, Burke said, "Let's go; they gotta cut that stuff."

Before Burk's hundred and eighty pounds of muscle and bone, the props back of the door gave way and it swung open. A little group of men, two corporals and a sergeant, sat in a ring about a burning candle, with mess cups and bottles. They met our entrance with an angry snarl. Other men in their bunks, interested by the racket and caught in the candle light, stared at us silently.

"You fellows'll have to turn in. No lights after ten and no noise. That's the old man's [meaning Major Colin] orders," said Burk gravely.

"Get in your bunks and I will ditch your glim."

"You go to hell," replied the sergeant.

"Ain't any use getting hard," stated Burk. "I got my orders, and if you don't think it's going out, you can just step over to the guardhouse with me."

"You put that light out and by God I'll put your light out, you lousy God damn acting jack, you, what do you think of that?"

For answer Burk stepped into the circle and picked up the candle and blew it out. From the darkness his voice said, "You guys get into your bunks, and pipe down," in a tone of mounting fury.

Outside, with a memory of that group with reason unseated by the day's torture, supplemented by the night's liquor, I said, "You just started something."

"I know, you stay here. I want to go around and see if all the other posts are all right. Don't go in for anything until I get back. I will bring Keef as I come."

I sat on the fountain, uneasy and fretful, until the crunch of feet announced the return of Burk.

Burk, sergeant of the guard Keef, and two sleepy privates came up.

"What are they doing now," asked Keef.

"Same old thing, you can't see any light but they are beginning to get noisy."

"No use monkeying with them," decided Keef. "We'll get the sergeant. I think the rest will behave."

Standing outside, in the quiet of that night, the tattoo of blows Burk rained on the door with a rifle butt seemed like a profanation. In the blackness they echoed back to us from the building opposite. There was no result, only from within. The sergeant called, "Well, come in, you bastards, if you must." After that, there was a shout of laughter.

All together we forced the door. It came away suddenly at the hinges and we all practically fell in a most inglorious pile.

In a silence broken only by the drunken laughter of the sergeant, we regained our feet, breathing heavily and audibly. Keef, with the simplicity of vast experience, put his hand on the sergeant's shoulder.

"You are under arrest. Come on," he said.

Steadied by that grip on his shoulder, the sergeant wavered to his feet, and with surprising meekness allowed himself to be taken outside, by the two privates and Keef.

For the second time that night, Burk picked up the candle.

"Now the rest of you pipe down," he said sternly. "if there is any more noise in this billet tonight, you are all under arrest."

He met each pair of eyes in that circle and shot a glance around the bunks. No one answered him and he turned to the door, where I was waiting and blew out the candle.

As I stepped out, a roar like the cannon's mouth ripped into the night and Burk, striking the backs of my legs, sent me flying on my face. I was up in a second, but Burk was still and quiet, lying pitched over on his side.

"They have shot Burk," I shouted, for my hand had encountered the slippery warmth of flowing blood.[11]

There followed a few minutes of exciting activity, then everything straightened out. Poor Burk died on the way to the dressing station[12] and, with our whole company on guard, we paraded that billet. Drawn up in a double line, only partly dressed and surrounded with guards, there presently began a strange inquisition. Major Colin, who had arrived with some of his staff, along with the officer of the day (Old Wapperjaw) almost at the time it happened, took full charge. Starting at the head of the first line, he shot a flashlight into the man's face and asked, "Did you shoot that man?"

"No, sir."

He repeated the same question to the next and the next, for the length of the two lines and every answer was the same.

There was an angry movement from the guard at the last man's answer, checked instantly by the major's steely glance. We all liked Major Colin and trusted him a long way.

Again we walked to the head of the line, and again the whole program was gone through, with exactly the same result this time as before. He went back to the head of the line and started over again. He repeated this a countless number of times. Minutes dragged into hours and still the answers were always, "No, sir."

The guards were shifted for relief; a new officer took the flash and the major's place, but the same program continued hour after hour. And for the line of weary men, there was no relief. We slept in snatches and always awoke to that never ending litany, the moving officer with his flashlight, and that sinking line of men.

The strain of that ordeal was telling on those men. The whole line was in steady motion, wavering on their exhausted legs. Some were crying in exhaustion, their teeth chattered in uncontrollable nervousness and they shivered in that hot night. At last came the end.

One of the two corporals who had sat in the ring by the candle, said fiercely to the other, "Own up, we have had enough."

As we moved away, a strong air set all the tree leaves whispering sadly and that night of ghostly quiet was gone. A faint gray light was stealing in and our guard was nearly over.

5

Behind the Lines — Beaugrenier

Seventy-seventh Company leaves Venault-le-Châtel on the morning of May 20, marches to Vitry-le-François where they load onto a train around noon and, around 4:30 in the afternoon, begin the journey across France, rolling by rail until 7:30 the following morning when they arrive at L'Isle-Adam north of Paris. They unload and march 22 kilometers to Marines and billet for the night. The next morning, May 22, they march another 13 kilometers to Beaugrenier in the Montjavoult Training Area. Here they will remain until the end of the month, drilling, refitting, reorganizing and undergoing extensive exercises in open warfare.[1]

Our Buglers

The following events take place in Beaugrenier in the Montjavoult Training Area, sometime during May 22–30, 1918.

We had in our company two buglers, as most companies do; musicians Slack[2] and Tilson.[3] Slack was an elderly man small, thin, with sunken cheeks and colorless eyes. His clothes were always scrupulously clean, but his appearance in them was something like that of an animated scarecrow. They caved in where they should have bulged out and lacked all identity to the human figure they covered. I mean, Slack could have turned his head in reverse on his shoulders and started backwards without anyone being any the wiser from the appearance of his clothes. Mentally he was...— but who ever bothered what he was mentally. He was just Slack. It was almost a shock to learn that he was really an "old timer" and had grown gray in the service. The war-time barrack-shed office in which he now polished the benches with the seat of his trousers, was only one in a long chain stretching round the world. Yet he seemed to have brought nothing away with him from his travels, beyond a little more flatness from the many benches.

Tilson, on the other hand, was a little incarnate spirit of the devil. Still in his "teens" he was as muscular as a tom cat. With a likable, freckled face, and a big, good-natured mouth, he had a sunny disposition and was seldom out of humor. His clothes and hair were always in disorder as if he had but lately emerged from some heated conflict and that was not infrequently the case. It was almost a shock to discover that he was an "old timer" also, and had been in service at various posts in the tropics. He was stuffed full of impossible lies about these places, but it was amusing to hear him tell them nevertheless. Tilson had one besetting sin, either brought with him from his Georgia home or acquired under the tropic sun. He was infernally lazy and a strong objector to early rising.

Once upon an evening dreary, our battered and mauled company dragged its exhausted self into a small town, well back from the lines, and went into billets. One-third of the company and three-quarters of the officers were already there before us, having taken no part in the work which had detained us. They were quite fresh and rested, and we were at that stage of exhaustion when men become difficult to handle or control, what cattlemen call "on the peck." Yet such are the amazing ways of military procedure; we were given the guard, while our rested and refreshed third tucked themselves into their little beds for a nice cozy sleep. Exhausted beyond endurance, we were given the delightful task of walking up and down the streets of that miserable little town all night to make sure no one committed a nuisance on our post. We had no other orders.

Well, the thing didn't go down. It couldn't. We had reached the point where authority meant nothing to us. Sentries got drunk and went to sleep on their posts, refusing to be relieved, and threatening to thrash anyone who tried to take their posts away from

The bugler, Tilson.

them. Others wandered off in groups to the brook at the edge of the town, and there, dangling their feet in the water, drank "*vin rouge*" until they fell over asleep with their faces to the stars.

Sergeants and corporals wearied out with futile efforts to get some order in the guard, gave it up finally, and got drunk to keep from going crazy. If there was an officer of the day, I guess he got drunk too, for no one saw him.

Now Trumpeter Tilson, who was of the rested third, had been assigned that guard because Slack was in the hospital, too weak to stand on his feet. Tilson took this severely to heart and absorbed much bolshevism along with his "*vin rouge*." This was Slack's guard, he averred, and "they" had no right or business to assign him to it. So he went "on the peck" himself and also to sleep.

Sergeant Sloan, also of the rested third, had noted the disorder of the guard. Rising early the next morning, he came over to the guard-house to see that reveille was blown on time and thereby save the guard from detection, if possible. Everyone in the guard-house was asleep when he arrived. Ignoring the rest he searched out Tilson and undertook to shake him into life.

Now, Tilson was never strong on early rising, at the best of times; few lazy people are. This special time, with his head full of last night's wine fumes and his own wrongs, he refused to get up.

Sloan promptly dragged him spitting and cussing out on the floor, and gave him his bugle.

Tilson, now fully awake, realized it was Sloan, not Gordon, who was sergeant of the guard, who was annoying him. He hurled the bugle into the other end of the room and began to struggle to get back in bed.

"You ain't the sergeant of this guard. You lemme go. You can't give me no orders," he roared.

"Listen Tilson, stop that." Tilson was trying to bite his hand. "Will you blow that call?"

"I won't blow nothing and you let me go. You ain't the sergeant of this guard."

"Listen, you fool, its six o'clock and you are supposed to blow reveille. I waked you. If you don't blow that call, I'll report you, so help me Christ. What in hell's the matter with you anyhow?" he asked irritably.

Tilson couldn't answer that, but with a final wrench he tore loose and began getting stiffly back in bed. Just before his nose disappeared from sight, he declared finally, "I ain't going to blow no more calls in this guard, I ain't."

Sloan shot a harassed glance about the room. It was a shamble. Men lay about in all attitudes of drunken sleep; the air oppressive with the odor of stale wine and drying vomit. No help here, and the minutes were slipping away. He thought of the other bugler and, going to the end of the room, he snatched up Tilson's bugle and fled for the hospital.

Poor Slack, with a temperature of a hundred and four degrees, and a mind full of hallucinations, accepted the bugle and led to the door, set it to his lips and blew; but ten devils from hell, the call he blew was "pay-day." Three times did Sloan stop him and urgently impress upon the shaking invalid that the call desired was reveille. Each time Slack would nod reassuringly and setting his lips to the bugle, begin again the beloved call of "pay-day." Finally Sloan let him go, wondering in his own mind how it would end.

Waking up about noon that day, I went over to the galley to see what were the chances of eating. A ring of men screaming with laughter near the kitchen attracted my attention. I went over to see what was so funny. It was Tilson. Three or four big, dirty cook boilers, a bucket of water, ashes, and soap and scrub brushes among them, and Tilson hard at work scouring one of the boilers. He was smeared from head to foot with pot black and his face was a study. He was crying in spite of himself, and, daubing away the tears, he invariably daubed on more pot black. Such another face you never saw. The more he daubed, the more the men laughed, and the more they laughed, the more he cried. It was pathetic. Of that wild guard on him alone did retribution fall.

Dizzy Lizzy

The following events take place in Beaugrenier in the Montjavoult Training Area in the last few days of May 1918.

Her real name was *Henries Jharkesa Chardnera*, or something like that, but to our outfit she was simply "Dizzy Lizzy," and in our short stay at that farm,[4] she endeared herself to every one of us. She appeared to be the entire motive force of that big farm and I mean it moved. Her day included such little things as rising, God knows when, feeding and watering the stock, cooking the breakfast for her uncle's family and the six German prisoners and their two guards allotted the farm, milking the cows, and then she would wash the breakfast dishes and be ready to go into the field for her day's work. Besides all of this, she had a lot of variegated pet animals and poultry to which she gave daily and personal attention. At night her duties became too multitudinous to enumerate. The mere thought of them makes my pen falter in exhaustion. Necessarily she was a traveler. She fairly flew from morning to night, hence the name "Dizzy Lizzy" with the added expletive "Full Speed Ahead."

At night she was always ready to sew our clothes, replace buttons, and cut our hair. She would jump in the door of the barn, in which we lived, with a gay little shout and then flash her eyes all around to see what we were doing. Sometimes we would be taking a bath. This would not disconcert her, but it would us. We would naturally have to throw her out until we were in suitable condition to receive a lady.

She was always merry and cheerful and would drag us from our heavy apathy, that had grown almost habitual with us, by her squeals and shouts of glee. If nothing else served, she would sing "*Madelon*" of which we were very fond, only she sang it in French, which we did not understand. She also worked with a will, an old copybook, and a stub pencil to master our language and tried at the same time to teach us her own.

Now I should love to describe her as a fairy princess, combining all the graces and beauties known to the visual world, but she was not. She had them all, but they were of the spirit. Her favorite character, "*Madelon*," was but a poor shadow to this living girl we all took so lightly. She was strong and active, but bent with hard manual labor; her face was plain, the skin colorless and rough from exposure, her hair scant and towey. Only in her motile gray eyes did her truly heroic spirit peep forth.

No, it was by sheer force of will, a will to please and help, she conquered us all, with not a bit of coquettish grace or charm, except what she burlesqued to amuse us, to help her out. We soon came to look forward to her coming and made much of her. Forgetful of her long day's work in the fields, we would keep her singing and dancing or screaming with laughter at our ridiculous French, until her uncle came to get her at midnight, and she was happy, happy in this endless self-sacrifice.

I used to make pencil sketches of her at her various occupations with some success, to the vast amusement of the gang. The most distinguishing feature of her costume was an apron made of Purina feed sack, decorated with usual red checkerboard. Her pride and delight in this garment were tremendous, partly on account of its being American, I suppose, and partly on account of the bright red pattern. I could always get a kick into these sketches by putting in the red squares with a piece of crayon. In spite of the obvious fact that they were caricatures, someone showed them to her. She was quite overcome with embarrassment at my showering so much honor upon her. After much difficulty of understanding on my part, she offered to "dress up" on the following Sunday if I would care to draw her. This, I begged her to do. I couldn't, to save me, picture Dizzy dressed up.

That Saturday night, in the light streaming from the open door of the farm house, the paymaster shelled out our frankies over a little table borrowed from the farmer, the whole proceedings watched attentively by the farm staff "*en masse.*" Even the German prisoners were allowed to come out and see. The men lined up alphabetically, lounged along the house wall awaiting their turns. In the security of a language not understood, they spoke with complete frankness concerning their wishes and desires. Their remarks were hard and to the point. It was rather amusing as the persons spoken of were all standing near but absolutely unconscious of being under discussion.

"I don't want to get drunk, I tell you," Private Mullen was saying, "I want a sweetie."

"Well, you will never get 'Black Eyes' ['Black Eyes' was the farmer's daughter], opined Private Moleskin."[5] "She can't see anything unless it's got tin bars on its shoulders."

"Maybe you better try Dizzy Lizzy or the Old Lady. You're not much on looks yourself, you know."

"I guess your last hope's the old lady, pard." Private Mills, late of Montana, regarded his neighbor with a grin of amusement "That Frenchman, Blanche, is riding herd on Dizzy."

"Then I shall try for the old lady, decided Mullen. "I like her best anyway. Her belly's so big and her legs so skinny, she looks like a pollywog."

Two or three times that evening in lulls in the racket at the cafe, Montana's

Dizzy all dressed up. This is the woodcut (there is no sketch).

remark came back to annoy me. I knew Blanche too well. A prince on the line in times of danger, behind the lines he was a rotter. Poor Dizzy to fall into his hands.

Sunday morning, sleep and a cup of coffee and in perfect bodily comfort, I must again take up my mental worry, yet what could I do? It was no business of mine. There were six visible crap games in operation and under a wagon shed the chaplain conducted divine services for the benefit of six soldiers. The similarity of numbers struck me as amusing but neither occupation offered any relief. Blanche was helping Dizzy with her morning chores and the sudden slackening off in her gait convinced me she had or soon would forget her promise to pose. I decided to get drunk on my own.

The cafe was empty and a Sunday quiet rested under the vine-trellised yard where the tables were. The sunlight fell through the leaves in patterns on the oak boards.

"*Cognac, une bottle,*" I yelled at the one-legged proprietor, who had finally answered my thumping on the table.

He stood staring at me for a long time, but finally decided I was sober and went away for the liquor, with a shake of his head.

A large iridescent "blue bottle fly" kept whizzing noisily about my head, making sudden hard landings on the table only to immediately launch itself into buzzing flight. It annoyed me. At last it landed too close, and with a bang that made my hand tingle, I smashed it to a repulsive jelly on the board. The action or the cognac suddenly relieved my mental tension, and I began to laugh until the tears stood in my eyes. Yes, of course, I was the blue bottle; a lot of good my buzzing would do. I would probably get slapped for my pains. Better let life take its own course. Some part of my mind, however, remained unconvinced, pointing out to me that I was following a drunken logic, but I clung to my new peace of mind and kept on drinking, staring straight before me.

Out of the gathering mist, Blanche materialized at my side.

"Well, you're a hot one, go off and get drunk by yourself."

"Oh go to hell," I invited him. Everything was becoming slow and rhythmic. He jarred upon me.

"Dizzy's all dressed up to have her picture drawed," he continued "I have been looking all over for you."

"Tell her to go to hell too," I heard my own voice say as I raised my eyebrows in an effort to focus my sight on him. He seemed to be getting larger and closer to me.

Then he said, "Say, kid, that fool girl has actually saved up eight hundred francs, so I am taking her to Paris to get married. Ha-ha, on her eight hundred, get me?" and he dug me in the ribs.

"You ought to be shot," I finally managed to articulate, but he had probably been gone a long time when the remark became audible.

I remained sitting there, the contents of the bottle going slowly down, and then suddenly I was being furiously shaken by someone. The day had somehow suddenly departed and only a faint pink in one quarter of the sky told where. Shorty was at my side. Over miles of space I heard his words disconnected and unimportant.

"Germans broken through. On to Paris. We to stop them. Company's formed. I made your pack, come on."[6]

He dragged me away, still only faintly comprehending the import of his words.

Rocking dizzily on my feet, with the world spinning below me, fully conscious of the situation now, I cursed myself for being drunk at such a time and fought to keep my equilibrium.

Slater pushed me back into the rear ranks where my weaving would be less conspicuous and said, "Hang on until after inspection. We are going in trucks so you will be all right."

He turned to the platoon. "Corporals report their squads."

"Second squad, one man absent."

"Hell! Who is it?"

"Blanche."[7]

6

The Attack — Belleau Wood

It is May 31 and the entire Second Division is on the move. Four days earlier, on the 27th, Ludendorff unleashed his third great offensive, this time against the French. Once again, initial successes are overwhelming. Twenty-five German divisions sweep across the Chemin des Dames, capturing Craonne, and crossing the Aisne and the Vesle. Soissons falls on the 29th and on the following day the Germans reach the Marne, capturing Château-Thierry and Dormans. Here they stand poised to march up the Marne valley some 45 miles to Paris. The Allied high command is in upheaval, close to panic. In the capital, where the rumbling of artillery is audible for the first time since 1914, the government makes plans to move to Bordeaux and residents flee the city in droves, a million in two weeks.

The British are in no position to slow this German breakthrough which threatens the two major railheads in the country, Paris and Amiens, as they are tied down in the north, while the French themselves are in a broken, disorganized rout. All the Allies have left are two untried American divisions, the First and the Second. No one expects them to do more than slow the German advance and perhaps buy some crucial time.

What the European allies fail to appreciate is that these two Yank divisions, though composed mostly of green troops, are led by Regulars, and overall are surprisingly able and tough. And what Allied intelligence has so far failed to discern is that the German divisions on the Marne are in terrible condition, plagued by dysentery and malnutrition, and that they have completely outrun their supply lines. They are very near the end of their endurance. Nonetheless, they are seasoned and shrewd, with several years of combat experience under their belts, and are masters at making the best of dire straits. They seize the high ground in and around the key area of Belleau Wood, and dig in in depth and in strength. Their artillery and machine gun emplacements are plentiful and well-ranged, while the earliest Marines to arrive have neither automatic weapons nor heavy guns. With the odds tilted heavily in favor of the German defense, the scene is set for slaughter.[1]

An Endless Line of Refugees

The following begins northwest of Paris in the village of Beaugrenier on May 31 and ends in the town of Saint-Soupplets on June 1. Virtually every witness who left a record of this journey describes scenes of chaos, with roads choked by disorganized French troops in retreat and endless lines of refugees, loaded with all manner of household goods, streaming away from the advancing German army.

I remember the sinking sensation of being detailed to remain behind. We had formed the company in the road before the farm at which we were billeted. It was night and the air seemed charged with the electrical thrill of oncoming danger. We had been told that the occasion was dire, only the fighting men were to go. Office force, galley and supply train were to come on afoot. The fighters were to be whirled in that night by truck and we were called out of rank to take up our old job as guard. We might later be thankful for it, but that night we were bitter and sore. We went back to the hay to sleep and avoid seeing the others depart.[2]

The next morning[3] was bright and sunny. A strange quiet rested on the place and a strange lassitude. We lounged about with nothing to do. Finally we went up to the picket line in hope of diversion. We could not get away from the picture of our company in the roar and crash of battle, with legions of onslaughting "huns," fighting like the heroes we knew them to be, powder-blackened and grim-eyed, but holding the line, and we back here moving indolently about in this trance-like quiet.

The picket line was equally overcome with inertia. A few tents and the long line of mules quietly eating hay crowned the top of a low hill. The skinners lay about in little groups on the grass swapping lies and jokes.

"Oh, you-all don't need fret yo-self, you-all get enough wah yet," Bole-weevil consoled us. We had been singing the blues about being left behind.

Finally a crap game started, and this kept us amused until the order came to get ready to move.

About noon[4] we did finally get underway and marched all afternoon. We arrived at some time before dark, in the edge of quite a large city.[5] We halted for a time at the side of the way across from a legalized house of prostitution. A French officer coming out noted us, lowered his head and walked hurriedly away. Some privates lounging on the steps waved greeting to us. A group of girls climbed to one of the window ledges to see *"Les Amériques."*

Sergeant Cuffey on the instant began to display himself. Cuffey was a headquarters noncombatant sergeant and the most conceited ass in the battalion. He wore officer's clothes, without the Sam Brown, of course, had a fat round face, and was red headed. He tried to get his nose, a snub one very much turned up, into everybody's business, but had a yellow streak of cowardice that made him back up from the lousiest mule skinner, if the skinner began to look dangerous, and yet in spite of all this and an awful propensity to brag, he was a likable sort of cuss too, maybe because he so continually made such a fool of himself.

Now he walked into the middle of the road and looked the train over critically, made several observations to the skinners, to which they paid no attention, and finally turned about to see if any of the girls were watching him. Here he did a little business on his own account, registered surprise at seeing girls. His face lighted up with surprised pleasure. He had not dreamed there were any girls within a hundred miles.

"Here's where I get a sweet kiss," he told us over his shoulder, as he walked toward the window. By now he had more or less caught the attention of the whole column.

The girl, slim and pretty, watched him approach with a smiling face, but when he took her elbows to draw her down, her expression turned to one of alarm. With sudden alacrity, she planted her foot hard and solid on Cuffey's chest, and kicking out, she sent him reeling into the gutter.

Cuffey regained his balance and stared in amazement while the girl with a frightened face, retreated hastily back through the window. The roar of laughter from the column was only downed by the order to advance.

At this town we entrained[6]; no mean task loading that whole column of wagons, carts and baggage on freight cars, but urged on by the officers we went at it with a will. The mules were the last thing to put on and offered the most difficulty. There was no loading platform so they had to be forced up a gang plank and into the cars. This they wouldn't do, instead, they would brace their front feet and squat with their back legs, right at the bottom, and no amount of pulling or whipping could induce them to go up the plank. Finally we evolved a system. Two of the biggest men would catch hold of each other's hands under the mule's rump, and the rest of us would push all along his sides. In this manner we would literally lift the animal off his feet and rush him up the incline.

Our activities at this time were furnishing great amusement to a little gang of English Tommys, perched on the yard fence, who, after the manner of the English, soon passed from laughter to jeers and personal comment. I will admit there was plenty of material for laughter incidental to our getting those crazy wild brutes in the cars, but we got them in, and we didn't need any comment from the English army.

"Wait 'til they are loaded. Wait 'til they are loaded," begged the stable sergeant,[7] for we had all had enough English satire.

Our tempers had not been improved by our task, and when the last mule had been heaved aboard, we turned with one accord — and that a grim one — on our tormentors. We were all armed with sticks with which we had been beating the mules and our intentions being so evident, the Tommys retreated over the fence and began a fighting retreat with rocks. One little bunch of our men, by sneaking up the fence, fell suddenly on their flanks, and in the disorganization that ensued, we managed to close with them. From then on their retreat was a rout, we whacking them mightily and well as we ran. The last we saw of them, their legs were still flying beneath them.

We only stayed on that train one night. Sometime after daylight the next morning we pulled into another large town,[8] and were told to unload. A lot of work for the ride we got.

The station yard was packed with people, and goods waiting for trains, but outside the big ornamental iron gates everything was perfectly quiet and normal. Garcons were taking down shutters, sweeping the gravel or arranging the small iron tables before the cafes. We were surprised.

We moved grandly around a big circular park, tree-shaded and grass-plotted, surrounded by big imposing

Top: "All day as we marched they streamed by with their set faces and queer conglomeration of salvage." Sketch.
Above: The woodcut of the sketch, the final product. Notice the people are going in the opposite direction. Unless the carving is reversed, the print will be a mirror image, which is what happened here. The heavy dark areas give a feel of desperation.

hotels. The sidewalks were gay with striped awnings and well-dressed people. Then we turned into a side street, and in three minutes we were in another world. A road full of frightened fugitives with their pitiful bundles of household goods and gods, bringing the war very close in their haste and exhaustion.

All day as we marched they streamed by with their set faces and queer conglomeration of salvage. At places they were forced into the ditches and fields, the road being banked with advancing soldiers and munitions. They did not complain but went on as best they could. The road wound through every variation of peaceful scenery, through picturesque villages, and over ancient stone bridges; by old churches and overgrown graveyards. Yet wherever it ran there moved this endless line of refugees. Toward night it began to diminish, finally falling away to only hurrying isolated groups, and we knew we were closing on the line.

On the Grounds of a Great Chateau

This takes place on the evening of June 1 in Château Marigny and the adjoining village of Marigny-en-Orxois, located about two kilometers west of Belleau Wood.

At dark[9] we turned into the park of a great chateau[10] and beneath the trees edging an artificial lake we camped for the night. Here we picked up the thunder roll of the cannon.

After supper, Tommy and I went off to the village.[11] At the chateau gate we found Ratting. There were French sentries here and he was uncertain if they would let us proceed, however, they did, without any remark.

The village was unlighted and abandoned, only occasional French soldiers hurried through. A threatening quiet brooded in its empty streets.

At the public fountain we were seized upon by two French soldiers, who, with much whispering and drinking of their thumbs, led us to an open cellar door and departed. We went down the stone steps to a large vaulted cellar, whose walls were lined with barrels and kegs and cases of liquor. It must have been the cellar of

"At the public fountain we were seized upon by two French soldiers..."

the village cafe, for most of the barrels and kegs had stop corks. We went from one to another, mess cup in hand, sampling each in turn. Twice we filled our canteens only to pour them empty again, because we found something we liked better. In a final decision between cherry brandy and Malaga wine, we all chose the latter, and after filling our canteens for the last time we departed.

The cellar of the village café. Woodcut.

Tommy, being somewhat the worse from his many samplings, we conducted back to the gate on his way to camp. The better to insure his early sobriety we gave each of the sentries a drink from his canteen, and starting him up the drive, we turned back into the town.

The chateau we found was being used as a dressing station.[12] In a lane leading up to it we came on a line of parked ambulances.

Passing a little group of drivers, one of them turned and said, "Hello Americans."

He was an American himself and had been two years in a French ambulance corps, hence the good English. We stood talking by his ambulance. He showed us several places where shell fragments had torn into the car.

"Two bad," he remarked. "I had two men killed in my ambulance the trip before last."

"What's doing up front?" we asked.

"Ah, the French are coming back as fast as they can, they evacuate towns before we can get the wounded out," he told us.

"Last trip we ran into a town that the Germans had; we thought the French still held it. There were only two of us but we turned our cars around and got out under fire. On the road we picked up a lot of exhausted Poilus that would soon have been taken."

We whistled softly at the direness of these tidings and the thunder roll in the distance became more menacing.

"The line," he presently continued, "is only about five miles away now. I would not be surprised if the Germans take this place by morning."

Again we fell quiet. We had been talking in whispers, I don't know why, and that oppressive, threatening silence gathered about us. To break it we gave our new friend, and the rest of the drivers, a drink of wine and in return they gave us cigarettes. At the end of this exchange an order was called to them, and with a hasty goodbye, our acquaintance ran with the rest of the drivers to start his engine.

"Day and night now," he called to us as the cars moved off. "Good luck," and he was gone in the night.

Coming in at the upper gate between two parked lines of some French staff automobiles, we ran into an illuminated Frog wearing a Croix de Guerre cord. We were all very convivial and embraced each other heartily, and, it apparently being his wish, did an impromptu dance together in the road. He kept assuring us over and over: "*Les Amériques sont bon homme du soldat.*"

He had probably learned what we did not know at that time, that it was our men who had stopped the German advance.[13]

After the dance, he took us to one of the cars and with much courtesy began ushering us up the steps into its interior. At that moment someone called and he answered. Hastily, not to say rudely, pushing us inside, with a cautioning shh-shh-shh, he dropped the canvas end, just as the crunch of gravel underfoot came up to the car.

Whoever it was stopped and there began an interminable conversation, carried on in whispers with our new acquaintance. They moved about crunching the gravel beneath their feet, but never got far enough away for us to duck out. Time dragged heavily. By the faint light that leaked in and our sense of touch we ascertained we were in some officer's car. There was a small bunk on which we sat, a desk, several metal cases, and a cabinet. Beneath the bed at one end was a small trunk, and under the head, merciful heaven, a basket of champagne. Our position continued to grow more and more irksome as time dragged on. Not only did we not want to be caught in some officer's quarters, but we were growing increasingly weary of sitting still on the edge of the bunk.

Finally, the whispering having ceased for some time, we decided the two outside had departed and each taking a pair of champagne bottles we got softly under the curtain and down the steps. We turned about to face a French officer and his Batman staring at us goggle-eyed in surprise. For a moment we stared too, then bowing to them gravely, the bottles clinking together musically in the process, we moved off at a leisurely pace up the drive. Out of view in the dark, we sprang upon the grass, where our feet would make no noise, and took to our heels across the park.

We crossed the lake by an ornamental foot bridge, stopping in the middle to dangle our legs and drink one of the bottles of champagne. We nearly strangled to death trying to catch the fuzzy stuff in our mouths and not waste any. In the excitement, one of the bottles got knocked off the bridge and was lost. Hiding the other two in our clothes, we rejoined the column.

Tommy had crawled under one of the carts and gone to sleep. The rest of the camp was listening to Sergeant Cuffey tell of one of his many amazing conquests with the ladies.

My brain, under the stimulus of the champagne, seemed to me to be just scintillating. I waited until Cuffey came to the end of his story, then said in a loud voice, "I think that's all a God damn lie," and retreated hastily into the train, followed by a roar of laughter.

The Watch

Pvt. Linn's movements following his night at Château Marigny are unrecorded, but within a day or two he will have returned to Seventy-seventh Company. On June 6th — a dark day in Maine Corps history, when they will lose more men in one day than they have lost in their entire previous history — Seventy-seventh Company supports the attack of Major Ben Berry's Third Battalion, Fifth Marines across a 44-yard open wheat field against the heavily-fortified stronghold of Belleau Wood.[14] Members of the Seventy-seventh Company will participate in two other assaults against Belleau Wood and the village of Bouresches over the next week or so. But this initial attack with Berry's battalion matches Linn's description most closely. The attack begins at 5 o'clock in the evening and lasts until sometime after dark. Advancing over open ground for the length of four football fields in the face of enfiladed machine-gun fire and artillery, Berry's battalion is completely chewed to pieces and never quite makes it to the wood. Under constant heavy fire from Belleau Wood, where the Germans have over 200 well-protected machine guns, the Marines lay flattened in the wheat, scarcely able to move, praying for darkness.[15]

It was the third night of the drive, and we were all pretty much done in. We crawled forward through a wheat field that seemed interminable, trying ever to come up on that phantom foe that always retreated before us,[16] yet strew our course with shells and bullets. Two days and two nights, almost without food, and sleep, or water, and under the most violent physical exertion.

We showed it. Our eyes were red rimmed and bloodshot, faces sunken and dirty, with streaks down from the eyes, where the over-driven excretion had tracked the dirt. Our hands were maimed masses of blood, powder-blackened and filthy. Our clothes were in tatters from the barbed wire.

We moved steadily forward under a nasty machine gun cross fire that mowed the wheat about us, and occasionally mowed us, in dogged determination, our mouths open and all wearing a fixed wrinkled grin of torture.

It was June and blazing hot. We had not drunk in six hours. Six hours on that burning chalkstone plateau, our bodies powdered and throats caked with dust, that rose in a veil about us at every movement. Six hours of unceasing exertion, and an agony of thirst. Then we stopped and stopping we slept.

From some far land, I was beaten into consciousness. A small radio-light watch was thrust into my hand by my neighbor. He said, "Watch one hour. Wake next man," and was asleep, in the act of stretching out. One leg was left still bent uncomfortably under him.

I groaned and looked at the watch. Both hands were on the one. Like most French nights, this one had turned bitter cold, and I was soaked to the skin with dew. The wheat was almost running water, but I was no longer thirsty, I was freezing.

I sat hunched up, hugging my knees, with my teeth chattering, and stared off into the darkness. It was unearthly quiet, after the roar of the past two days. On the far horizon, three fires sent up columns of dim red light, but both sides had apparently exhausted their flare guns, for the darkness remained unbroken.

Back of me, somewhere in the wheat, two wounded men were moaning steadily, and just before me, the stark face of a dead German stared up at the stars, with open eyes. One of the wounded men moaned with a steady hoarse regularity, with each rasping breath, and the sound he made was ghoulish and could not be located. It came now from here, now from there. Sometimes it seemed to come from the sky overhead, and again from the earth beneath me. The other one whimpered in a thin high falsetto tone, at times giving a hideous burlesque of a child laughing. They were long drawn out and climbed steadily in key until the last high note broke. At each break, you knew it was that soul's last sound on earth, but each time as your nerves let down in relief that racking cry would begin again, and through it all ran that hoarse, steady moan of the other. These two sounds alone broke the stillness beneath the stars.[17]

What hell of pain could wring such sounds from a human being? Well, I would probably find out soon enough, and I looked at the dead German. In the starlight his face looked calm and composed. I had started out envying live rats, now I envied a dead soldier his rest and peace.

Staring into that still face in that awful hour, unable to see the good I did, and racked by physical agony, I would have gladly changed places with him. For him it was all over and there was peace.

I shook the man next to me into life. "Watch one hour. Wake next man." My hour was done, and I was asleep.

Top: "The Watch." Drawing. "I sat hunched up, hugging my knees, with my teeth chattering, and stared off into the darkness."
Above: The woodcut of "The Watch."

Holding Up the "Y"

After having participated in several attacks on Belleau Wood and an attack on Bouresches, the Marines of Seventy-seventh Company would remain in the line until June 23, when they were relieved and marched to a wood one kilometer east of Montreuil-aux-Lions where they bivouaced.[18] Linn's and "Tadpole's" visit to a YMCA hut behind the lines takes place sometime just before that relief. Linn's statement that the infantry was "making war history these past twenty days" is no exaggeration. Headlines about the Marines at Belleau Wood stopping the German drive and saving Paris had appeared around the world and made them — during late June and early July — the most celebrated regiment in the war. Considering the ordeal these two Marines had undergone in the previous three weeks, their reaction upon being refused service by a punctilious "Y" clerk is understandable.

Into the continuously shifting line of graves,[19] from which we fought on a certain front, came word that a "Y" had opened behind a battery of artillery, about two miles behind us. At that time we were in desperate straits for tobacco, and that was a fighting front, and cigarettes were the one relief to our over-strung nerves. We diligently saved all our butts until we had enough for a new cigarette, smoked the dry quids of the chewers, anything in fact, that was tobacco. There was no fastidiousness in that inferno.

With the consent of the corporal, a little slight man with an enormous head, "Tadpole," and I undertook to sneak back and find that "Y." The fighting was all at night so we traveled through the perfect quiet of a spring day, once we were back out of sniping range. The woods were a maze of tender greens and song birds twittered and sang in the boughs. Except for some engineers burying dead bodies, you could hardly have believed this ground was nightly the scene of the wildest human conflict.

We found the "Y" and our jubilation knew no bounds.

"How much can we buy?" we asked.

"One of each thing," we were told.

"All right, give us the limit, please."

Two little piles were quickly accumulated before us. Each contained one can of tobacco, one pack of cigarettes, one plug of chewing tobacco, one cake of chocolate, and one pack of cookies.

We were counting out our frankies to pay, when the secretary said, in a conversational voice, "Why, you boys are out of the infantry, ain't you?"

Now the infantry had been making war history these last twenty days, so we proudly acknowledged we were. Almost on the instant the counter was bare. To our blank stare, this man said, "I am attached to the artillery, I can't sell to infantrymen."

"At that time we were in desperate straits for tobacco..." Woodcut.

In words that would have brought tears to a glass eye, we told that man of our privations and necessities at the front. We pleaded with all the eloquence of despair, but he would not let us have a thing. Then we got mad. Our tempers were not of the best just then, and the sight of all that stuff and the need at the front was too much. After a short conference together in whispers, we came back to the counter and presenting our automatics, we said, "Put that stuff back here or we will blow your God damn head off."

The secretary dived under his counter, but his runner had fled for the guard. The guard arrived, so we did nothing. Behind the guard came a captain of artillery. The secretary's nose again appeared above the counter and he began to put his case to the officer. From the drift of his harangue, it was evident that he expected the officer to have us tied over the noses of a couple cannons that were being fired frequently and given a ride on the next shell going out for what we had done to him. The captain now turned on us, very military, very hard eyed, but no fathead artillery officer ever got us "Yah-yahing." He undertook to give us the third degree.

"We are out of a company in action on the front, and you undertake to hold us here on any crazy charges of a fool of a 'Y. M. C. A.' man that we haven't hurt or taken a thing from. You will pretty soon find yourself in a hole," we told him.

So great was our prestige at that time that this dignitary, after considering this a moment, invited us to get back to that place where we were so much in demand, and not to come back either. We went.

When we told our adventure back at the front, it was only the absolute necessity of not leaving that prevented the platoon from going back en masse and annihilating that "Y" man and his store; and the artillery too, if they offered any interference.

Six or seven days later, Tadpole and I, now serving as runners, had an occasion to go back through that wood on the morning following a night of hard fighting. We arrived on the spot from which we had been so ignominiously routed, but what a change was there. The artillery was gone, its dead unburied. The trees that had camouflaged it were uprooted and shattered. Fresh turned shell holes were everywhere. A shattered and mangled gun carriage and a pile of dead artillery men told of one direct hit for the Heinies.

The "Y" hut was still there, apparently unhurt, but strangely quiet. We approached it and leaning on the counter looked in. On the floor lay the secretary, with one side of his head half cut away. We regarded him with complete indifference; he was just another stiff now. We helped ourselves free gratis to his supplies and went on with our message.

7

The Line — Soissons

Very shortly after Linn and Tadpole pay their fateful visit to the Y south of Belleau Wood, on June 23rd, Seventy-seventh Company is relieved from front line positions in Belleau Wood and Bouresches and is marched to a wood just west of Montreuil-aux-Lions where, over the next few days, they are joined by the other companies of the battalion. Here they remain until July 4, when the battalion is moved to a wood surrounding a chateau just south of St. Aulde. The following day the battalion occupies reserve positions between Bézu-le-Guéry and Villers-sur-Marne, where for the next ten days they dig trenches, construct machine gun emplacements and string barbed wire in anticipation of a large-scale attack which never materializes.[1]

Also during this period the men of the Marine brigade rest, refit and receive replacements. During the previous month the Second Division sustained nearly 10,000 casualties and they are now badly in need of some serious R and R. The war, however, waits for no man, and the soldiers of the Second Division are soon to have their sojourn of peace and relaxation cut short.

On July 15, Ludendorff unleashes his fifth offensive, code-named "Friedensturm," against French and American positions, attacking with 43 divisions along a 50-mile front, from east of Reims south to the Marne. The Marine brigade, bivouacked on the Marne, has their sleep disturbed in the pre-dawn hours by the German barrage, audible upriver from the other side of Château-Thierry.

As it happens, General Foch, supreme commander of the Allied forces, has already planned a major counter-strike with the purpose of reducing the huge German salient. He places eighteen divisions in the hands of the notorious French general Charles "the Butcher" Mangin, renowned for achieving his aims whatever the cost in the lives of his own soldiers. Among the divisions under his command will be five American divisions, including the Second.

With virtually no warning or time for preparation, Second Division head-quarters receives orders on the evening of July 15 that they are now under French authority and that they should make ready to move within 24 hours, destination unstated. The Second Division commander, General Harbord, will later write: "A division of twenty-eight thousand men ... had been completely removed from the control of its responsible commander and deflected by marching and truck through France to a destination unknown to any of the authorities responsible either for its supply, its safety, or efficiency in the coming attack." The last-minute preparations and the secrecy are meant to ensure a surprise attack but their practical effect is to stretch the physical and mental endurance of the men and officers of the Second Division to the breaking point.[2]

The next day, July 16, Headquarters, Sixth Machine Gun Battalion, receives orders to assemble that same evening at the Bezu-Montreuil-Saint Aulde crossroads at 5 o'clock and make camp for the night. At 4 in the morning of July 17, the battalion loads onto a convoy of French camions and disappears northward into the darkness. The supply train follows on foot.[3]

The Terrible Night March

The following begins early the morning of July 17 when the Marines of Seventy-seventh Company are picked up by camions at 4 A.M., with their machine guns, ammunition and accoutrement, at the crossroads of the Ussy-Lizy roads just outside of Montreuil-aux-Lions. They ride northward for eleven hours, in extremely uncomfortable conditions, until arriving at a point about a kilometer and a half south of Taillefontaine at 3 o'clock in the afternoon. Here they get off the buses and march into the Bois de la Taillefontaine where they make camp. Then at about 10:30 that night, they begin marching northward on the Villers-Cotterets-Soissons road through the ancient royal Forêt de Retz.[4]

This night will be especially horrendous. There are 28,000 men of the Second Division on this march towards Soissons, as well as numerous other divisions, American, French, Moroccan, Senegalese, and others, all jammed together on a single highway through the Bois de Retz, during a ferocious thunderstorm in pitch blackness, in a sea of mud, with falling tree limbs injuring and even killing soldiers, absolute confusion everywhere, men separated from their units, nearly every unit lost without maps, mixed up with other units, and most of them badly off-schedule. It is impossible to know who is where at any given time.

Finally, at 3 A.M., the men of the Sixth Machine Gun Battalion arrive at the northern edge of the Forêt de Retz where, due to total exhaustion, they are permitted to stop and sleep along the road for about four hours. Then at 7 the next morning, July 18, according to the battalion history, they continue their march to Verte Feuille Ferme where the companies receive their combat missions.[5]

We were dumped from a line of trucks on the roadside. We had been riding all night (16th and 17th) and up until then — about three o'clock in the afternoon — the trucks had been full of men and equipment and that ride had been more of an ordeal than a respite. There had not been space for us all to sit down at one time and we had been jounced and banged about unmercifully on the rough roads. Yet we had managed to catch some sleep in short, interrupted naps.

From the roadside we climbed a wall into a meadow field, crossed it and the brook at its border, and arrived at the base of a great forest-clad hill.[6] This forest teemed with life and soldiers of all nations. There were French batteries, limbered and ready to go forward; English tanks and tank corps; Italian engineers; Polish and Belgian infantry; and Bengalese and Sengalese and Chinese, all milling through these trees, intent upon their own affairs and going up or coming down that enormous hillside.

It took the better part of an hour to gain the summit. The day was blazing hot and we breathed a sigh of pleasure when we got there. We were told to prepare our suppers and rest; at midnight we were to go in.

Over little fires of hastily collected sticks, we soon had bacon sizzling and the appetizing odor of boiling coffee in the air. It was a picturesque scene. Our whole company camped in a glade of that forest, squatting in groups around the squad fires, cooking their suppers beneath those enormous old forest trees.

Then we all spread our blankets for a nap we never got. We were called away to make another trip to the bottom of that hill for more ammunition. We left everything on the ground for we were promised our nap when we got back.

There was a great deal of delay getting the ammunition. Half of the company had probably regained the hilltop before we even started to climb, my squad being the last to receive its consignment. The daylight was rapidly failing and great inky blue storm clouds were rolling up into the sky as we again crossed the meadow field. The heat of the day had not abated at all, only now it was murky and enervating. We began that long climb through the twilight woods with about sixty pounds of ammunition on our shoulders. We climbed slowly for we were tired, and the air was heavy and dead. Beneath those enormous trees and the gathering cloud-bank, it was almost night already.

Halfway up there came a blinding flash of lightning that turned the tree leaves and boles to silver, then an ear-splitting crash of thunder. In the lull that followed, as though that had been an arranged signal, all the bugles on the hilltop burst into frenzied cry of assembly. Again the lightning flashed and the bugles' clamor was lost in the mighty thunder roll of the heavens that followed. Then down came the rain, roaring on the leaves above our heads.

We mended our pace. Everyone was madly hurrying up the hill. It had grown quite black and only when the lightning flashed could you see at all. In desperation of ever gaining the summit with our loads, we threw the ammunition away and hurried on, gasping for breath, the perspiration streaming down our bodies. Over our heads the storm crashed on and the rain roared in the tree leaves. There was almost a stampede now. In the darkness and confusion we got separated from our comrades and there was nothing to do but go it alone.

Gaining the top of the hill at last, in the blackness, running into men and horses and falling over piles of supplies, I sought our glen and my company. In the blackness and storm everything seemed changed. I thought I found the glen but I could not find my arms and equipment. I was lost.

All about me men were yelling for companies and companies calling for men, but I could not find mine. For a time I ran madly about, falling down and getting up, desperately yelling for my company and only answered by the jeering crashes of thunder from above. Then I took a plunging header into a tree and only my helmet prevented knocking my brains out. This sobered me down.

There were dozens of companies all about me. They were all going to fight. What difference did it make which one I fought in? As soon as the first men fell I could arm myself and someone was sure to fall before I would be in need of a weapon. This was reassuring and I was debating whether I should join a company of Highlanders who were calling their roll near me or hunt up a company of Americans, when in walking forward I ran hard into a company standing quietly across my path. A voice, familiar to me, cried, "Jesus Christ, guy! You damn near cut off my ear with your helmet."

It was my own company; my chum had brought along my equipment in the faint hope of finding me and I was again armed and in my place. I don't suppose I had been a hundred yards from them at any time, yet in the roar and blackness it was little short of a miracle that I found them.

We had thought that we were nearly at the front. That proved a mistake. Somehow we forced ourselves into a road already packed to overflowing and started forward. Such a mad jam of struggling humanity would be hard to conceive. Soldiers, horses, trucks, cannon, caisson and tractors, jammed so tightly together we literally trod upon each others' heels. It was miserable work. We would go for a while, then everything would come to a packed stop, and we would wait and wait, then forward again for a while, then another stop and another wait. Aggravated, tired, never able to swing into a lasting stride, we went on hour after hour, without rest or cessation. At every road intersection, the jam became greater as more men, horses, and trucks, literally hurled themselves into the congested mass.[7]

This occurred somewhere near the end of the night-long march through the *Bois de la Retz,* on the night of July 17–18, because in his narrative Linn mentions a dead German gun crew, such as he shows here, and because on that march most men of the Second Division ran out of water and suffered terribly from thirst.[8]

The roadway was rough and irregular, cut into ruts and mounds by the engines of war that had gone before us, and covered with slithery mud from the rain that still fell heavily. In the blackness it was impossible to see where your feet were going and so we lurched and wallowed and staggered. It was impossible to fall, we were so packed together, but added to all the other trials of that march was the buffeting one received from his fellows in their floundering.

My chum, shoulder to shoulder with me, nearly drove me into insanity. I know now he must have been forced to walk in a rut, but he continually struck my shoulder, throwing me out of stride and at times causing me to stagger when he caught me off balance. At first it was only annoying, but its continual repetition as we dragged on hour after hour raised in me a burning fury of hatred. My mind dwelt continually on the joy it would be to draw

Left: "There came a flash from the hedge before us and Sergeant Murphy's helmet rang like a bell." Sketch.
Right: The woodcut of Sergeant Murphy down. "Murphy walked slowly around in a circle, looking into the sky, then he fell in a pile."

my bayonet and at his next buffet drive it through his side. Over and over in my mind, I enacted this scene, seeing his agonized lurch and distorted face in the faint light as he sank beneath our feet, to be trampled to a formless pulp in the roadway. And yet, such are the queer workings of the human mind, at daybreak seeing his face drawn with the agony of exhaustion, I took his rifle from him and added it to my own load.

Soon after daybreak (of the 19th) we left the road and deployed for action. We had come up on the line at last, some four hours later. A short rest was imperative, we could hardly drag one foot after the other. While we rested, we rifled the packs of the dead for our breakfast. Then forward again.

That morning, crossing an open field, a retreating German infantryman fired a cannon at us point-blank. He must have known something about artillery for he succeeded in loading and firing a smashed and abandoned cannon, whose crew had all been killed. There came a flash and roar from the hedge before us and Sergeant Murphy's helmet rang like a bell, then the shell exploded half a mile behind us. Murphy walked slowly around in a circle, looking into the sky, then he fell in a pile.

Falling seemed to bring him to, for he popped up on the instant. That shell in passing had crimped the edge of his helmet.

Hurrah for the Frogs!

*This section appears to overlap the previous section, "The Terrible Night March,"
as both describe the night of July 17–18, though relate different incidents. In the
previous section, the narrative ends sometime after sunrise of the 18th, after the
terrible night march through the Forêt de Retz has ended. This section, however,
rather than beginning where the previous section leaves off, appears to turn the
clock back a few hours so that we are once more on that terrible march. It is as
though Linn cannot permit the trauma of that ordeal to pass with only a single
telling, but must dwell upon it again.*

Oh, the God-forsaken memory of the night hike, when night succeeded
night, through endless eons of suffering, until the actual arrival on the scene
of battle was almost a relief. Exhaustion long past movement was phlegmat-
ically automatic and mentality so numbed beneath waves of physical weariness
as to be no longer interested in relative merits of life or death. Hour after
hour of unrelieved monotonous exertion while the rains of heaven poured
down; when the only dry spot on your body was the top of your head, and
you went on and on, step after step, while your load grew heavier and heavier
as it absorbed the water. Nothing to see but blackness and rain; only the road
to feel beneath your feet. Nothing comes nearer, nothing is left behind. You
stagger on through ruts and stones, while your muscles are burned away and
a faint wonder arises in your brain at this thing you call your body, which
goes on when you have long since stopped.

At the gray dawn of such a night, we defiled into the woods at the roadside and literally fell asleep.[9] Some of the men did not even drop their packs,
but fell asleep still in them. As I pitched, exhausted, prone, I felt the rain
strike hard and cold upon my face, but even as my mind encompassed the
idea of shifting my helmet to meet this new condition, I was asleep with the
act unaccomplished.

Hours later, through a tortuous lane of unreality, where fire gave no heat
and food could never quite be eaten, consciousness came struggling back into
the wet and stiffened thing, lying in the mud, that was I. All about me men
were undergoing the same process. It still rained and in the gray and curtained
light, we stared strangely at one another and no word was spoken.

My chum next to me was abstractedly examining a malodorous brown
smear across his collar and face. He examined a finger test of the substance,
with a grave aloofness, found his worst fears realized, and seeing us watching
him, remarked, "I knew I smelled it, but I hoped I wasn't in it." The thing
struck me as funny and I essayed to laugh, but on the instant my jaws became
unmanageable and struck up such a burst of independent chattering that we
all went off into fits of hysterical laughter.

Left: "My chum next to me was abstractedly examining a malodorous brown smear..." Drawing.
Right: Notice the rain and the desolation of the place are much more prominent in the woodcut.

Not far off was a French rolling kitchen with a fire burning in it and we descended upon them. With our teeth chattering in our numbed and soaked condition, no word was asked or given. The French soldiers warming their hands at the blaze, in tacit sympathy moved aside to give us room, and oh, the unalloyed joy as we thrust our arms into the blaze and felt the life once more creep down those stiffened members, felt the blessedness of warmth as our jaws relaxed and then once more came under the control of our wills. As we thawed into life, the French became more vivacious and joining in the circle about the blaze began to talk to us. Their cook gave us each a scalding drink of black coffee and we were restored. I say, "Hurrah, for the Frogs"— they were real comrades to fight with.

A French Band at an Old Chateau

This episode takes place on July 18 while the Sixth Machine Gun Battalion is spending much of the day resting in reserve. Information regarding the battalion's location is contradictory, but Linn and at least part of Seventy-seventh Company appear to be camped in a wood near the famous Château de Pierrefonds.[10] For the Fifth Marines, the ordeal of the attack on Vierzy is already underway, while for the Sixth Marines and Sixth Machine Gun Battalion, the ordeal will begin the next morning, before dawn. But for now, Linn and his chum Ratting are

Another crap game. Woodcut.

enjoying a peaceful hiatus at a beautiful old chateau in the French countryside, listening to music.

I lost all my money in a crap game, sixty some francs, and got up from my cramped position, feeling discouraged. Not at the loss of the money, that was just so much paper gone, but with the discovery that I was disqualified for any further play. The loss of this distraction, this escape out of the reality of life, was dispiriting.

For a time I stood watching the play as fortune or misfortune followed the clicking ivories for the different members of that group. Some score or more of men in a tight, enrapt circle, with a few French soldiers standing around as spectators. These later followed the interchange of piles of money with almost protruding eyes. The stakes were fairly high, probably two or three hundred francs were won or lost on the pass. There was no enjoyment watching others play, so I turned my hopes to new fields of diversion and strolled away.

Ratting joined me and we left the grove in which we were camped for the day and walked over to the chateau nearby. We had arrived at daybreak, after hiking all night, slept until noon, had our dinner, and were now killing the afternoon. As soon as it was dark we would go forward again. We were in some doubt as to our reception, as we crossed the lawn, for we knew the chateau was headquarters for some French outfit.

We met no opposition and strolled idly along the graveled walk to the front of the great rectangular pile of masonry. A straight facade of stone with square holes for windows in monotonous regularity, unrelieved either by blinds or awnings. A sort of uncovered stone porch ran along the front, its steps descending to a great flagged ellipse in the center of which was a mirror pool, now dry and empty.

We sat on the raised edge of the pool and regarded the building with disapproval and it, supremely oblivious of us, stared blankly at nothing. Two bright silk guidons fluttered at the door and a lounging chasseur-de-alpine on guard were the only relieving items in the view. Heavy afternoon peace drowsed over everything and the faint continuous boom of distant cannon only emphasized the quiet. We were too much depressed to criticize and sat on, inert and voiceless.

Two or three times I noticed it and then turned simultaneously with Rats to say, "Do you hear that music?"

We strained our ears to listen and presently picked up again the faint rhythmic beat of a drum, with some trace of accompanying melody.

"A band," we both ejaculated in wondering surprise. "Right under the Heinies' guns too; that's French nerve for you. Let's find it."

We descended a broad stone stairway into a sunken garden where the peace of ages seemed to dwell. Marble statues of fauns and nymphs peeped at us from screens of bushes and fall-saddened breezes alternately ruffled all the leaves above us into music or left them mute and still. We gained the end of the garden and climbed another stairway to the level of the drive, just before the entrance gates. Here four great stone posts stood guard, their ornamental iron gates standing open on a long avenue of maples. At each side there were stone lodges, doing duty now as a galley and barracks for an outfit of chasseurs. Two of these latter lounged smoking before the barracks, and before the galley a large monkey on a chain was hopping about some boxes and baskets of supplies. We went over to examine him.

Discovering us suddenly he made such a furious rush at us we both backed up automatically in some uncertainty as to the amount of liberty his chain allowed him. At the end of his leash he stood braced and glowering at us and we stayed on staring at the animal in voiceless uncertainty. We were troubled which was the monkey after all. Neither its savagery nor foolishness equaled ours. This damnable little brute was making madmen of us on this somnolent dreamy afternoon.

"Parley." The French cavalry was most apparent during the Battle of Soissons, and nearly every member of the Second Division who described the battle mentions encountering French cavalry.

The plump pink-faced cook came out and, probably to amuse us, gave the monkey a bottle in which he had put some wine. Very deliberately the animal accepted the bottle, seated himself comfortably, drew the cork with his teeth and drank the wine. Then he handed back the empty bottle. The cook cocked his head on one side and smiled at us as though to say, "Smart, don't you think?"

We did not think so. Oh! The enviable monkey. Oh! The stupid monkey who kept him chained and gave his blood and life for the privilege. In another minute I should have screamed or cursed to find relief, but just then the band started to play, near enough to distinguish the melody.

After two or three deep breaths in which we got our feet back on the earth we turned away.

In a grassy open dell a little way below the gate, we found the musicians, probably at practice. They were all alone, seated on camp stools, the leader standing before a music rack. We picked a grassy bank drenched in sunlight and lay down near them.

Half dreaming, lost in thought and melody, with the hot afternoon sun beating full upon us, and flashing in dazzling areolas from the polished instruments, time slid unheeded by. The music which had been progressing by fits and starts and much explosive language from the leader finally swung into a good rhythm and proceeded uninterrupted to the end with some dash and vigor. There being now a definite pause and as the whole band had observed our arrival, to show our appreciation and encourage them on, we applauded with a good deal of spirit. To our surprise the leader turned smiling to his audience of two and bowed in the most formal manner.

For a short intermission we lay on our backs blowing cigarette smoke into the unclouded dome of heaven, then turned on our elbows as the baton rapped smartly on the steel rest. This time they played "*Madelon*," beloved of the soldiers of that time.

> "She conquers one and all,
> Yet favors none at all,
> And as the wine goes through
> Their veins, they say,
> Oh*, Madelon...*"

This time, at the conclusion, our applause was generous and sustained, helped out by three or four chasseurs who had lounged in during the piece and joined us on the bank. This time the conductor gave us three bows and then, turning back to his men, said something that set them all searching through their music. While they hunted, the leader consulted his watch and looked up into the sky, puzzled. The sun no longer shone and in the pause a soft, sad little breeze ran ruffling through the bushes.

Again the master rapped smartly for attention, held a short pause, then to a full sweeping gesture, the band swung into sound. The tune they played this time was "America." Involuntarily we burst into applause and the director turned slightly toward us to smile and nod. As he turned back, the bank beyond raised in a cloud of smoke and a detonation like the cannon's mouth sent the musicians sprawling on the ground, their music lost in the mighty roar of the explosion. Another explosion shook the hill above us at the chateau.

"The departing hum of a Gotha came faintly to our ears..."

Amid the sound of falling earth and breaking tree limbs we heard the frantic blowing of a bugle.

From the shelter of the woods we looked back but the glade was empty. The musicians, casing their instruments as they went, were all hurrying toward the gate. In the comparative quiet, for the bugle had left off blowing, the departing hum of a Gotha came faintly to our ears and the occasional boom of an anti-aircraft gun taking a shot at it.

The day had changed completely; heavy clouds blackened the sky, and as we came up on the drive a cold drizzle struck our faces. Coming back through the sunken garden the place had the feeling of a sepulcher. The marble statues looked cold and aloof, far from life.

Some hours later, as we waited for the last lingering departure of light, in the edge of the woods a mile below the chateau, a company of chasseurs carrying stretchers, each with the white band and red cross on his arm, came swinging down the road in the now-pouring rain. As they came opposite to where we lounged voiceless and depressed at the side of the road, I recognized our band of the afternoon. The steady, stern-faced man at the head was none other than the smiling wielder of the baton.

They passed in silence and after them we too drew out upon the road and moved off silently into the night. My mind went back to the monkey stuffed with food and wine, comfortably curling up for his night's rest.

Caught in a Crossfire

In the early morning hours of July 19, at 4:30 A.M., *Seventy-seventh Company is ordered into Vierzy in a reserve position behind the Sixth Marines. However, at 8* A.M., *two platoons of the Seventy-seventh, including Linn's, are sent in support of the First Battalion, Sixth Marines, on the western outskirts of Tigny.11 Linn's account begins sometime later that morning, and describes the assault on Tigny.*

Behind the crest of a hill we lay as tight to the ground as we could stick. We were in a nasty box, caught in a crossfire of our own and the enemy's artillery. The air above hissed with flying bullets from the German maxim, that plugged into the ground or our bodies, as the case might be.

We had outrun our schedule as usual, and our own artillery, instead of lifting to clear away before us, was drilling the hillside on which we lay, with holes, and our bodies with metal. How many of our own men at that spot were killed by our own shells, I would not like to say.[12] So we lay praying that at least our own fire would raise; the German fire was heavy enough. While shells came screaming in from front and back, tearing up the ground and rolling over the men like inanimate bundles of rags, we lay with our faces thrust hard into the dirt, slightly contracting our features as each shell scream ended in a roar and cloud of blown up earth and smoke.

Then forward.

From the crest of the hill, all hope of descending that shell-beaten, exposed slope alive looked impossible. The earth fairly danced beneath a hail of exploding "eight-eights."[13] We ran straight into that fire. In no order at all, we ran down that hill. Who fell in that run, we neither saw nor cared. Throw-

Headquarters U. S. Marine Corps

ADJUTANT AND INSPECTOR'S DEPARTMENT

Washington,   January 11, 1919

92368-FVF

Sir:

I am directed by the Major General Commandant to inform you that a hospital report has just been received from
abroad regarding your son, Pvt. Louis Linn, Marine Corps.
as follows:

Entered Base Hospital 27 from command July 19, 1918
Diagnosis: Gun shot wound, chest.
Disposition: Returned to duty, Aug. 15, 1918.

This is the first information received by this office of
a casualty in the case of the above named man, and it is quite
probable that you have already received same direct from him.
However, as there are many instances in which the relatives
have not received the information, this office is sending out
the reports in all cases.

Yours respectfully,

Captain, Assistant Adjutant & Inspector.

William E.Linn,
    McLean, Va.

Notification sent to Linn's family.

ing ourselves into the ditch that edged it, we thrust our rifles through the
hedge, on its bank, and began to fire. We were in action again and that was
some relief.

By noon we had taken the town in the valley.[14] That was our objective.
We lay in the drain of a road now, on which enemy shells cut queer antics,
jumping and skipping about on its hard surface. The sun wheeled slowly
across the sky, and still we were kept in our ditch, while what had been a picturesque little town disintegrated into a smoking mass of rocks and tiles and

"We were in action again and that was some relief." Woodcut.

broken timbers under the steady downpour of German shells. We were still kept so tight to earth, we were unable to guess how badly the company had been hit.

About four o'clock, our relief divisions being pushed in behind us to go on with the drive, the German fire let up on us a little and began to worry them. We were able to ease our cramped joints and sit up. There were plenty of shells still whizzing about, however.

The first house with only a walled vegetable garden separating it from the road behind which we crouched had a pump on the wall facing us. We all eyed it with thirsty longing and each time the house was hit prayed for the safety of the pump. The pump came through safely, and it being my turn, I took four canteens and made a dash for the pump, running through between shells.[15]

With all four caps off, I was holding the canteens all together under the flow of water with one hand and pumping with the other, a clumsy and not efficient operation. Then two furtive Frogs, also in search of water, showed up. One of these began to pump, while his companion and I filled canteens. By the time mine were filled, some fifteen or twenty men, encouraged by our success, had collected there. With the intention of returning the favor done me by the Frog, I offered to relieve the man at the handle, so he could fill his canteen.

"My buddy's filling mine, I'll keep her going."

What happened next I can neither tell nor understand. Some higher sense made me conscious of black death above that well. I fled in mortal terror half back across the garden and plunged down, conscious of a roar behind me. A minute later, when the whizz of flying metal stopped, I looked around. Only a gaping hole still smoking, the shattered stock of the pump, and a pile of debris of rocks and human bodies remained. Two or three, of the twenty or more, had life enough left to struggle weakly on the ground.[16]

With our thirst satisfied, we were next conscious of ravenous hunger, and as if in our necessity we created the thing we needed, word came down that a Red Cross man had by some miracle gotten into the town with bread and syrup. To prevent any concentration, we were only allowed to go two at a time, if you cared to go at all. Going meant running a shell gauntlet a couple hundred yards along an exposed road.

My turn came with Tadpole, and we successfully made the run. There were men before us, from other companies, and we waited our turn. A soldier knelt beside the road by a sack of bread, busily slashing a loaf into slices. As each slice fell, a greedy hand snatched it away. Beside him knelt the Red Cross men with an open can of syrup between his knees. Upon each of the snatched pieces of bread he daubed a spoon of syrup. Our concentration on this procedure was enormous. Everything terminated so suddenly and quickly in this life, even to live to eat a slice of bread and syrup was a great step gained.[17]

There came a crashing detonation. I felt the road fly beneath my feet, then strike my hands and face. My helmet went clanking away before me. There was a yell of "Gas!" and almost instinctively I was pulling on my mask, my head still dizzy from its contact with the road. All of this in the space of a second of time.

Thus engaged, I saw Tadpole hastily stuff the bread the soldier had been cutting into the syrup can, which had been knocked over and was running its precious contents on the road. On top of this he stuffed his raincoat, then snatched out his gas mask and dived into it. As a guard for his safety, he told us later, he held his breath.

Help had arrived and put masks on all the wounded. The Red Cross man and his assistant were both dead. The shell had exploded almost between them. Tadpole and I were slightly burned under the arms and legs, by the gas, but we ate the bread and syrup, after some cutting and skimming.

Later in the afternoon the fire had slackened still more and we were now sitting on the side of the road or the ditch. I had just poured tobacco into a cupped paper when before my amazed eyes the tobacco suddenly leaped away

Top: "By noon we had taken the town." Drawing.
Above: Woodcut of the drawing. The explosions look like flowers. They are more prominent in the woodcut.

of its own accord. Simultaneously I felt myself traveling rapidly through space, then the crash of my fall. I was up again almost on the instant, dizzily staggering in the road. Something wet and hot was running down the side of my face, into the corner of my eye, and into my mouth and along my chin. I had just the sensation of a sharp stick being stuck in my back. It was not so painful as annoying. I kept asking to have it pulled out.

Someone caught my elbows and dragged me into the ditch. Someone else had pulled out my first aid kit and torn it open. I was still groggy in the head and could not identify persons about me. With the feeling of the bandage going around and around my head, it came to me that I was hit.[18]

Sergeant Sike[19] was bandaging my head and neck, then my back.

This done, the same kindly hand washed the blood off of my face with my canteen water and gave me a drink. The cool water and the drink completely brought me around. Thereupon I proceeded to give an exhibition of nerves. I became perfectly furious. I expressed my determination to kill every "God damn German" on earth and went hunting through the debris for my rifle. I couldn't find it, so I wept. The stooping over must have sent the blood to my head, for I fell over. I was helped up again and with someone steadying me staggered off to the dressing station.

To me it was a long and agonizing trip to that station, but we got there. My helper wedged me into a seat on the staircase in the hall. He gave me an encouraging pat and asking me to give his love to the mademoiselles of gay Paree departed.

I sat on that step a long time. The whole stairway was a ladder of wounded men, and they sat all around the hall with their backs against the walls. The worse off ones lay full length on the floor. The whole house seemed in a like condition, but no more of it was within my vision. Nothing was done for them, and they were all mute. A strange dull apathy rested here, where one would naturally have expected a great deal of bustle. A surgeon occasionally strolled somnolently among these suffering men, smoking a cigarette. He regarded them with the aloof abstraction of some foreign matter such as vegetables. The stream of wounded never ceased to arrive. They were brought in and either sat or laid down, according to their condition, and those who brought them departed without a word. Occasionally the surgeon would come out of his trance long enough to direct where one of these arrivals be put, but he would immediately revert into it, without so much as a glance at the soldier he had arranged for.

Outside, the sun, a great red ball, was dropping down to its setting on that hot summer day, but there was no movement of the air and the heat of midday still lingered in that house. Staring out of the door, directly before me, the bright colors of a staff pennant caught my eye. Near it was a group of French officers, their red-topped hats and two-colored uniforms making a

Beaurepaire Ferme. A U.S. Army Signal Corps photograph taken on July 19, 1918. On the evening of this same day, Pvt. Linn would arrive here, badly wounded, on the back of an ammunition truck.

pretty spot of color against the gray of the buildings.[20] There came a scream in the sky and the spot was gone in an upburst of dirt and smoke. This settling and eddying away disclosed the blue uniforms mixed with dirt of the road and contorted into uncomfortable positions that remained strangely still.

An American water cart, a tank on two wheels, pulled by two mules and driven by a skinner, crouching far forward, and urging his tired beasts to greater speed, turned into the road. For a second a black hole made a perfect bull's eye in the tank and then the whole thing dissolved in whirling smoke and reappeared as a pile of debris at the roadside. The two mules were down, one of them trying valiantly to rise, the other quite still. At the side of the road, one wheel all alone spun around and around on the side of the hub, slowed down and finally became still too.

My eyes ached, hot and burning, yet I could not close them. I was sick and weary and my head throbbed like a beaten drum, but I could not relax. I could not shut out my consciousness of life. I remained sitting on that step in that hot breathless hall catching my breath, gasp after gasp, until I felt that unless I escaped I should surely die.

An empty ammunition truck[21] stopped at the door and everyone able to stand the ride was offered the opportunity to go back. The truck was soon filled. I was lifted to a seat on the sloping tailgate. The driver said to us, for we were in a line across the board, "You fellows hang on. I am going like hell now and I can't stop to pick you up if you fall off."

We said we would and both of us kept our word. When we had about reached the end of our endurance and I had been for some time speculating on whether I would have enough life left to crawl out of the way of the next vehicle if I intentionally fell, the truck drew up before a farm house[22] at the roadside and stopped.

We were helped out by many hands, the owners of which said kind or amusing things to us, and taken through the gate of the farm yard and up to the door of the house.

The soft twilight of a midsummer day was settling now into dark. Figures moved about through the semi-obscurity to the soft trilling of crickets. Beneath a shed, the Red Cross had a fire going and were busy cooking soup. They offered us this in little tin bowls, also chocolate and cigarettes, but few of us accepted.

Inside the farmhouse, by the light of a couple of lanterns, a surgeon and two orderlies were busy upon their tasks. We were taken in one at a time and the bandages put on by our comrades were cut off and fresh bandages put back. A ticket was made out and tied to each man like a side of dressed and inspected beef. After this some were told to go back and get on the truck, others were put on stretchers and carried away.

When my turn came, I suddenly discovered I had lost my voice. Straining to my utmost, with my lungs pumping like a pair of bellows, I managed to whisper my name, rank, company and division. I caved in during my bandaging and the task was completed with me sitting weakly astride a chair, holding the back. I struggled up when it was over and started for the door, without waiting for an invitation. It was not that I had any great love for riding that truck, but my nerve was gone now and I was in mortal terror of the guns. I wanted to get as many miles between us as possible before I stopped. Besides I had noticed the surgeon nod for a stretcher and I was afraid it was for me. I was sure if I were put on a stretcher, I would die. The orderly caught me in two steps.

To my whispered assurance that I was all right the surgeon said, "Why sure you are. You just lie down for a while and you'll feel stronger. There will be plenty more trucks."

The stretcher with me on it, was carried away and presently put down in company with many others, under a huge canvas fly. It was night now and the stars twinkled brightly all along the edge of that canvas.

I lay fighting for my breath. Each respiration required a willed effort on my part. Next to me was a French soldier thrashing about on his stretcher and moaning continually, "*D'eau, d'eau.*"

But no one gave him any. After a while he essayed to get up and, balancing himself for a second, fell heavily out on the ground with a moan.

Someone came and put him back on his stretcher. I tried to get their attention to tell them what he wanted, but all ability to make a noise had left me now, and they departed. In putting him back on the stretcher, they had reversed his position, and his feet were now to my head. He continued to thrash and moan for water, and in his thrashing he kept kicking me in the head and shoulder, where I was wounded, with his great hob-nailed boots.

I could not save myself. I could only turn away my face and bear it. He kept this up for some time, muttering inarticulate words, dispersed with moans of "water." Finally after a last flurry in which he split my lips and cut my ear, he straightened out and died.

At some time during the night[23] my stretcher was taken up and placed in an ambulance with three others and we were driven until daylight. We were then put down again in an open field.[24] As the daylight increased and the morning mist dispersed, a whole field of banked stretchers was disclosed to view. We lay there all day staring up into the sky. The fierce heat of the sun brought on a kind of torpor in which suffering was lessened, but the whole field moaned in concert. I didn't moan. I couldn't make a peep.

In the afternoon a thunderstorm broke over us.[25] The lightning flashed and forked, and the thunder boomed in mimicry of the guns. We were soon soaked to the skin from the torrents of rain, and our stretchers made little tubs of it for us to lie in.

This, however, was rather pleasant and reviving, as most of us must have had some fever. The usual bitter cold French night setting in and the rain continuing was not so good.

On the brow of the field above us were a number of big tents, almost like a circus. Into one of these I was eventually carried that night and placed upon an operating table. A whole line of these ran the length of the tent, with wounded soldiers on them all and busy surgeons and orderlies at each. The place was full of glaring light, the odor of ether and stale wounds. Overhead the rain drummed steadily on the canvas.

Again I was bandaged. As the stretcher bearers took me up from the table, the surgeon said, "Don't take him back out in that rain. Find some place for him in here."

I was put down in a corner of the tent, by what I thought was a pile of salvage. From time to time, more was added to this pile, and the dull thud of its falling catching my attention, I looked at the pile with more attention. Salvage indeed, a whole pile of miscellaneous arms, legs, feet, hands, and all the variegated salvage that may be lopped from the human frame, in a great mound that continued to pile up.

Two days later, in a base hospital,[26] where I had been X-rayed and marked out like a land plot, with little black cross marks, indicating likely spots to dig for iron, I awaited my operation in a hall beside the operating rooms. I had much company for the hall was lined with patients. Busy nurses and orderlies flew about administering hypodermic injections and ether. This place ran day and night, and had been going at that speed for a week, under pressure of the drive.

From one of the operating rooms there issued a great fat surgeon with a face like a full moon. His apron was one mass of blood stains from chin to waist. He reminded me so forcibly of meat butchers I had seen in the market that I lay grinning at him. He was lighting a cigarette and happened to notice me; the fact that I was grinning caught his attention, and he regarded me more closely. Finding I was grinning at him, he leveled his cigarette at me and said, "Just for that I'll take you next."

I often wondered if he did. Well, after that I had nothing to worry about.

8

Hospital — Angers

The following four reminiscences take place during Pvt. Linn's hospitalization and recovery in Angers, following his wounding outside of Tigny during the Battle of Soissons. The first two take place in Base Hospital 27, while the last two occur outside the hospital, in or near the town of Angers. Linn enters the BH 27 on July 24, 1918, and will be returned to duty on August 15. All four accounts occur during this three-week period.

Linn's experience of Base Hospital 27 is far from pleasant, and occasions a good deal of bleak commentary and complaint. On the face of it, this is hardly a surprise. He is, after all, recovering from a serious shrapnel-inflicted chest wound, a circumstance that would foster a pleasant disposition in no one. But Linn may in fact be more fortunate than he realizes. Base Hospital 27, according to the great majority of soldiers who passed through it during the First World War, was "the paradise of the wounded man," famed for its Romanesque architecture, its elegant table furnishings (left behind by earlier tenants, Roman Catholic priests), and a very tolerable cuisine which occasionally included such smuggled delicacies as stuffed quail or a golden Anjou wine. But most particularly, Base Hospital 27 was renowned for the expert and tender ministrations of its nursing staff, most of whom hailed from Mercy Hospital in Pittsburgh, Pennsylvania.[1]

The Nurse

Our night nurse, in that hospital, was a big, clumsy Bridgety sort of a woman. She was far from the age I could call a "girl," with a face as hard as a wall of the "Tombs." She had a pair of hands as big as boxing gloves, and she handled them and us with about the same gentleness and lightness you can see any full grown bear demonstrate in a zoo. It was as much as your life was worth to get that lady to change your position.

One night when most of us were asleep, she came in to give us our daken irrigation.[2] Each of us had from two to a dozen little rubber tubes, like worms, running into our wounds, and at regular intervals, the nurses injected a liquid called daken into these tubes. On this occasion Bridget advanced upon us, a lantern over her arm, for the ward was in darkness, with her syringe and bottle.

The first man awoke from a sound sleep with a yell. "Ow-ow, stop! Jesus Christ! Ouch!"

We all burst out laughing at his racket and Bridget told him to stop swearing or she would report him. None of us worried very much about being reported, but we all had a healthy dread of getting a wallop from one of those hams she wore on the ends of her wrists. The man reduced his complaints to whimpers and she advanced to the next bed.

This bird was wide awake and anxious. He got his first shot with a yelp of agony, and almost succeeded in jumping out of bed in spite of a busted leg. Bridget caught him, and he got three more shots, then he broke down and wept. Bridget was in her glory; if she didn't taste happiness that night she will never know it, in this vale of tears.

Up until now I had been roaring with amusement at the howls of anguish from my ward mates, but only one bed now separated me from Bridget, and I began to feel uneasy. Daken irrigations were entirely painless. We had been getting them all through the night without even waking up. Something was certainly wrong tonight. As she advanced on my neighbor, I said very undiplomatically, "Nurse, you must have the wrong bottle."

The nurse.

She told me to mind my own business. I did that by watching to see what effect this elixir would have on my neighbor who was the most quiet alive man I had ever seen.

He looked like the popular caricatures of "Old Man Temperance League," a round coconut of a head, with a little dry frizzy hair above his ears, long red nose, and cadaverous jaws. He had not said a word audibly since he had been put in his bed, so far as anyone had heard. The only convincing evidence we had of his being alive at all was that he took aboard all food given him.

Bridget loaded her gun and gave this sound economist his first shot, everyone watching breathlessly. It was a tense moment, even Bridget hesitated to watch the result. Into that death-like silence there now came from the bed a line of despairing detonations from its occupant's stomach, then silence. While the rest of us thrust our pillows into our mouths to stifle our laughter and shook with hysteria, Bridget gave the poor wretch four more shots, her lips pressed hard together in fury, but elicited no further sound. Seriously, I thought she had killed him. I gathered up the ends of my tubes with my good hand and lay on them. This move had not escaped Bridget's eye.

Throwing back my cover, she said, "Now, just let go of those tubes, young man."

I said, "Nurse, you are not going to get any of that stuff into me 'til you look what it is."

"I know what I have," she said in an exasperated tone. "Let go of those tubes."

Handicapped with the bottle and syringe, however, she could not shake me loose.

Another patient.

"Maybe you know, but I don't, and I'm getting the dose. Will you hold the lantern so I can read the label?"

Probably thinking that the quickest way to end the dispute, she did, and we both read "Alcohol."

I didn't say anything but looked up into her face.

She stormed, "That's better than daken," and went away for the right bottle.

When she came back, I said in a pleading voice, "Can't you start on some of the others, please, Nurse, you have probably got the formaldehyde."

"If I hear another word out of you tonight," she cut in on me, "I will box your jaws."

I subsided.

Rudberg

I remember the orderly we had in one ward. His name was Rudberg. To us he was anything but that — Redbug, Bugberg, Hugbub, Iceburg, Lugburg, and some hundreds of other variations, were for us a happier appellation. He was a short, dumpy boy, with a fat serious face, dark brown eyes and a mouth about the size of a button-hole. His short duck legs were encased in trousers much too big for him, the seat down almost to his knees. He was kind-hearted and anxious to please, but a clumsier, more awkward poor mortal I never saw.

It was his nightly task to put out the lights and every night when he did it we used to put a candy can barrage on him. By blowing out our breath with a hiss and whistle, we could imitate a shell screech and for some reason we always derived great joy from bombarding poor Rudberg to the accompaniment of this imitation shell din. The cans striking the iron beds and walls made their own bangs. Rudberg, having pulled the switch, would fly for his life, while the invaders threw cans and shouted with laughter. He was actually in terror of us and could never be induced back into the ward for an hour or more, no matter how imperative our needs.

One bright moonlight night we were all awakened by a tremendous jarring explosion at no great distance. We sat up to listen. In the quiet that followed, while we were wondering if "Big Bertha" were turned around on us, or if the Germans had somehow jumped over our line, we picked up the wavering hum of several Gothas. German aeroplanes and a moonlight night, bombing, of course. We listened, wondering when they could let down another egg. They seemed to have gotten directly over our heads and stuck there. Their planes hummed and hummed, but did not move away from over us. Lying there helpless, wondering if the next bomb would come crashing through the roof on top of you was pretty nerve-racking.

Then down came the next, landing in the courtyard, just outside our wall and giving us all a bounce. Pieces of rock and iron came shattering through the windows and fell about the ward. Two more bombs followed in close succession, one going into a hospital building and so finishing off a lot of poor fellows already pretty far gone.

The hospital was now in an uproar, doctors and orderlies were flying about like mad, making for the bomb proofs. Rudberg, with a lit lantern over his arm, was running up and down the ward absolutely distracted. Ever so often he would dash out in the yard on his way to the bomb proofs, but invariably losing his nerve, he would come flying back in again.

I yelled at him, "Put out that light, you damn fool. Don't keep running out there waving it at the Heinies, unless you want to get hit."

He snatched the lantern from his arm and started to blow it out, but three more bombs came down with consecutive crashes. He dropped it on the floor and dived head-first beneath the nearest bed.

The lantern broke in its fall and oil running out by the wick began to flame wildly. We all started yelling at Rudberg to put it out, but no amount of yelling would bring him out from under that bed. To add to the general hilarity, the man whose bed Rudberg was under had gotten a crutch and kept trying to poke him out. His two neighbors obligingly threw everything they could lay hands on under the bed at him yelling, "Bang! Redbug."

"Bang! Hugmug."

One of the men able to walk finally had gotten up and smothered out the fire before it caught to anything. At last they made it too hot for the badgered orderly, and he made a scamper for the door, his teeth chattering together in his terror. He reached it just as the nurse and doctor were coming back in and collided violently with the latter. The doctor said, reassuringly, overlooking the collision, "It's all over, Rudberg, they are gone now."

The nurse coming in said, "Why, Rudberg, did you stay with the men? I think that is splendid. You ought to get a decoration." Then she turned to look at us, for we had suddenly burst into a perfect howl of laughter.

A Conversation

One blazing hot summer day I toured Angers on foot. I stared at its cathedrals and over its bridges, and gaped at the front of its hotels. The ward master at the hospital had finally decided I was well enough to be trusted on liberty and secured me a pass, good from twelve to six. I tried to make the most of it by walking all over the city. Both of us made a mistake.

At about three o'clock in the afternoon I mentally pulled myself up to inquire just where I thought I was going. Just what was I looking for in these hot, endless streets? More cathedrals and hotels? Just what was it I was expecting to happen to me? I had certainly worn the edge off staring at architecture and strangers. I realized suddenly that I was very tired and hot, and rather shaky from my sojourn in hospital. It came upon me now almost as a blow, that I still had several miles to walk back to that hospital before I should be done with this liberty. I tried in vain to recapture my zest for this excursion, but it had flown now. I was only conscious of weariness and the oppressive heat and glare. What a sell, this liberty.

"Nothing ever happens to me," I mused bitterly. Considering that I had recently been an interested participant in the greatest war of history, this was hardly true, but the thought in my mind had reference to my never having any of those lovely romantic adventures that the heroes of fiction are so continually beset with. Looking about me at the stupid or stolid faces of the people I was inclined to doubt if they did, either, or if anyone did in fact. Actual life was rather a flat affair, even for a soldier in wartime.

I abandoned this line of reverie here and decided to go across the street to a cafe and get a rest and something cool to drink.

Seated at a little iron table on the sidewalk in the shade of a striped awning, I loosened my tunic collar and began going over in my mind what I should like to have, but the necessity of ordering never arose. The end of a wooden club landing with a light tap on my table and remaining poised there on its nose took my attention. My eyes traveling up from the club encountered a sleeve band marked "MP."

At this point a rasping voice drawled, "Well! Aren't you sittin' pretty."

From these gentry I expected nothing pleasant, despite the fact that I was an exhausted soldier convalescing from wounds. I looked at this person to try to ascertain what I was up against.

"Let's see your pass," he snarled out of the corner of his mouth.

While my hand sought out the piece of paper and extended it to him, we looked at each other steadily. If it was only the matter of a pass I could easily satisfy him. He was a big, square-shouldered mutt in a faultless uniform and Stetson campaign felt, only his face had too much jaw on the bottom of it.

He made no movement to take or read the pass, only leaning on his club, continued to scowl at me with an angry contemptuous sneer. I had never done anything to him, never even seen him before. I sat looking gravely at him, wondering what it was in me that excited such animosity in his breast.

The sneer suddenly left his face and pointing at my throat he stormed, "Button up that coat!"

"Ah! You have saved your country's flag," I told him, complying however with his command.

"Now get out," he directed, indicating the street with his club.

"What for?" I demanded.

"Because I tell you, that's what for. This cafe is for officers only."

"Do you know of one for privates only?" I inquired, lamely covering my retreat.

To this he deigned no reply, and I moved off humiliated by the glances from the civilians at the other tables.

"What a sell, liberty," I mused bitterly. "Can't even buy a drink."

Stiffening myself up as best I could, I started out to walk back to the hospital and be done with the whole thing.

I walked and walked and walked, that hot afternoon, until I thought I would drop in the street. Finally I found myself in a bare, unshaded street, on which the sun beat mercilessly. Lined on each side by mean houses built clear to the sidewalk, that street stretched clear away to the horizon. A regular nightmare street. I had a slight touch of vertigo just looking at it and leaned against a telephone pole until the feeling passed.

When I opened my eyes again an American soldier had appeared from somewhere and was standing on the pavement a short distance away. He had noticed me and we moved toward each other, the only visible humans in that vast extent of sun-swept thorough-fare.

"Is this the way back to hospital?" I asked, when we had come up to each other.

"Yeah, right on out." He nodded up the street with his head.

"But, my God, I can see five miles. Do we have to walk all that?"

"Not more than a mile farther. You'll see the hospital down a cross-street. You could have ridden up to that next street over on the cars and saved yourself this much of your walk, the way I did."

"It's evermore hot and I am thirsty. Do you know where we can sit down and get a drink?"

My new acquaintance scanned the street a second, then said, "We can get a bottle of cider up here a-ways. Come on, I will split one with you."

The door we presently entered set a small bell on a coiled spring above it to jingling hideously. We entered a small, mean little cafe, with an ugly zinc-topped bar, behind which, on dirty shelves, were some doubtful-looking bottles of liquor. I looked at my companion. This certainly was not very promising. He, however, had seated himself at a small deal table with an air of being at home, so I came over and joined him. The bell had left off ringing finally and in a silence broken only by the droning buzz of some flies, going round and round on the ceiling, we waited for some service.

After some variegated thumps and bangs in the rear of the building, as though several heavy pieces of furniture had to be moved to get to us, the curtain over the rear door was put back and a lean, angular woman came through. I had looked up hopefully when the curtain moved, but the sight of her sharp nose and scrawny neck put my interest to rout. I gave our order.

Two cloudy glasses and a bottle of cider were presently placed before us. But what a sad travesty on what we called cider this stuff was. A bitter, sour liquid with a flavor evenly crossed between soaked pine shavings and the lees of a wine keg. We each took a drink without any great enjoyment and then hastily lit a couple of cigarettes to get the taste out of our mouths.

Then we lounged down on our elbows and proceeded to get acquainted.

"What ward are you in?" I was presently asked.

"Twenty-six."

"I am in evacuation. I will be sent back before long," he declared, staring somberly into his glass.

I said nothing and after a long draw on his cigarette he looked me in the eyes and said, "I am afraid to go back."

After a minute, I found my voice and staring at the ugly bar said, "Yes, it is sort of terrifying after the quiet of hospital, the smiling nurses, regular meals and soft beds. You can't sort of believe, just over the hill, thousands of men are devoting their lives to killing each other, in an inferno from hell, and that it is expected of us to get well and go back."

"I don't mean that," he interrupted me in a slow, even voice. I had looked at him when he spoke, and he continued, looking squarely into my eyes. "I mean, I am afraid to go back. Don't you understand? Afraid of getting hit; I am afraid of the guns, of the yellow faces of the dead, their sightless, staring eyes. Haven't you seen them, where they had gone round and round, clawing up the ground with their finger in their agony; then finally died with their faces to the sky? Haven't you?"

"Sure."

"Something's happened to me. I've gone yellow. When I think of the wh-sh-ht-bang" (here he cleverly imitated a shell come in and explode), "the rat-tat-tat whis-s-bang" (he now had a realistic mimic war roaring in that miserable little cafe — machine gun, rifle, grenade and shell roared and crackled about our ears — and the proprietress regarded us gravely from the door, but went away; he stopped suddenly and took a drink, then finished his sentence). "I get weak, sick inside. I am afraid, so what's the use lying about it?"

This man spoke like my own conscience. I had a desire to hug him to my heart in sympathy and understanding. Instead I shifted my gaze to my wine glass, and began to turn it slowly around on its base. He seemed to be waiting for me to speak, so I philosophized, "There isn't much use ever lying to yourself, but it sometimes helps your neighbor. You pretend a lie and he thinks, 'My buddy's not afraid, so I won't be either.' That's a lie too but it may help him stand up to have his brains dashed out and not cower in the bottom of some hole despising himself, but all in one piece."

"Listen, guy! I am serious. I took a liking to you and told you all this, maybe because I thought you felt that way too, but now I don't know whether you're jeering at me or not. Are you?"

"Sure I am afraid," I admitted, "terrified, but I am going back and so are you. We won't take a job here to stay back and we will go forward when the word comes, even if it's to claw circles of agony in the mud with our hands. We won't claw safety out of a dog-robber's job here, because we are that kind of fools. Doesn't that help a little?"

"Say! I'm sick of heroics."

"Life's just sort of a gesture, so you might as well make a grand one as a dud."

"Aw, snap out of it," he snorted. "That bunk is all right for you with a convalescence in front of you, but not so good when a guy is holding out a rifle for you to limber up to. Wait 'til you are ready for the front again, then tell yourself that for me."

I was grinning at his vehemence and he began to laugh himself. The rest of the cider was divided between the two glasses and we pledged each other top and toe. When the glasses were down he said, "You have kidded me into a better humor all right, but tell me, what do you do? No kidding."

"What do you mean, what do I do?"

We had risen from the table and stood looking across it at each other.

"I mean, how do you meet fear?"

"Jesus Christ, guy! I have just told you I don't. I am just as terrified as you are, or more so."

"Well! How do you go on?"

"Be a fatalist. You are either going to get it, or you are not. You can't help yourself. There is no use trying to reason, so turn to something beyond yourself: God, if you believe in him; destiny, if you like; or just plain duty to your brother man. Give them the responsibility of what happens and go ahead. It's amazing how you will be carried on, like a log on a wave. You are carried forward by a force you do not understand yourself. Tell me, haven't you experienced that yet?"

"Ah! Sure. I know that force — cognac. Come on, buddy, let's go from here or we will be late for chow."

"You go to hell!" I retorted and all the way back I tried fruitlessly to decide which of us had been kidding the other.

An Idyllic Interlude on the Loire

The following takes place in the days immediately before Linn is recalled to duty on August 15, on the river Loire, presumably within or just outside of Angers, but its exact location and identity must remain a mystery. It appears to be someone's private garden, perhaps belonging to some benevolent private citizen who has opened his or her home to convalescing soldiers. If every other section of Linn's memoir reads like a forced march through the Inferno, this one is a peaceful vision of Paradisio. It is luminous, lyrical, and, in its inevitable transience, profoundly poignant.

I remember the lazy Loire flashing in the sun over its ripples, under green banks. Young girls with skirts, high kilted above lovely bare legs, wading in the shallows, enjoying the coolness, while younger brothers and sisters nearly naked or entirely so tumbled about them like little living Cupids. And the old men with snowy locks and time-marked features drowsed on the banks above them, while the Loire sang its song of summer days and summer ways, under softly swaying leaf fronds.

And we, the living, who had so lately come through the portals of battle, hand in hand with death, harassed by memories of our comrades falling all about us, the acrid odor of burning powder in the air and the impact of biting iron in flesh, lounged indolently and impassively in that old garden for a while. We asked for nothing more than to sit and admire young girls we would never know, old age that we should never attain. They were equally beautiful in our eyes, equally endeared to us. Like thirsty sponges, we soaked up those soft sweet voices from the river, and while our eyes devoured their lovely forms, devoured the lazy summer quiet of those afternoons and the happy song of the river, at the back of our minds was the knowledge that on the line the cannon still rolled and our parole was short.

We lay prone on the soft green grass or sat with arms about our knees, smoking endless cigarettes in an impassive quiet that rivaled enchantment. It was dangerous to do too much talking in that garden of peace. One word too much sometimes shattered a soldier's nerve completely and the quiet would give place to an explosive outburst. A tale of love, of home, of hope, when oaths would crackle madly like rifle fire in that quiet air, and finally the racking sound of a grown man sobbing softly with his face in the grass, and each of us avoiding the eyes of the others, and saying nothing until the soft swish of departing footsteps through the grass brought some relief. Life for us was under the sword, and those days were golden coins that we clung to like misers. Those two girls, sweet, quiet and beautiful, who daily welcomed us to their garden and daily gave a smile and words of liquid music to each, were like the creations of our fondest dreams. In pastel-tinted summer dresses, their ribboned hats of golden straw tossed negligently upon the shadowed grass, they were surely the synthesis of all that is beautiful and good in life. They were, to us, the living symbols of a life beyond all hope of attainment. Ours was a life of hardships, brutality and death, and these hours were stolen sweets from an existence not our own.

I do not even know their names, those two. I was taken to that garden of dreams, by another soldier, the afternoon following my return to the hospital; down a rocky, winding lane, overgrown with honeysuckle, through an open gate and along a path by the river, to where a little group of soldiers lounged beside two girls under great elm trees on the river bank.

One girl lounged negligently in a lawn chair of striped awning, an open book in her lap, the gossamer thread of a burning cigarette rising from a hand on the chair arm. The other girl sat demurely upright on a rustic stool, busy over some needlework.

My soldier led me before the lounging one, smiled, and said, "*Bon jour Mam'zell*," with a nod to me, "*Mon ami*." Then he walked away to the river's edge.

Mam'zell regarded my gold sleeve chevrons with a pair of beautiful gray eyes, raised them to mine and smiled. "*Asseyez vous*," she said.

"*Merci*," I replied, and sat down before her, and we regarded each other with smiling impoliteness.

To the beauty-starved soldier, she was ravishing, and I laid my heart in tribute at her feet, while my eyes took a most careful inventory of her person and apparel. All the beauty of refinement, taste, and personality were there in this slim girl, from the ribbon lacings and dainty feminine tucks at her throat, to her dainty little white shoes. A far cry from the rough trapping of a private of the line.

Even the advent of refreshments did not break the exalted quiet of that place. We were given lemonade and cookies by the second girl, assisted by some of the soldiers. Conversations were monosyllabic affairs. Only the highlights of sentences were spoken; intuition must fill in the rest. Whole paragraphs were left suspended on a word, and fancy might complete them as it chose. The futility of words seemed an accepted law here.

Half-dreaming before my goddess, I sat watching her slender swelling white-clad ankles, until moving, she changed her position and recrossing her knees, gave me, seated at her feet, a moment's vision of delicate, snowy underclothes and faintly pink flesh in curves of alluring beauty.

Unavoidably I looked up into her face to meet eyes that told me that I had been detected in my theft. I could neither look sorry, nor feel it, and so we remained looking seriously into each other's faces. Then smiling faintly enigmatically into my eyes, she inclined her head and those great gray eyes slipped free of mine.

That was my first day. The first bead of the golden rosary that slipped so swiftly through my fingers. Daily we gathered in that garden, beneath those old trees for those golden afternoons. Afternoons of life for many of that little group. The Loire running fast down across its shallows, loitered for an hour, softly lapping that old garden bank. Like an impersonal goddess our "Beautiful One" welcomed us to her garden. Like eaters of hashish we dreamed away the hours, and like disembodied shadows we went voiceless back to billets when the day was done. Strange as it may seem, there was no competing for favor and no jealousy. We were really as aloof as our divinity. We felt the aloofness of certain extinction.

Sometimes I made sketches, lying on the grass, in a spirit of bitter revolt against my lot, drawing intentionally crude, with features left out, like faces in our dreams, or caricatures of our absurd antics, and looks in the great maelstrom of destruction. All the time I drew, the rest watched me steadily and when completed and torn from my pad, they snatched the sheet and studied it with intensity of interest I could not understand. Rudely snatching the sheet from each other, they almost tore it to pieces. Stranger still, they wished to possess these drawings and begged for them, offering me anything they had in exchange. I did not draw a great deal, only in certain moods, and then it was for my own relief. I willingly gave them the drawings. I wanted no mortgage on the morrow, each setting sun was the end of a life.

Yet life is devious and this very drawing led me into a mortgage on the morrow, for while the second girl was quite as much interested in the drawings as my comrades, and herself made me a little pair of worsted "Lucky dolls" in exchange for some, my "Beautiful One" hardly paid them the courtesy of a glance, and never expressed a wish to have one. In spite of myself I was piqued and did my best to make her recant, and I always met defeat. I put my best into those bits of paper, trying to infuse into those black smears of pencil all the living fury, the needless hell of war.

I was so engaged that last afternoon, when a voice said gently, for even bad news must be quiet in that garden, "Back to billets, fellows, we are leaving for the front."

The dream was done. Our hour had struck. Soundlessly our castles of joy slid down in ruins at our feet and slowly we arose to go. Oh! The hell of going back. Only the returning soldier may know. Then those old elms looked down on our final adieu, for the import of the message had been explained to the girls. A little pale, they were giving a smile and handclasp and some final word of cheer to each as we parted.

I still held my sketch book, and as I stood waiting, looking at the unfinished sketch, the queer little game of hope I had played, and lost in the face of death, seemed sad and pathetic. I gathered up the page in a crumpled heap and tossed it down the bank of the Loire, thrust the book into my pocket and said my good-byes.

We were to leave at four in the morning, to steal away unnoticed like the Arabs in the verse. Lights were put out at the regular time, but no one cared to sleep. We sat about in little groups, faces dimly seen at intervals by the glow of our cigarettes, drinking sour wine and talking in strangely peaceful tones. The first shock was over and we knew the way our feet had before them.

At four o'clock, our column, like an army of shadows in the eerie light, defiled upon the street on our march to the railway. We had expected to leave the townspeople asleep in their beds, but we received a surprise. They banked the sidewalks as to witness a parade. The girls, the matrons, the old men, the little children and the maimed, derelicts of war, all there, to cheer our leaving with a smile. Truly we were proud that they liked us so well.

As the column advanced, moving between those lines, a rain of softly whispered words of love and cheer enveloped the lines and beat softly into our ears, to the steady crescendo of marching feet. Soft hands reached out to touch our swinging hands. Rough hands, with fingers missing, engulfed ours for a fierce squeeze, yet never a word above a whisper, never a light, not even the glow of a cigarette in all that throng.

We moved on through that strange scene, assailed by a chaos of feelings that came too fast for analysis. Then we were opposite the little crooked lane, and in the faint colorless light of dawn, we saw our two friends, muffled in capes, standing upon the curb. They watched the passing soldiers with fixed smiles, picking out and nodding to each of our little group. Then, as our eyes met, a hand was thrust into her dress and a crumpled sheet of paper was pressed across her breast. My last unfinished sketch. She saw that I recognized it, and while I drank my last look into those unfathomable gray eyes, she folded the paper and slipped it into her bodice above her heart, and stood with her hands pressed on it, looking steadily at me, her lips forming the words, "Un souvenir."

I watched her until her outline was lost in obscurity, then turned back to the task of being a soldier.

9

With the Company Again — Camp de Bois de l'Évêque

Upon discharge from Base Hospital 27 in Angers, Pvt. Linn rejoins Seventy-seventh Company on August 16, 1918, at Camp de Bois de l'Évêque, an enormous French training post located along the highway between Nancy and Toul and overlooking the river Moselle. The camp consists of "maneuver grounds, numerous Adrian-type barracks, and ranges for various kinds of firing equipment: rifle, machine gun, pistol, trench mortar, antitank, grenade, and artillery."[1] During the month that Linn was hospitalized, the Marines of the Second Division had occupied a "bon sector" near Marbache, on the Moselle. Here, for the most part, they rested and recovered from the twin catastrophes of Belleau Wood and Soissons, their first extended period of quiet since the previous May. Now, just as Linn rejoins them in the Bois de l'Évêque, things are picking up again. Replacements are being received by the thousands, training regimens are undertaken in earnest, and there is talk of a new offensive in the offing. From mid–August to early September, the Second Division is encamped in the Sixth Training Area, centered around the village of Colombey-les-Belles, with individual units rotating in and out of Camp de Bois de l'Évêque for five-day periods of intensive training. The Sixth Machine Gun Battalion is camped right in the Bois de l'Évêque itself during this time.[2]

Back to Duty

This episode takes place at Camp Bois de l'Évêque, on and immediately following August 16.

One day in the early fall, I rejoined my company at a rest camp. I was sent from the office down a long street of portable barracks to "B-14." A number of men, perfect strangers to me, regarded my entrance with indifference. Some mistake, I decided, and stepped out. I tried the next barrack with the same result. I came out and started back to the next above, when a voice said, "Hello Jim, you still alive?"

I regarded the speaker with a grin of uncertainty.

"Well, Jesus Christ, you don't even know me," he yelled.

We had met in the middle of the street and had gone into a bear's clinch, holding each other as if about to start a wrestle.

"Who in hell are you, anyway?" I inquired. "You sound sort of familiar, but damned if I know you."

"I'm Robinson! They made me a new face in the hospital. How do you like it?"

"Your own mother wouldn't know you," I told him, staring in wonder.

"Golly, I'm glad to see you back," he went on. "Mighty few here now you will know, all replacement. Pop Sikes[3] is here. Most of the old gang are in his platoon. We will get you in it."

"How about the officers?" I asked.

"All new Looeys. We still got 'Old Woppjaw.' You can't hurt that sucker, he stays too deep."

"Major Colin's gone; seven typewriter bullets through the chest.[4] Major Wallack is in charge.[5] Your friend's back from 'O. T. C.'[6] Got a 'Sam Browne'[7] on so he's out of your reach, ha-ha. He sure ran you ragged for a while, Jim! Too bad you didn't plug him that morning in billets."

"Well, here's what's left," he said, and we entered the barracks.

Half an hour later we turned out to answer mess call, still talking volubly. It was amazing how many things we found to compare notes on.

"Not much use going," declared Moler. "Chow is just a formality in this place."

"We are going to start eating again next Thursday," said Renet.

"What head do you get your dirt from?" inquired Robinson.

"By next Thursday I will be broke of the habit," averred Moler.

Once more I was lined up for food in the old familiar manner. Mess kit in one hand, canteen cup in the other, cutlery stuck in my legging. That was "manners" in service. The whole galley crew was still intact and despite the rush of activity, they all gave me the glad hand of welcome, even the head cook and mess sergeant. I was quite overcome with emotion, but one hand held up all the food I had gotten and didn't notice the weight either.

A piece of beef, the size of two of my fingers, a boiled potato about the bulk of a golf ball, two slices of bread and a cup of coffee, was each man's ration, and Hoburna had announced generally to us all, "There ain't gonna be no seconds, either."

"Ain't nobody had nightmares from overeating here," averred Renet. "I am hungry enough to eat a cheek off Hoburna's rear end right now."

Next day we went out to drill but after doing squads east and west a few times, we were too weak for the manual of arms so everybody lay down.

For dinner we each drew four hard-tack, two pieces of bacon and a sack of tobacco.

After this rather sketchy repast we were called back to the drill field to witness a demonstration of something new, "incendiary bombs."[8]

At the upper end of the drill field was a road cut down about three feet lower than the field. On the bank thus formed were massed the privates. The road was reserved for officers only. In the field beyond were the specialists who handled the bombs. A couple of hundred yards on down this field was a growth of young pines that were to represent the enemy. The bombers planned to lay a barrage before these pines, behind which we could advance without the slightest possibility of being seen.

We had no great interest in this new contraption. Experience had taught us these variegated devices usually flivvered when most needed, or else got in our own way and were no help at all.

Still it was more fun to watch these birds shoot off fireworks than do squads right, and besides, the groups before us offered no end of material for wise-cracks. Jests flew about on that bank, while we waited, to which the officers in the road tried to remain contemptuously oblivious.

Everything worked lovely. The bombs exploded into beautiful flowers of fire-tipped smoke. The pines disappeared as if a curtain had been dropped in front of them. It actually looked like a curtain. A solid wall of smoke without a loop-hole. It stuck together, too, hugging the ground and in no hurry to disperse. We all applauded the success of the demonstration.

The officer in charge now came forward, pleased with his success, and holding one of the bombs in his hand. He informed us the bomb was also valuable in stopping the enemy's attack. Thrown into their ranks it caused them to become disorganized by being blinded as well as burned and could not be directed. These bombs could be thrown by hand, he explained, and he invited a fat old major of ordinance to throw one.

Now that major could not have had very much experience in throwing anything but dirty looks, for although he gave the bomb a mighty sling, he sent it on a returning parabola up into the sky above.

A stampede of officers started on the instant. That bomb was bound right back to the spot from which it had started, and those officers wished to leave that spot. The major who had thrown it took to his heels down across the field where the bomb should have gone. The rest of the officers were caught between the spot where the bomb would certainly fall and the bank where we stood. They charged our bank like a football team, yelling "Give way." We only braced ourselves for the onset.

The novelty of actually having our officers before us in time of danger inspired that whole bank like a flash to keep them there. And I say with pride and joy that not one got out of that road before the explosion.

The fight was short, but hot while it lasted. Those birds were scared pink. A stiff adjutant undertook to crawl through my legs. He got his head through and then hung up, like a jinned rabbit. He lost his balance on the bank, and couldn't push forward and his helmet caught behind my legs and wouldn't come out, and he couldn't get his chin over the helmet-strap to free his head, so there he hung. He was pretty red in the face and foolish-looking when I let him out.

Nothing much really did happen when the bomb did explode. Very little of the fire reached us and on the moment we gave back with a will. Those officers charged up the bank, then, slapping out spots of fire, pretty red and flustered, and knowing in their own minds that they had behaved like a pack of fools. The worst of it was they knew there was no possibility of retaliation. We had only behaved as stupid privates are supposed to behave.

As we went happily back to billets afterwards, Renet said, "After that it will be hard-tack and water for supper, gang."

The Bee-Hive

Some days later, sitting on my bunk, I was joined by Ratting, who wore an air of great mystery. After looking carefully around to make sure that no one was observing us, he leaned close to me and asked, "Do you know anything about bees?"

Such a question after so much preparation took me by surprise. I had expected at least some proposal to assassinate the captain. I burst into a roar of laughter and answered that I knew it was damn painful to be bitten by one.

Then I asked, "Say! Are you trying to kid me?"

"Sh-sh-sh!" He dug me violently in the ribs with his elbow to make me stop laughing.

"Listen, fellow," he proceeded, "do you know how to get the honey away from the bees?"

"I know several ways," I assured him.

"Listen guy, no damn monkey business. Do you?"

"Well, I tell you I do. Have you some for me to take?"

Again Ratting looked carefully about.

"You know, I don't trust that Corporal Hughes. He's a squealer," he declared, looking darkly at the corporal. Then turning back to me, "Listen, don't tell a soul, will you?"

"I don't know anything to tell. What's this nonsense about bees anyway? I think you have one in your bonnet."

"Say, fellow, if you know how to get the honey, we're going to steal a hive from that farm up the road."

Ratting here eyed me critically to see what impression his proposal had made.

"Huh! Who is?" I demanded.

"Why, you and me and Simmes."

I regarded him a minute and said, "I tell you Rats, as hungry as I am, and I am real hungry, I don't care much about stealing a poor Frog's bee-hive. I would have to kill the bees for us to get the honey."

"Poor Frog, hell!" snorted Ratting. "That bird has made a fortune out of this camp. His charges are outrageous, because he's the only farmer here. Even the Frog soldiers say he ought to be ashamed for robbing us so."

"Well, if it is like that, I am on. When do we start?"

"If we can make it, we had better go tonight. They are starting things up front and we ain't much longer for this place."

Simmes being ready for immediate action, we agreed on the coming night and I went off to the dressing station to get some sulfur from an orderly I knew pretty well.

Late that night, armed with sulfur rags and a rubber poncho, four of us slipped through the sentry line and getting on the road advanced on the farmer's bee-hives. At my request, Renet had been added to the party and made its fourth member.

The hives, in a high-walled yard next the house, presented some difficulty to our program but we finally found a place where a number of rocks had fallen out of the wall and by climbing a little way up a tree that grew beside the breach we got upon the wall. Then we muscled ourselves down into the yard as noiselessly as possible. We stood in a little group, listening attentively. The breach was much nearer the house than we thought safe to get, but the windows on this side were all dark.

I was suddenly struck with a new worry. "Have they got any dogs?" I whispered.

"Yes, but so many soldiers come here, I don't think they will bark," whispered Ratting.

"They will bark if we make much noise," opinioned Renet, also in a whisper.

The farm still remained wrapped in quiet, so we advanced on the hives, and what hives they were. As big as dog kennels. We groaned in spirit as we surveyed them. The four of us, however, succeeded in lifting one from its bench and carrying it over to the wall, heaved it up in the breach and two of us then held it while the other two scrambled back over the wall. We moved the hive forward, then they held it while we scrambled over.

At this interesting moment came the ring of footsteps on the hard road. We set the hive hastily down on the ground and Renet and Simmes sat on it for camouflage.

The bees were getting fretful at so much rocking about, and a few of them came out. In a low voice I warned the others not to yelp if they got stung.

By this time, the sounds were almost upon us, and as the night was very light, we watched with beating hearts to see who it would be. If it was some of the farm people or the Gendarmes, we would be in for it. Two French soldiers came into view and we all breathed with relief. They slightly checked their step on seeing us but we said nothing and they went on, with a few curious glances back at us.

As soon as they were by, for no French soldier ever stopped at that farm, we again picked up our dog kennel of bees and carried it across the road and a short way into the field. Ratting wanted to carry the hive a mile away, but the rest of us had enough of lugging that bee bungalow about.

With an entrenching tool we made a hole, fixed and lit the sulfur, and set the hive over it. Then, covering it with the poncho, we banked the edges with dirt and went back to the roadside while we waited for the bees to perish.

Then we went back to that hive and fell upon it like four famished honey bears. In the dark we ate everything, bee bread, young bees, comb, old bees and honey. We had been in too big a hurry and not all the bees were dead, but we never found this out until we got them in our mouths.

At each fresh sting, we only groaned and kept on eating. Gee whiz! but that was grand honey.

Finally stuffed to repletion, we each filled a bacon tin with comb and returned to camp. By the time we got there our mouths and tongues were so swollen we could hardly make a sound, but perfectly content, we turned in and went to sleep.

The next morning we judiciously dispensed to Top one bucket of honey and although the Frog raised merry hell we heard nothing about it. He took his revenge by jumping the price of wine to double what it was.

That day I met the Top in the company street. He said, "Ha, Jim, not back a week and into rascality already, huh?" I grinned impudently and asked, "Did you get some of that honey, Top?"

For answer he took a wallop at my jaw, which I sidestepped, and then went on his way chuckling.

Marching in Strange Company

The following episode takes place during the northward march by the Sixth Machine Gun Battalion made between September 3–8. At 9 P.M. on the Third, the battalion leaves Camp Bois de l'Évêque and hikes about 12 kilometers to the Forêt de Hayes, arriving at 1 A.M.

At 9 the following evening, September 4, the battalion leaves the Forêt des Hayes and hikes about 21 kilometers to the Bois St. Gengoult, arriving at 5 A.M. on September 5. It is probably on this particular night's march that the following takes place. Linn describes crossing a pontoon bridge and the only sizeable river the battalion crossed was the Moselle, a few kilometers to the northwest beyond the Forêt des Hayes.

They remain in the Bois St. Gengoult until the evening of September 7 when, again at 9 P.M., they leave the wood and hike about 6 kilometers to the Bois des Hayes, arriving at 2:30 A.M. Here, near Manonville, about three miles south of Limey and close to the front lines, they will remain until the afternoon of the 11th, preparing machine gun barrage positions, bringing up ammunition and consolidating it into dumps, reconnoitering front line positions and making preparations to lay down a machine gun barrage on enemy positions on the 12th, the beginning of the Battle of Saint-Mihiel.[9]

I remember one night, or rather the wan small hours of one morning, hiking along in an agony of sleepiness. I would have given my soul to have been able to lie down and go to sleep. I would continually fall asleep walking, and would nap until I stumbled and fell against one of my neighbors. This would partly rouse me, and I would march along until again overtaken with slumber.

At one of our periodic halts for rest, I crossed to the opposite side of the road to sit on a pile of cracked rock, put there for road repairs. It was not that the rock made a comfortable seat, but because the slant of the pile lifted the weight of the pack from my weary shoulders that I chose that seat. I must have slept as soon as I sat down.

Some noises awakening me, I looked up to find the company in motion, and hastily scrambling to my feet, I fell in the first blank space that came opposite me. I figured that since I had joined the company in motion, I was now at some point below my correct place and at the next halt could regain my old place. I drilled peacefully along.

Then I got a jolt. We marched out on a pontoon bridge that even my sleepy intellect remembered having already been over that night. Only now the remains of the old bridge had changed over from my right to my left. For a minute I puzzled, then thought, "Heavens and earth, we are turned around and marching back on our old tracks." But this did not seem very reasonable.

At this point memory gave me a chilling stab that brought me wide awake. I remembered I had crossed the road, leaving my company, to sit down, but had only jumped up to join this one. In other words, I had left a marching company on one side of the road to join another on the opposite, hence going in the opposite direction.

By peering closely into the sleepy faces of the men about me, I was soon convinced that I was in a strange company. We had by now reached the end of the bridge, and falling out of rank, I stood aside to let them march away. Then I turned about to hoof, for the third time, those weary miles.

10

Going In Again — Saint-Mihiel

Wounded Again

*On September 12, in the first major action of the war under American command,
ten divisions (216,000 men) of the First American Army under General Pershing,
supported by four French divisions (48,000 men), launches an attack on the Saint-
Mihiel salient against 75,000 Ger-
man troops under Lt. Gen. von
Fuchs. The Allies advance five miles
along a twelve-mile front in heavy
rain...[1] The assigned objective of the
Second Division is to take the towns
of Thiaucourt and Jaulny and continue to the northwest another six
miles or so, until their line is
straightened out. The Third Brigade
of the Second Division leads the
attack, with the Twenty-third
Infantry on the left and the Ninth
Infantry on the right. The Fourth
Brigade of Marines follows in support, with Seventy-seventh Company joining the Third Battalion,
Fifth Marines on the Ninth
Infantry's right flank.[2]*

"I remember the eve that a big drive was to
start." Woodcut.

141

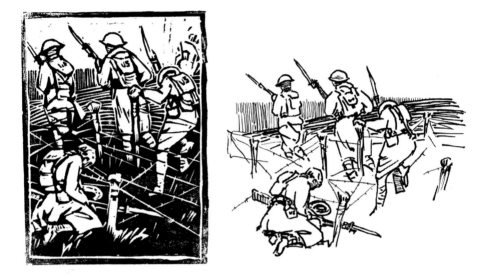

Left: The barbed wire jumps out against the dark background of the woodcut.
Right: "Then we ... were ... streaming out the passages already cut through our
barbed wire..." Drawing.

We were not at all superstitious in the way of being afraid of ghosts or
the dead. We were in such close and continual contact with death that far

from being afraid of it, we even lost our
respect for it. "When you are dead you
are done." "Watch the live ones, the
dead won't hurt you." They were our
maxims. Still we were mostly fatalists.
If you were going to get it, nothing in

Left: The "French whippet." Drawing. *Right*: The "French whippet." Woodcut.

"The trench had literally been torn open from end to end..." Woodcut.

high heaven or low earth could save you. Death struck in such amazing ways. What did catch our attention was that it so frequently warned its victims. Some presentiment, somehow they always knew.

I remember the eve[3] that a big drive was to start. We were to be in the first wave[4] and had come up behind the trenches and waited in the pouring rain for night to go to our stations. We were in a wood[5] and I walked a few paces aside and leaned against the bole of a great forest tree. Many and strange are the thoughts that run through your mind at such a time. Flashes of faces long forgotten or never seen, yet vivid and alive, strains of music elusively sensed, yet not really heard, feeling and sensations of movement and rest.

Dreaming in this way, my mind was clear away from the fields of war when a voice said clearly and distinctly, "You will be hit."

"What?" I asked aloud in surprise.

My mind instantaneously made a comparison of the two speeches and told me I was wrong in supposing the first one had been aloud. Yet until I had spoken, my mind itself had thought the first speech had been heard. Who or what did speak, interrupting my mental train of thought, I do not know.

Yes, I would be hit.

We were to be the first over. We were, therefore, of course, the last to arrive. In a deluge of rain we came to the end of the communicating trench, holding to one another's coats to keep from getting lost in the blackness. Occasionally a cannon spoke from the German lines. Otherwise the rattle of the falling water and the slosh of our feet in the mud made up the only sounds to be heard.[6]

We were stopped for a time at the entrance to the trenches[7] and as we stood looking gloomily into the rainy night, a roar like the end of the world burst suddenly upon our ears. Our whole side of the horizon suddenly leaped into a flashing stupendous uproar. A wavering, vibrating light, like the aurora borealis, crept up across the sky and as battery after battery added its crash to the prevailing din, the whole universe seemed shaken to one mad crash of explosion.[8]

Although we were prepared for this, its arrival was so much more than we had expected, we instinctively tensed our bodies expecting a blow. The sound was so great, to be heard it was necessary to shout in the face of your listener, and even then it was doubtful he would understand.

The weird and ghostly light had now brought everything into visibility and through it the pouring rain looked like stripes of metal tinsel or some unreal effect of artificial scenery.

We were now in a great hurry and floundered through the churned up mud of the trenches, tripping and falling in a wild scramble to get to our places.[9] To add to our difficulty, the trenches were banked with men who had to flatten themselves against the sides to give us passage. But we got there at last, covered with mud and panting from our exertions.

Once we were in position,[10] our haste to get there seemed rather needless, for we remained idly in the downpour for a long time. Behind us the thunder roll of cannon-fire seemed ever to increase. The whole sky screamed and howled with the passing shells. A few German batteries were firing and the explosion of their shells about us was almost lost in the greater volume of detonation.

Then we received the order and were scrambling up the trench face and streaming out the passages already cut through our barbed wire to form a ragged irregular line of battle.[11] There was little danger at this time, with such a bombardment on their lines small chance of any rifle fire being directed at us. Their artillery was almost as helpless under that stupendous cannon work.

Just before their entanglement we lay down to wait for the artillery to raise its fire and while we waited an incendiary smoke screen was laid down as further protection when this happened. A line of French whippets[12] was coming up behind us. Where they had sprung from we

Dragged back to life. Woodcut.

could not guess, but their value at this time was tremendous. Some thirty yards of barbed wire entanglement barred our way and we counted on the tanks crushing it down.

At the point where we crossed, without the least opposition, the first line of enemy trenches, I don't think a man had been left alive in them. The trench had literally been torn open from end to end, its sides blown in, its emplacements shattered. Only maimed inanimate bodies mixed with the debris lay across our path.

At this point our tank foundered. These trenches were enormously deep and wide, regular tank traps, and further increased by the shell craters in them. The little whippet failed to bridge it and went down on its tail with its nose cocked up in the air. The more it squirmed and twisted the lower it sank.[13] Finally its driver and gunner climbed out to look the situation over. The driver made a gesture so significant no words were needed. Only a Frenchman could have done it, a little shrug, a cant of the head, and an elevation of the palms, and he had written his "finis" to his career. This gesture, on a field of battle.

We moved over to go through behind the next tank and there was some concentration at the place. Above our heads there came the roar of a plane and the next second rending detonation. I felt a sensation of spinning madly, then a plunge into blank nothingness.[14]

Finally I became conscious of someone worrying at me, but as if I were a long way from the spot being worried. The mental me seemed to have slipped quite free, or almost so, of my physical body, and I tried to keep it so. For I seemed to be in some place I did not want to leave.

Finally, in spite of myself, however, I was dragged back into the punctured and bleeding body, lying in the mud. I could not recapture my memory of the place where I had been. Yet it had been a place or condition of unearthly beatitude. Only the faint memory of that heavenly felicity stayed with me.

"This one is still alive," said a crude voice, insistently pulling at me for some reason I could not guess. I gave up my dream and knew I was still alive, but the knowledge gave me no pleasure. I knew, or felt, I would be better off dead.

11

Hospital Once More —
Neufchâteau & Orléans

When Pvt. Linn and six other Marines are wounded by a concealed grenade east of Limey on September 12, they would have been carried to the advance dressing station in a well-protected house cellar in Limey where their wounds are cleaned and dressed and where they will remain for the rest of the day and night. The next day, the 13th, Linn is moved about five kilometers to the south, to Field Hospital #1 in Noviant-aux-Pres.[1] Later that same day he is moved again, probably by ambulance, 25 kilometers to the south to Base Hospital #45 in Toul, which is also serving as an evacuation hospital.[2] The next day, September 14, he is evacuated, probably by hospital train, to Base Hospital #66 at the Rebeval Barracks in Neufchâteau. Finally, on September 23, he is moved again, probably by hospital train, to Base Hospital #202 in Orléans, where he will remain until late December.[3]

Operation

The following most probably takes place on late on September 14, at Base Hospital #66 in Neufchâteau. Linn is in need of surgery after his wounding on the 12th, and from that time until now he has been shunted from one dressing station or field hospital to the next, as medical personnel attempt to evacuate him to a facility sufficiently equipped to provide him with the procedure he requires.[4]

I remember waiting in a courtyard. It was late at night and we had just been taken from the train.[5] It was cold and the stars sparkled sharply. The stretcher bearers had deserted us, and we lay waiting our turns, staring into the sky above or at the dull gray facade and occasional lit window of the huge

147

building across the court. Figures moved about the yard but that abstracted unreality of the small hours made them shadowy and unreal. Then I was on the operating table. Faces bending over me and a steady flow of sound. Words, clinking of glass, snipping of shears and a multitude of uncatalogable sounds vibrated in my head. My nose was full of the stench of dakin, ether, iodine and the stale smell of mutilated flesh.

Pain mounted in dizzying waves as deft hands tore away the blood and time-stiffened bandages. An orderly, nurse and doctor were busily at work. Yet they never glanced at my face, nor appeared to be conscious of the fact that I was a human being. As soon as a wound was exposed, the surgeon fell upon it with probes and bits of dipped gauze on little shiny pinchers. The nurse stood by, handing and holding, and the orderly went on undoing new bandages. I watched them, dizzy with pain, catching spasmodic gasps of air between hurts.

The surgeon and nurse were working on my thigh and I desperately, as one grasps a dentist's chair, still held, with my one good arm, the all-too-scant skirt of my shirt across my body. But my hand was in the way and the surgeon tried to thrust it aside. Hardly conscious in the pain, of what I was doing, I clung to that shirt and he was forced to break my hold. Then for once, he looked at my face and said, "What's the matter with you? You're no Scotsman."

A new nurse appeared at my side, loading the heavy, pointed, blunt syringe for an "ATS." injection.[6] "Operate," I heard the surgeon say, between waves of ache.

Jocko

This begins immediately after Linn's surgery on probably the 15th or 16th of September, 1918, at which time he is still at Base Hospital #66 in Neufchâteau.

I "came to" from ether one time to find myself in the main building of a big base hospital. I had gone from one of the board barrack annexes that morning to the operating room, and was much surprised at finding myself in new surroundings. It was just at noon and the ward was full of bustle and confusion, the rattle of plates and cutlery, and much conversation.

Becoming conscious of something behind my head, I rolled up my eyes. Peering down at me was the queerest apparition one could want to see; a round coconut of a head, low-browed with a roach of stiff black hair coming down nearly to the nose, above little, very round, cloudy black eyes, set in a dark hairy face. These eyes held the same bright inquisitiveness to be seen in

THE AMERICAN RED CROSS
NATIONAL HEADQUARTERS
WASHINGTON, D. C.

BUREAU OF COMMUNICATION
W. R. CASTLE, JR., DIRECTOR

Jan. 18, 1919

My dear Mr. Linn:

    I wish to confirm the telephone conversation had with your office last night.

    Cable from Paris reports Louis Carlesle Linn, 77th M. G. Bn., wounded right arm, right thigh, awaiting return to duty.

Very truly yours,

Wm S. Lewis

Assistant Director

Mr. H. A. Linn,
704 Hilts Bldg.,
Washington, D. C.

wsiaae

Notification of Linn's second injury.

the eyes of what their owner so much resembled, a monkey. After a time, becoming annoyed at this continual scrutiny, I said, "Well, Jocko?"

For answer, he drew back his lips to expose his small yellow teeth and making a little monkey-like clicking in his mouth he took hold of an iron tension rod that ran up by his bed and shook it furiously. His impersonation was perfect and I laughed in spite of my sickness. Thereupon he gave over his antics and inquired if I wanted some dinner. No, I did not want any dinner. He then proceeded to notify the nurse who happened to be in the ward that I "had come out of it."

The nurse presently appeared at my bedside, a lovely young girl, perfectly adorable in her crisp, neat uniform. She looked just like the heroine out of a war romance, and so she was, only I did not happen to be the soldier of the piece. She leaned down with a smile that was worth being wounded to see, and said, "Well, now, what have you got to say for yourself?"

This was too ambiguous for me to attempt an answer, so I smiled back and asked if I could have a drink.

"Not yet. We will give you one before long," she promised, and went away.

From that time forward I was continually under the observation of this man behind me. Squirm as I would, he would always find some position from which he could see all I did. He seldom spoke, but he simply had to see everything I did. If I explored my Red Cross bag, it must be done with him noting carefully what I had. I am convinced he read most of my mail over my shoulder, in spite of me. He worried me so, I would have liked to choke him.

He not only watched me, he interfered in all my concerns. Mostly this was done maliciously, but he was just as willing to do me favors. He woke me every morning to tell me my breakfast was getting cold, although he knew perfectly well I never ate any and hated to be awakened in the early morning. I had trouble getting to sleep at night and to overcome this, I used to, on the

A fresh dressing. Woodcut.

pretext of having a bad cold, get three or four doses of a medicine called "Brown's Mixture" that had or was supposed to have a narcotic in it. My system was to get one dose from the day nurse just before she went off, another from the night nurse when she came on, and a third from the orderly. Well, this monkey behind me would frustrate my plans two out of three times by blowing on me.

If I took revenge on him, such as walloping him with my Red Cross bag, containing my penknife, belt buckle and other heavy articles, or threw my spittoon at his head, he would never retaliate in kind. He would shake the tension rod and chatter furiously, making all kinds of monkey faces at me, until I would forget my anger and begin to laugh.

One night I was awakened from a most hideously realistic dream, of being back in the carnage, and found my bed surrounded by the surgeon, nurse and ward master, and orderly. Jocko of course was peering over my shoulder. They all regarded me with anxious intensiveness. I became a little startled and asked breathlessly, "What's the matter?"

"What's the matter with you?" asked the surgeon. "Why were you groaning and howling so?"

"Was I groaning and howling?" I gasped.

"We thought you were dying."

I looked pretty foolish, I expect, as I answered, "Oh! I was having a nightmare."

It was their turn to gasp then. After that they burst out laughing.

"A nightmare — so that's what had us all startled out of our wits, was it? I think we should give you a beating," declared the nurse, pulling my nose.

"I think we should beat this artillery man," declared the orderly, getting Jocko by the ear. "He caused all the trouble by calling us."

"Please don't call me for any more nightmares tonight," begged the surgeon, departing. "I am a very weary man."

When they had all gone, I turned to the crestfallen Jocko. "Messing with me some more, eh? Well, you sure made a monkey of yourself this time."

Armistice

At the time of the Armistice on November 11, 1918, Pvt. Linn is in Base Hospital #202 in Orléans, having arrived there September 23.

Right across from me was a fish-faced "Down Easterner," who complained all the time, in a nasty nasal whine. He received double the attention of any of us, but nothing was ever satisfactory. In a room full of desperately hurt men, he must be babied and attended to, as though he alone had to put up with a little suffering.

If we laughed or talked after lights, he would whine in a voice just missing sobs, "I can't sleep. Taps is went. Pipe down."

We all received our wages in that hospital or were loaned an advance on them, and we were able to buy a lot of stuff to help out the rather rough fare served us. This bird, however, would never spend a penny, but he would stare at us so hungrily when we ate candy or fruit, we would have to throw him some so we could eat our own with any enjoyment.

Linn's letter home from the hospital after his right eye was wounded and his eyes had been bandaged. He was afraid he would be blind.

We all despised him and his everlasting whining complaints. With the exception of Jocko, we all ignored any conversation he offered. I will have to admit, the only talk he ever got out of me was an order to quit his whining and pretend he was a man. Jocko, however, would answer his questions, call orderlies and do other favors for him.

One morning an atmosphere of excitement pervaded the ward. It was known that an armistice had been agreed upon and would be proclaimed at noon. Then noon struck and immediately all the bells in town began to ring. The boats on the river and all the factories blew their whistles and the great organ of the cathedral by the hospital began to play. Four years of bloodshed and carnage was to come to an end at last. From the streets below came one mighty roar from the combined voices of humanity mixed with the barking of dogs and blowing of automobile horns. Whether the people sang or just yelled or did both, it was impossible to tell. It all blended into one great roar, mixing with the ceaselessly chiming bells and the thunderous chant of the great organ. One mighty surge of sound, proclaiming victory.

Everyone able to move about had fled the ward to share in the excitement of the streets. Miss Lucian was fussing about the "Howler" who of course as the rest of the world grew happier became the more fretful and unhappy. All morning long it had been one thing after another. He couldn't eat his breakfast. He wanted something else. His bed hurt him. He wanted his feet rubbed. Orderly, nurse and doctor gave him special attention. Jocko watched him with untiring attention, his little round, muddy brown eyes shooting from one person to another about the "Howler's" bed as they worked to ease him.

His confounded peevish whining spoiled the music and bells and everything. In desperation, I said roughly, "Ah! Nurse, stuff a wad of cotton in that baby's mouth, and tie a bandage over it."

The "Howler" immediately started in on a long preamble, that if I hurt like he did, and so on and on, finally ending in sobs.

Miss Lucian presently came over and leaning down above me said softly, so no one could overhear her, "Don't say mean things to him, Jim, he's dying."

She pretended to fix my bed while I looked at her, conscience-stricken. I had never thought of that. Then she went quickly away.

So a little later in the afternoon, while the air rang with the joyous clamor of the bells, and groups of happy, singing people went marching through the streets to the victorious blare of bands, the little screen of death was put about the "Howler's" bed and he breathed his last and became forever as quiet as anyone could wish.

12

Bits of Life and Death

Neither the time nor the place of the following four episodes can be ascertained. Linn himself could not remember when or where they occurred, which is why he placed them at the end of his memoir in a separate chapter. Even though they are not part of Linn's chronological narrative, and exist in a kind of disconnected limbo apart from the main memoir, Linn clearly considered them important enough to include, and it is not hard to see why. They are arresting and poignant stories that stand on their own merits. Though they reveal little of the history of Seventy-seventh Company, they reveal much about the nature of war, from the tragic to the absurd, and therein lies their value.

The Prisoner

There are certain events of those days, little scraps without sequence, that haunt my memory. I have lost the part that went before, or what came after, only the events themselves remain as vivid as if only just enacted.

I remember one hot mid-day, eating lunch at the side of the road, in company with a French tank corps, just outside the gates of a war wrecked village, during a big drive. We sat about in the small triangles of shade afforded by the tanks in little mixed groups, French and American, they sharing our food, we their wine.

At the opposite side of the road were lined some thousand or more German prisoners, just captured, in a column four deep. The American guard, opposite us, was deep in conversation with an officer, his bayoneted rifle resting on the toe of his shoe. These prisoners eyed our food with hungry longing, but since they would soon be back where food was plentiful and we would equally soon be on the line where food was scarce, we ignored their visual appeal.

When we were about through, however, one of the French soldiers gathered up a handful of scraps and, walking over to the prisoners, gave them to a very hungry, exhausted-looking German boy. Receiving the scraps, he began stuffing them into his pocket but from this pocket he first removed something that glittered in the sunlight; a watch almost certainly.

Just above us was a parked American staff automobile with two soldiers on the driver's seat. When the metallic flash occurred in the German boy's hand, one of these soldiers hopped out on the road and walked slowly across to the prisoners, without attracting the notice of the guard.

Coming up to the German boy he regarded him smilingly for a minute, then suddenly thrusting his hand into the lad's pocket, snatched that shiny something out and running back to the car, jumped in.

The prisoner who had just received an act of kindness from his captors and was in no way expecting treachery did not seem to realize what was happening until the American lad turned away. He started then to pursue him, calling out beseechingly in German. The other prisoners, realizing the danger, caught his clothes and dragged him back into their ranks. He then tried to attract the guard's notice, finally pulling at his sleeve.

The guard, who was still talking to the officer and had seen nothing of what had happened, stopped his conversation for a minute to push the German boy roughly back into the ranks of the prisoners. He then turned back to the officer.

Who can tell what sentiment of attachment that watch had for its owner? After a minute of fretting, the boy again left the ranks and took hold of the guard's sleeve. At the touch, the guard wheeled and the next second had driven his bayonet through the boy's breast. He fell forward upon his knees and then over on his side as the weapon was jerked free of his body, but from his contorted lips there came no sound. A few slight tremors shook him and he lay quite dead in the dirt of the road, staring open-eyed into the burning sky. The guard turned back to the officer and they resumed their conversation.

Benjy's Story

A line of trenches we once held ran through the wrecked remains of a little village, going under the houses and behind the walls of the last line of buildings. The church had been razed to the ground with the exception of the lower half of the steeple. Our predecessors had used this little vestibule room now banked about by piles of rock and timbers for an officers' quarters, and it was fixed up quite snugly.

It had chicken wire bunks, a table, several chairs and a wood stove. Its walls were a veritable picture gallery of nude or semi-nude female beauties, cut from the pages of various periodicals of rather doubtful reputation. Their place here in a church vestibule was only another of the vagaries of warfare.

For those of us who were in on it, this place became a sort of club, where we came when not on duty in the mud of the trenches, to smoke cigarettes and get thawed out at the stove. One night a little group of us lounged in this retreat, milling over the news of the day, the most important of which was the daring theft of a bathtub from the Germans by some enterprising Yanks. The Germans had the tub in a brook just before their lines; now it was in the same brook, but just in front of our lines. The gentlemen engaged in this venture claimed the whole German army had chased them back across "No Man's Land," and only given over the pursuit when they had dived through their barbed wire, like a lot of rabbits, and closed the gap.

"It was Benjy, here, who first found that tub," averred someone.

Corporal Benjy regarded us with a pair of humorous blue eyes and his lips began to go up at the corners. Benjy was a four-foot American-born Dutchman, with a long upper lip, a turned-up nose and a serious expression, camouflaging a very humorous disposition.

"That's where I caught my square-head," he said. We were incredulous, Benjy was such a little fellow.

"Well, I hope to do something unmentionable in your mess gear," declared Benjy.

"He did for a fact," averred the first speaker. "Tell 'em about it, Benjy."

We all drew up to hear the story, for Benjy was a favorite entertainer. He made a desperate gesture and began.

"One evening, right after we came to this hole, Lieutenant Poe[1] came up to me and said —"

"Is that Looey any relation of Edgar Allen?" someone of a literary trend here interrupted.

Benjy's Squarehead.

"If he ain't, he ought to be," replied Benjy. "This one is crazy enough to be Edgar's mother.

"He said to me, 'Corporal Benjy, I want you to take a couple men and go over and catch me a German tonight. I want to ask him some questions.' Just like that. Say! If that bird had asked me to borrow a plane and go up and pick him a few stars I wouldn't a'been knocked any flatter. A fat chance I had with two men catching a live Heinie. I was a lot more likely to catch a dose of lead poisoning.

"As he turned away, Poe said, 'Come to my billets when you bring him in.' I said, 'Yes, sir! When I bring him in I will.'"

"Well! That night we three fools crawled over to the German lines, nose-diving into shell holes each time a star shell went up. We —"

At this point the narrative stopped while we listened to the voluminous double crash of a huge railroad cannon that the Germans brought in every night to fire on us. Soon after the boom of the gun, we would hear the shell, as big as a G. I. can, singing up in the sky. It seemed to travel quite slowly, although, of course, going like a streak. It was easily possible to trace the parabola of its course by the sound. Then down she came with a rending detonation that shook the earth, and dug a hole you could put a haystack into. We all looked back to Benjy and he resumed his account.

"We was wandering up and down in front of the Heinies' entanglements, with not the slightest idea what to do next, when we hears someone fetch a groan. We crept up on the spot where the sound had come from and there was a squarehead, hunched over this tub, holding handfuls of water to his forehead and every once in a while fetching a groan. We held a consultation, whether we should creep up to him and knock him cold, or shove a gun in his mug. He looked pretty sick, but you never could tell. We finally —"

Again the narration left off, for that tremendous "boom-boom" and again we listened attentively for the shell scream. When we picked it up it was coming decidedly more in line with us than we found comfortable. Our well-trained ears informed us that that shell was going to hit close.

It seemed to come slowly, but its time of transit was short. Its screaming descent was directly for our refuge. Too late to run now. It being impossible to locate definitely the spot of its fall, you could be just as likely to run beneath it as away from it. With tightening muscles and suspended breath, we drew back hard against the walls, our eyes set in our heads, while we listened to the death song of that descending avalanche of iron and explosive.

The air crackled into a mighty roar and a mighty thud shook the ground beneath us. The candle gave a wild flicker and expired and in complete darkness. We waited for the crash that would start us on our road to the next world.

But it did not come. The shell had been a dud. However, we departed quickly from that building, that now had half a ton of fused explosive beneath it. I never did hear the end of Benjy's story.

At Loggerheads with Moler

One time our squad, on a hotly contested advance, found itself dangerously near out of ammunition. We were all so nearly exhausted that the corporal merely looked from one of us to the other, without the heart to order any of us to go back for a new supply. Finally he asked, "Ain't there two of you able to make it?"

Moler and I, the huskiest men left, undertook the task. We finally made the nearest ammunition dump, and wiring a case of cartridges to a pole to carry on our shoulders, we started back. The faint gray of dawn was beginning to creep in, but the light of the guns still flickered in the sky as we plugged wearily along on our return. Stray bullets sang about us and occasionally shells tore up the ground, but we were too numb with exhaustion to mind them.

Then we reached a long barbed wire entanglement and we had missed the opening.

"It's higher up," I said.

"It's on down," contradicted Moler.

"You been veering off to the left ever since we started," I pointed out. "I knew you would make us miss it."

"Like hell! You been pretty near prying my neck off pulling me to the right I know where it is, it's on down."

"Don't be such a damn fool, Moler. The opening's above. If you don't come on we will have daylight catching us."

"Don't be a fool yourself. The opening's on down and that's where this ammunition's going."

"It is like hell, it's going up."

"It's going down."

"It's going up."

We stood for a time, glowering at each other, then Moler started off to drag me and the ammunition on down the entanglement. I began to pull in the opposite direction and for a time we had a tug-of-war, now pulling the case a few steps one way, then getting it pulled back the other.

Our fury and exasperation with each other was almost choking us.

A dud?

Finally, as if upon a concerted signal, we set the box down and went at each other with our fists. While shells exploded and bullets whistled about, we thumped and beat each other with what remaining energy we could master. We were, however, so lean and hard of face and body and so weary of arm that in spite of our thumping no damage seemed to result. We gave over our fighting and sat down side by side, on the case of ammunition.

It was Moler who cut the knot of our difficulties. When we had somewhat regained our breath he said, "You won't carry it down and I won't carry it up, so we got to push it through."

"Through it goes, then, brother," I agreed. And though we pushed it at the expense of some torn clothes and torn hide, we got it through and went on our way, the best friends in the world.

One Dead Soldier

At a bare, sun-bitten crossroads one time, I saw a dead soldier lying in the dirt of the roadway. On his arm he wore the red band of a messenger. Overtaken by a Greater Messenger, he now lay just out of the wheel tracks in the road, powdered with the dirt of each passing vehicle. He was however, beyond all care of that. Near him three officers stood talking together. They were in good spirits, laughing and striking their legs with their canes from time to time. Some were officers of the S. O. S. for they wore caps instead of helmets.

Presently one of them turned and spit and it just missed landing in the dead soldier's face. Probably for the first time, the officer then noticed the corpse. It was nothing to him. He started to poke it with his cane as one pokes some inanimate bundle. He did, however, restrain this impulse and turned indifferently back to his companions.

A few minutes later a truck whirled around the road intersection and the officers stepped hastily back to assure their own safety. In doing this, the officer who had spit indifferently stepped upon the dead man's hand and stood there until the truck had passed, crushing out the fingers with the heel of his boot.

And somewhere this lad had friends and relatives who loved him well. A mother, maybe, who had nursed him at her breast. What would they say and how would they feel to see such needless indignity to one who had paid the supreme price of his life.

And these fine officers would go safely home to reap the reward of glory, earned by the sacrifice of these poor lads with their faces in the dirt.

How that crossroad, the dead messenger, and the clean officers with their canes did burn itself into my memory. The poor, fond fool lying dead in the road.

13

In a Casual Company — Orléans

On December 21, Pvt. Linn is transferred from Base Hospital #202 in Orléans to a casual company (number unrecorded), also in Orléans. Here he will remain until the first of February 1919, when he will be transferred to Casual Company #994 in St. Aignon. The following evidently takes place in the casual company barracks in Orléans.

Paris at Last

We were quartered at the time in old stone barracks in a fairly large city,[1] but that's all the good it did us. We were virtually prisoners. When we got tired of looking at the four square walls of our room, we could go over to the window and stare at a great square parade ground, on which a December rain beat steadily. Meantime, the drip from the eaves played a monotonous dirge in the puddles below.

The weather was too bad for drill and all liberty had been stopped.

The reason was, we had received an issue of raincoats to meet the bad weather, but on the first rainy day thereafter, when we fell in for drill, we had no raincoats. Everyone's raincoat had been "stolen." Now we paid for it.

Truth here forces me to acknowledge that the residents of that town were keen buyers of American raincoats. Fifteen francs was the price and no haggling. Now we had no liberty and it was coming on Christmas.

At some time in the afternoon the new guard roster was posted and to add to the normal vexations of life, I found my own name blossoming on it. The Devil, there was nothing for it.

I must have been on the second relief, for at two o'clock next morning I went on watch for the second time. I had spent the intervening hours shooting crap with the prisoners, somewhat to their sorrow, since I had most of their frankies in my pocket when I departed.

Now I was overcome with a desire to sleep. I had certainly envied the prisoners as I left, turning in to the hay.

My post was guarding a line of parked trucks under an open shed. The rain had stopped and it had turned cold. I was cold, sleepy and tired. An electric light burning with an icy abstract brilliance in the cold black night, swinging before the tool shed door, sent out long sharp spikes of light to my sleepy eyes. It had a loose reflector above it that made a tiny rattle to each gust of the wind. That was the only sound that broke the death-like stillness.

Now, parked in that line of trucks, was one American limousine, beautifully upholstered and cushioned. Each time I passed it, temptation assailed me anew. Time dragged terribly. The door was unlocked. Having gone so far, I climbed in and sank to my eyes in the soft cushions. In the stillness I could easily hear anyone approaching, and hop out, but the door let in a lot of cold. Finally I closed it.

A violent pitch brought me back to my corporeal body and the realization that I was being whirled along. A sun well up was alternately flashing into my eyes over the roofs of passing houses. "Holy mackerel!" This was the limousine I was in.

From the next corner, having slowed up to turn, that car sped on away, leaving me to contemplate its diminishing serial number, standing on the curb. Some passing Frogs viewed my maneuver with surprise. I was simply dizzy with horror. One moment it is midnight and I step into a car to while away my watch, and the next it is sun-up next day and I am standing on the curb of a city street, five miles from barracks. Who relieved me? What happened to my post? The guard? I went to the nearest cafe and had a drink. Then I ordered a cup of coffee. Here was a fine kettle of fish. I must think this out. Nothing helped, however, and after two cups of coffee, and three of cognac, and much head scratching, I was as much involved as ever. I was beginning to be light-headed from so much drinking and thinking. At that moment, in blew Private Tulley.

We went out to breakfast and after he had listened to my story, he found the solution. I couldn't get out, so I had as well go on in. That afternoon we went to Paris, "AWOL."[2]

Epilogue

Home — USS Tiger and Quantico

A Blow for the American Soldier

This begins on February 6, at La Havre, France, and ends at Quantico, Virginia.

At Le Havre we were loaded on an empty freight ship[1] bound for America, a casual company late of St. Aignon.[2] The boat had only awaited our embarking and left immediately. In a little silent band we stood at the iron deck rail as the ship slid out past the breakwater. As the mists of distance closed in, we took our last look at France and wondered if we would ever again in this life return to her shores. All about the ship the following sea gulls screamed mournfully, sounding like nothing so much as a rusty pump squeaking. We went below and started a crap game.

About noon of our twenty-second day at sea, we came between Capes Charles and Henry and after two exciting years abroad again beheld our homeland. The boat came to anchor just off Newport News, and I tried to remember just how I felt when leaving on that far day with it all before me. But I could not recapture the sensation at all. I had forgotten.

We found the camp in an uproar. There were some two thousand wounded and returned veterans there before us, and we were overwhelmed with the tale of their grievances. It seemed that the home guards resented the appearance of the vets' gold chevrons, which in a way put them in a class with the Boy Scouts. The officers who were all stay-at-homes were almost as bad.

The vets had been graded into companies and put to work, while the post companies did nothing. Those who had good legs did the guard duty.

If their legs were hit they were put in the kitchens as galley rats. Those not so badly hurt were set to work cleaning the streets and gutters and doing other necessary camp work. The only task the home guard kept was guard duty, to see we did not infringe or evade established orders.

At six o'clock, when there was liberty, some of us started off for town. At the bridge we were stopped by the MP, although men were going out of camp.

"There ain't no liberty for you fellows," the MP sneeringly informed us.

"Why not?"

"Never you mind why not, them's the orders on this post."

"Is the post quarantined?"

"Naw, anybody can go except you guys. You gotta stay in, see."

"How can you tell which ones to stop?"

For answer the MP pointed contemptuously to our sleeve chevrons and division insignia.

We walked a short ways back, then, taking out our knives, removed the offending bits of tinsel. It was galling, but we were then allowed to leave camp unchallenged.

One evening coming up from the hydroplane landing on the river, in company with another vet, I got into my first trouble. As we walked along, talking absorbedly about planes, we passed a lieutenant who was on the opposite side of the street. Neither of us did more than notice a figure pass. We were too absorbed in our conversation.

"Stop!" someone called.

"Stop, you two!"

At the second challenge we looked about to see who was being ordered to stop. It was for us. A shavetail, the one we had passed, strode up to us and stalked around to put himself directly before us. Here he set his feet well apart, placed his hands on his hips, set his teeth, and compressed his lips. This was all exactly after the approved manner of all good heroes in war movies, when they have the enemy where they want him. We regarded his maneuvers with cheerful curiosity.

"Ha-m-m," he grated out. "Didn't you men see me?"

"We did notice someone pass," I replied gravely.

"What?" he yelled.

"Why us?" I answered.

"You say 'Sir,'" he roared at me.

"Sir."

"Why didn't you salute me?"

"I didn't recognize whether you were an officer or not, Sir," I answered.

This was half a lie, for a soldier separates men and officers at a glance, but it was as near the truth as I could get, short of ten minutes of explanation that would probably not be understood. I was beginning to get mad myself now, and bit off my words as sharply as he did. This catechism from a little squirt not dry behind the ears over nothing was too much, even if he did have a chip of tin on his shoulder.

"Is there anything wrong with your eyes?" he demanded.

"Yes, I got them hurt in France, where the war was," I shot back at him.

"What?" he fairly shrieked.

"A shell," I shouted back.

For a minute I thought he was going to have apoplexy, then he got out a little book and wrote down our names and companies.

We were court-martialed and fined one month's pay apiece.[3] The officer who pronounced the sentence said, "Maybe this will teach you to show the proper respect for your superiors. You are not in the trenches now." I hardly need say he had never been in them.

Some days later our affairs had come to a head. The camp was practically in revolt but a passive one. We simply refused all duty except eating our meals. We had not returned home to have the life browbeaten out of us. We would bring the war home with us first.

We were ordered to attend a talk by the commander of the post. The whole overseas contingent was there, over two thousand men.

A number of officers, majors, colonels and captains took their places on the stage of the auditorium where the assembly was held. Then the commander came on, a nice pussy-mouthed old fellow, stuffed to the eyebrows with self-importance and officerial superiority, but about as much of a soldier as a nanny goat.

He came to the front of the stage and without preamble began, "I am hearing a lot of complaints about you men and I mean to have it stopped."

"Hurrah!" shouted some soldier in the hall. After a glare in the direction of the cry, he went on.

"There may have been some laxity in the observance of military etiquette abroad owing to the irregularity of conditions, but I want you men to understand the war is over and the license of the trenches is not to be tolerated here by your superiors. An officer is a man set above you by the United States government and a private — "

"Is just a God damn flunkey for these superior officers, eh?" someone in the auditorium cut in on this great person.

"Who said that?" he bellowed, his jowls shaking on his tunic collar.

"What does it matter? We all mean it." One of the men stood up to face the stage and went on. "We have enough of your damn superiority. We never saw any of it displayed on the front. This is America and supposed to be a free country, where all men are equal and we are citizens of that country. You happen to be hired by the United States to direct us. Now suppose you direct us according to their wishes and not according to your own insufferable self-conceit. We want decent treatment and a square deal and mean to have it if we have to fight."

"Officer of the day, officer of the day."

"Yes, sir."

A little fat slob of a captain came bustling down into our midst.

"Arrest that man."

"Yes, sir."

"Sergeant of the guard."

"Well?" inquired the sergeant.

"Arrest that man."

"There is no guard to arrest him with, sir, we are all here with him."

"I will break you to the ranks," exploded the captain.

"Thanks, sir, I will accept the favor."

The sergeant took out a knife and began to cut away his chevrons.

"Two days later in a little group of prisoners..."

A roar of laughter shook the hall, intermingled with shouts of "Pull in your ears, fathead, you are going through a tunnel."

Then an event happened that we had not prepared against. The lights went off. We had stationed our own men at the switches to see this did not happen, but a smart officer had scuttled over to the powerhouse and thrown the whole place into darkness.

We went back to billets, thrilled with the joy that we had struck our first blow for the freedom and dignity of the American soldier. In fancy we saw our uprising spreading from coast to coast, successfully changing the position of a soldier from a degraded menial to a respectable position, his right and proper place in a democratic country.

Two days later in a little group of prisoners, I was set to work unloading coal from coal cars.[3]

A short distance up the track lay a special train banked about by hundreds of our fellows. They were dressed in new uniforms, resplendent in gold braid, bound home on a month's furlough with two month's pay in their pockets.

They had sold us out for two month's pay and a month's leave. When we had staked our liberty on securing their honor, they had chosen a month's leave.

Following the incident in the auditorium, a notice was posted that all the overseas men who could show they had not been concerned in the recent disturbance would be given two month's pay and a month of leave. With no support now, the rest of us were gathered up and put in prison. Yet we had the satisfaction of knowing that it was our sacrifice that had gained them that much.

Coda

As It Might Have Been

I tried not to look servile. I did not feel so, but we are all actors and instinctively play the parts in which we are cast. I am sure I looked servile.

The place was the guard-room: my last forever. The time: my discharge from the service of my country. I stood listening to the terms of a dishonorable discharge, as they slid through the thick lips of a too-well-groomed officer. A great fat slob, stupid and stolid, with pouched underlids to his eyes, and knock-knees, a regular bogle, but wearing the bars of a captain.

The guards, off-duty, sat on their cots with averted faces or dropped heads. They would not meet my eyes. They seemed the only clean, wholesome things in the room, and I wondered what was passing in their minds.

My eyes roved over the bare walls of the board barrack, stopping at the clock ticking steadily on the wall, on again over the rack of rifles, whose feel I knew so well. I detoured to the wainscoted ceiling to avoid seeing the incubus before me, then I brought my eyes back to the immobile men. What did they think? What did I care?

The reading came to an end. The corporal of the guard advanced to me with open penknife and began to cut away my buttons, those buttons imprinted with the eagle of liberty and the stars of bravery. He took off my hat, my divisional emblem, then paused, uncertain. I wore four gold bars, two for the years in a foreign land and two for bloodshed on a foreign soil. At a nod from the captain these also were cut away. He then looked me over, but there was nothing else.

"Conduct this man to the boundary of the United States reservation. Give him this paper. Stay and see that he leaves." So spoke the captain.

We stood on the ties of the railroad track.

The corporal said, "Here," giving me the paper, "you will have to walk to the next station, this one is on the reservation. It is only a couple of miles."

167

"My three ghosts go with me." Woodcut.

I turned about and walked slowly forward. I did not think, I did not feel. I stepped on tie after tie, wrapped in apathy. Yet, strange to say, I was not alone. Three men walked with me, step for step, in sympathy and understanding: a soldier of France, a soldier of England, and a soldier of Russia. In broad noon-day light we walked slowly forward, talking together, but only one shadow fell across the ties, only one voice disturbed the quiet, and those were mine.

Notes

Chapter 1

1. "Parris" was spelled with only one r during the war.
2. Major Edwin N. McClellan, USMC, *The United States Marine Corps in the World War* (Washington, DC: Government Printing Office, 1920), p. 25. Thanks also to Jim Broshot, Matt Taylor, Jerry Beach, Carol Waldron and Kurt Johnson of the University of Kansas World War I Discussion List.
3. The identity of "Sgt. Slater" is uncertain, but he will show up again in "Boxcar Pullmans," "In Billets Again," "No Man's Land" and "Dizzy Lizzy." Among Linn's fellow recruits at Norfolk was one Robert Slater from New York City and, like Linn, he will be assigned to the First Machine Gun Battalion at Quantico (later re-designated the Sixth Machine Gun Battalion), and will serve alongside Linn throughout much of the war as a member of 77th Company. So perhaps the "Sgt. Slater" of the memoir was actually Pvt. Robert Slater. Why Linn would choose to "promote" his friend in the memoir is anybody's guess, but it might explain why the Sgt. Slater of the memoir seems to hang out with privates and corporals more as a casual buddy than as a superior in rank.
4. Bradley E. Gernand, and Michelle A. Krowl, *Quantico, Semper Progredi, Always Forward* (hereafter *Quantico*) (Virginia Beach: Donning, 2004), pp. 62–88.
5. Captain T.J. Curtis, USMC, and Captain L.R. Long, USMC, *History of the Sixth Machine Gun Battalion, Fourth Brigade, U.S. Marines, Second Division, and its Participation in the Great War* (hereafter *History*) (Neuwied-on-the-Rhine, Germany, 1919), pp. 5–6.
6. "Kranski" is probably Pvt. George Oranski, #108299, who was with Linn at Norfolk. He will be wounded during the first day of fighting at Belleau Wood. He will rejoin the company at Camp Bois de l'Évêque on August 18. (The same day Louis will return from hospital.) *Muster Rolls*, George Oranski.
7. The "Bridge of Sighs" would have been the sturdy wooden footbridge which was the only way in or out of Quantico. It crossed over a storm runoff which was designated on old maps as the "River Styx." Both names reveal a similar fatalistic humor. In Roman mythology, it was across the River Styx that the ferryman Charon carried the souls of the newly dead into the Underworld. The Bridge of Sighs refers to the elevated bridge of the same name in Venice, leading to the interrogation rooms in the Doge's palace. The view from the bridge was the last glimpse of the outer world viewed by convicts before entering prison, hence their sighs. Gernand and Krowl, *Quantico*, p. 67.
8. The battalion (Headquarters Detachment, 77th and 81st Companies), loaded onto trains at Quantico at 6:00 A.M., December 8, 1917. Curtis and Long, *History*, p. 6.
9. Linn's memory is mistaken here. It was not the next afternoon, but still the same day. They did not travel all day and night and into the next day on the train, but arrived at their

destination — Newport News — at 3 in the afternoon of the same day, December 8. Curtis and Long, *History*, p. 6.

10. The USS *De Kalb*. Formerly the German raider *Prince Eitel Frederich*, built in 1904, 15,000 gross tons, the *De Kalb* was one of 120 German ships interned in the United States at the outbreak of the war with Germany. The German skeleton crews aboard these ships attempted to render them unfit for transport service — at least until Germany had time to gain an advantage in the conflict — by damaging them in ways which were critical but not obvious: smashed cylinder heads, scored bearings, and the like. Inspection of the *De Kalb* disclosed no apparent damage, and she was placed into transport service. Altogether the *De Kalb* would make eleven successful crossings to France, loaded to the decks with doughboys. Not until the end of the war would the sabotage be discovered — the Germans had sawn one (or possibly both) of the ship's two screw shafts four-fifths of the way through, and filled the cut with grease to conceal it. Information initially derived from a newspaper clipping dated 1930 found among the papers of Alpheus Appenheimer, Headquarters Detachment, Sixth Machine Gun Battalion. See also Paul Schmalenbach, *German Raiders* (Annapolis: Naval Institute Press, 1977). Thanks especially to Brooks A. Rowlett of the University of Kansas WW Discussion List.

11. It was actually several days before the *De Kalb* was at sea. It did not leave Newport News for three days, anchoring at the mouth of the James River to take on coal, then leaving on the 11th to steam north to arrive in New York Harbor on the 12th. There it remained at anchor until joining the convoy and sailing for the open sea at 8 o'clock on the evening of the 14th. Linn's conversation with the two seasoned sailors at the deck rail probably occurred that same evening. Curtis and Long, *History*, p. 7.

12. According to the diary of Sgt. Peter Wood, #108011, of 81st Company, the *De Kalb* entered the Gulf Stream on December 16. Lt. Peter P. Wood, USMC, *Diary of Lt. Peter P. Wood, USMC, 6th Machine Gun Battalion, 1917–1919* (hereafter *Diary of Lt. Peter P. Wood*) (Bangor, Maine: David Sleeper, 2001), p. 12.

13. "Renet" is probably Pvt. Charles P. Renick, #108305, of Cumberland, Maryland. He will serve in the 77th Company throughout the war. *Muster Rolls*, Charles P. Renick.

14. December 27.

15. The primary American destroyer involved in this action, according to an entry in the diary of Pvt. Alpehus Appenheimer (Appenheimer, Unpublished diary), was the USS *Jenkins*, DD-42 operating on escort duty out of Queenstown, Ireland. German naval records show no U-boat losses for this date, so the unidentified U-boat evidently survived the encounter. (Gudmundur Helgason, "U-boat Losses, 1914–1918," uboat.net. See also Gibson and Predergast, *The German Submarine War, 1914–1918* [Annapolis: Naval Institute Press, 2003], Appendix III, p. 374). In the table "Contacts of Transports and Cruisers with Enemy Submarines" (found in Vice Admiral Albert Gleaves's *A History of the Transport Service: Adventures and Experiences of United States Transports and Cruisers in the World War* [New York: George H. Doran, 1921], pp. 167–171), there is no mention of any contact with a U-boat by an American vessel on this date. However, the encounter is recorded in the diaries of Pvt. Appenheimer, Sgt. Wood (*Diary of Lt. Peter P. Wood*, p. 13), Pvt. Herschel V. Lane (unpublished diary, by permission of Lane's granddaughter, Laura Hall), and in the memoir of Sgt. Daniel Morgan (*When the World Went Mad: A Thrilling Story of the Late War, Told in the Language of the Trenches* [Boston: Christopher Publishing House, [1931], p. 20), as well as in Pvt. Linn's memoir. Of these four independent witnesses, Herschel and Linn state that the U-boat fired a torpedo at the *De Kalb*; Wood, Morgan and Linn state that the *De Kalb* fired at the U-boat; Wood describes in detail which of the ship's guns were employed; Wood, Morgan and Linn state that the *Jenkins* and other destroyers pursued the U-boat and deployed depth charges against her (Morgan reports that an oil slick was spotted); and Appenheimer and Wood identifies the primary defending vessel as the USS *Jenkins*. Particular thanks to Jim Broshot, Peter Beeston, Geoffrey Miller, Marcus Poulin, Ric Pelvin, Niall Ferguson and Mike Yared of the University of Kansas World War I Discussion List.

16. December 28.

17. "At 5 P.M. on Dec 31st, all troops disembarked and marched to the railroad station. Entrained at 6pm and proceeded to the training area." Curtis and Long, *History*, p. 7.

Chapter 2

1. Curtis and Long, *History*, p 7.
2. Appenheimer, unpublished diary.
3. Despite a major effort by the AEF, involving many shiploads of equipment and men, to supply their own railway needs so as not to burden further the already overtaxed French railway system, the movement of American troops during the war was accomplished almost entirely on French narrow-gauge trains. William J. Wilgus, *Transporting the A.E.F. in Western Europe, 1917–1919* (New York: Columbia University Press, 1931), pp. 372–.
4. These small French boxcars were designed to hold 40 men or 8 horses or mules. The Americans, generally somewhat larger than their French counterparts, found 40 an impossibly tight squeeze. The boxcars came in several designs, some with a hard bench along the wall, others without; some with open windows just below the ceiling, and others without. All designs had a sliding door on either side, the same as American boxcars. The wheels were set towards the middle, rather than the corners, so that the cars tended to rock end-to-end. All in all, they were a misery. Laurence Stallings, *The Doughboys: The Story of the AEF* (hereafter *Doughboys*) (New York: Harper and Row, 1963), pp. 40, 178.
5. "Moler" is possibly Pvt. Daniel Millar, #108285. He will appear again in "Bits of Life and Death." He will be wounded by shell fire at Blanc Mont. *Muster Rolls,* Daniel Millar.
6. "Frog" is doughboy parlance for "Frenchman."
7. Linn is close, but a bit off the mark. Germainvilliers is in the *Haute-Marne Department* ("department" is the French equivalent of "province").
8. Linn is essentially correct in this observation. Manure was the key to the fertility of each farmer's fields and the size of his harvest. To the American army, on the other hand, these same manure piles were a potential source of contamination and sickness, and medical officers made it their business to have all such piles removed outside the village limits. Marine teamsters were assigned the task of loading the piles into wagons and dumping them indiscriminately outside the town, with no deference shown to issues of individual ownership, causing the villagers a great deal of difficulty and inconvenience. Needless to say, this policy resulted in considerable ill will toward the Americans.
9. The elderly villager who so bewildered the Marines was simply the town crier, a kind of walking newspaper, and a common fixture in rural villages across Europe since at least the Middle Ages. It is surprising the Marines didn't recognize him for what he was, since town criers had been equally common in American towns and villages during colonial times, and had survived into modern times in children's stories, folklore and grade-school primers. In any case, to have followed the poor fellow around with raucous hooting and applause must have provided the villagers with yet more conclusive evidence that the Americans were essentially just a mob of rowdy loonies.
10. "Cob" is probably Pvt. Harold S. Cobb, #108228. During the difficult night march on Soissons, he will become separated from his unit, and eventually transferred to 137th Company, First Corps Replacement Battalion at Noisiel. He will never return to the Fourth Brigade. He will continue serving in the Marine Corps until 1921. *Muster Rolls,* Harold S. Cobb.
11. "Hern" is probably Pvt. George H. Kern, #108269. *Muster Rolls*, George H. Kern.
12. Germainvilliers.
13. "Frankies" is soldier slang for French francs.
14. "Garden" is possibly Pvt. Max Gordon, #108248. *Muster Rolls,* Max Gordon.
15. "Zhim" is "Jim," as pronounced by the French. "Jim" is the name Linn has given to himself in his memoir.
16. "Cpl. Burk" is Cpl. Stanley Zyglarski (Zygloski, Zyglerski), #108208 of Buffalo. He joined the Marine Corps in January 1915 and trained at Norfolk. Prior to America's entry into the war, he served in Marine detachments aboard four different naval ships. He will serve with 77th Company until he is murdered by another Marine in May 1918. His identity will be established conclusively in "An Assassination." *Muster Rolls*, Stanley Zyglarski.
17. "Mess Sergeant Hoburna" is almost certainly Sgt. James Koberna, #108180. He will appear also in "Horseradish" and "Back to Duty." In addition to being a mess sergeant, he also serves as a gunnery sergeant, and will go on to win the Silver Star Certificate for actions at Blanc

Mont and another SSC and *Croix de Guerre* with Palm for action in the Meuse-Argonne. George B. Clark, *Decorated Marines of the Fourth Brigade in World War I* (hereafter *Decorated Marines*) (Jefferson, NC: McFarland, 2007), p. 226. *Muster Rolls*, James Koberna.

18. "Sgt. Sike," referred to by his men as "Pop," is almost certainly Sgt. Alfred G. Slyke, #108185. He will appear again in "The Arrival" and "Back to Duty." He joined the Marine Corps in 1910, served at Manila and Vera Cruz and in Marine detachments on board nine different naval ships. While in France with 77th Company, he will receive a commendation for valor for actions on the Verdun front and be decorated again at Blanc Mont. By war's end he will be awarded the Navy Cross, the distinguished Service Cross, two Silver Star Citations and the French *Croix de Guerre*. During the heaviest fighting at Soissons "Sgt. Sike" will pull the badly wounded Linn to safety and attend to his wounds, very likely saving his life. Sike will die of an unspecified ailment on November 4, one week before the Armistice. Clark, *Decorated Marines*, p. 235; George B. Clark, *Devil Dogs: Fighting Marines of World War I* (hereafter *Devil Dogs*), (Novato, CA: Presidio Press, 1999), p. 50; Harry R. Stringer, ed., *The Navy Book of Distinguished Service* (Washington, DC: Fassett, 1921).

Chapter 3

1. Randal Gray with Christopher Argyle, *Chronicle of the First World War, 1917–1919* (hereafter *Chronicle*), 2 vols. (New York: Facts on File, 1991), pp. 144–154.

2. Entraining table: "Moves of the Second Division (less Artillery) from Third Area to New Training Area," Attached to General Orders No. 23, Headquarters Second Division, AEF France, March 10, 1918 (hereafter General Orders No. 23) in U.S. Army, *Records of the Second Division*, 9 vols. (Washington, DC: The Army War College, 1927).

3. General Orders No. 23, *Records of the Second Division*.

4. This depot is at Nancois, a few kilometers north of Ligny-en-Bar. General Orders No. 23 stipulates that all trains will stop at Nancois for an hour so that the men can receive a hot supper.

5. The Russians who befriend Pvt. Linn are almost certainly from the First Battalion of the *Legion Russe*, under Colonel Gotua, and are probably on their way from Toul, where they have had a period of rest and refitting, to the front lines near Amiens where, shortly, as part of the Moroccan Division, they will suffer terrible losses. Originally these men had come to the Western Front as part of the First Russian Special Brigade, sent to France by the czar in early 1916, and subsequently participated in the "Nivelle attack" of April 16, 1917, in the Fort Pompelle region.

With the outbreak of the October Revolution later that year, many of the Russian soldiers in France mutinied, with the result that the entire Russian brigade was demobilized by the French government and dispersed across France into various labor and internment camps. A number of the Russian soldiers, however, refused to mutiny and, under Colonel Gotua, demanded the right to keep fighting on behalf of the Allies against the Germans. By mid–December 1917, their petition was granted and they were formed into the *Legion Russe*, as part of the Moroccan Division. My thanks to Richard Spence of the University of Kansas World War I Discussion List for information regarding the *Legion Russe*. See also Jamie H. Cockfield, *With Snow on Their Boots: The Tragic Odyssey of the Russian Expeditionary Force in France During World War I* (New York: St. Martin's Press, 1998).

6. *With Fire and Sword*, published in 1894 by Henry Sienkiewicz, is a popular historical novel of Poland and Russia.

7. Curtis and Long, *History*, p. 9.

8. *Ibid.*

9. "Our captain" would have been either Capt. Louis R. deRoode, commanding the 77th Company in March 1918, or second-in-command Capt. Augustus B. Hale, Curtis and Long, *History*, p. 5.

10. The liaison officer would have been a French officer.

11. "When the 6th Regiment of Marines reached Camp Massy [*sic*] near Verdun they found

a secretary established in a cowshed by the side of the road. He had 'secured' several wonderful boilers from headquarters and for six weeks he filled canteens with hot chocolate for officers and men tramping by." William Howard Taft, *Service with Fighting Men: An Account of the Work of the American Young Men's Christian Association in the World War*, 2 vols. (New York: Association Press, 1922), Vol. II, p. 122.

12. Camp Nivollete.

13. Curtis and Long, *History*, p. 10.

14. Camp Joffre, somewhere close to Eix. Precise location unknown. *Ibid.*

15. This was almost certainly a 60-cm-gauge light railway train, probably a French Decauville. Linn appears to remember the locomotive as rather smaller than it actually was, but in other respects his description is accurate. These narrow-gauge trains were used extensively around Verdun (and elsewhere on the Western Front) to bring supplies, men and ammunition from standard rail and canal heads to within about three miles of the front lines. (Steam locomotives did not approach much closer than that as their plumes of steam and smoke made them easy targets for German artillery.) At about the three-mile line, depots were established from which supplies for the front were carried forward by wagon or by rail, using small gasoline locomotives or horses or mules. I am indebted to historians Niall Ferguson, Peter Foley and Len Shurtleff of the University of Kansas World War I Discussion List for this information.

16. Curtis and Long, *History*, p. 10.

17. The *Tunnel de Tavannes*, a single-track railway tunnel on the Metz-Verdun line which ran for 1400 yards beneath the Meuse Hills, just to the west of Eix. During the war it was expanded to include barracks, dressing stations, storage depots and command posts, and was of sufficient size to accommodate upwards of 4000 men. See Alistair Horne, *The Price of Glory: Verdun 1916* (New York: Macmillan, 1962), pp. 303–05. I am also indebted to Peter Farrell-Vinay, David Heal and Len Shurtleff of the University of Kansas World War I Discussion List for the identification of this tunnel.

18. Linn probably means a "210" rather than a "410." The German army employs a variety of 210 mm caliber shell pieces. Thanks to Jim Broshot of the World War I Discussion List.

19. Curtis and Long, *History*, p. 10.

20. The town is "Eix," about ten kilometers east of Verdun, in the Moulainville Sector. Seventy-seventh Company is positioned in support of Third Battalion, Fifth Marines. Linn is not alone in misspelling Eix with an "A." It is misspelled "Aix" in Appenheimer's diary as well.

21. Both photographs and drawings from the war depict roads camouflaged in this manner in the vicinity of Verdun. Very likely such camouflage was in use all along the Western Front. Long elevated burlap banners were strung on poles along roadways where troop movements occurred, in order to obscure the sight of them from enemy artillery spotters and planes.

22. "Sgt. Blanche" is probably Sgt. Benjamin Blanchard, #108509. He enlisted in Boston in April 1917, did his basic training at the Navy yard in Philadelphia, joined 23rd Company, Fifth Marines in June 1917 and was promoted to corporal in July and sergeant in August. He served in various companies, but remained always in the Fifth Marines. In November 1917, Blanchard sailed to France with 43rd Company, Fifth Marines and was made stable sergeant, in charge of the company's horses and mules. Finally, in February, Blanchard joined 77th Company where he began serving as a transport sergeant. On March 22, 1918, while 77th Company was at Camp Nivolette, Blanchard was reduced in rank to private on a charge of "incompetence." He will serve with 77th Company until the terrible night march on Soissons when, like so many other Marines, he will become separated from his unit. He is reassigned to another company — the 75th Company, Sixth Marines. During the fight at Blanc Mont, he will receive a gunshot wound to the head, but will survive. *Muster Rolls*, Benjamin Blanchard.

23. The identity of "Horseradish," the main subject of this chapter, is uncertain.

24. "Humfers" is possibly Pvt. Arthur Humphries, #108260, from Atlanta, Georgia. He did his basic training at Norfolk. In December 1915, Humphries was promoted to corporal and to sergeant in the Central, Eastern and Southern Recruiting Divisions until October, when for reasons which are unclear, he was reduced in rank to private and transferred to Headquarters Detachment, First Machine Gun Battalion at Quantico. In December he joined 77th Company. In February 1918, in Germainvilliers, Humphries was tried for disobedience of orders and ordered to forfeit a portion of his pay. He remained a private in 77th Company until the Armistice,

after which he will work his way back up to sergeant. He will remain in the Marine Corps until 1922, being reduced in rank to private and working his way back up to sergeant two more times. *Muster Rolls*, Arthur Humphries.

25. "Norton" is possibly Pvt. George P. Nordin, #108293, who trained with Linn at Norfolk. He will serve with 77th Company throughout the war and the Occupation, until his return to the States in August 1919. He will be awarded the Silver Star for actions at Belleau Wood. *Muster Rolls*, George P. Nordin.

26. "Simmes" is possibly Pvt. Harold B. Simmons, #108311, who also trained with Linn at Norfolk. At Belleau Wood, Simmons will repeatedly venture out under shellfire and in plain view of the enemy to repair telephone lines, for which he will be awarded a Silver Star Certificate and a *Croix de Guerre*. Like Linn, Simmons will be wounded by shellfire near Tigny on July 19, during the battle of Soissons. His name does not appear on muster rolls until December, when he is listed as a patient in a New York hospital. He will serve in the Marine Barracks, Navy Yard, in New York until November 1919, when he will be honorably discharged. *Muster Rolls*, Harold B. Simmons.

27. "Brown's Mixture" is *Collis Browne's Chlorodyne*, an over-the-counter remedy for bowel complaints which contains morphine and which is sold in a "little unbreakable bottle [that] stows away in any small pocket." In advertisements of the day (i.e., *London Times*, 12 August 1914), soldiers are urged to keep a bottle always at hand in their kits, and families are encouraged to give them as gifts to soldiers on their way to the front. Thanks to Jim Clay of the *Great War Forum*.

28. One of the muleskinners in that supply train, Alpheus Appenheimer, will later tell his children and grandchildren about driving his team and wagon through shellfire while carrying supplies to the front lines. According to Appenheimer, the Germans would "walk" the explosions down a stretch of road where the supply wagons would be coming up to the line. By watching the explosions approach, timing the intervals with his watch, he could calculate the distance gained by each shell (all the while holding his four mules steady). Appenheimer would position himself as close as he dared to the approaching explosion and, as soon as it hit, drive his team hell-for-leather through the hovering smoke to be safely under the trajectory arc of the next shell. Thanks to Clay Appenheimer, Dorothy Schmidt, Don Schmidt and Mitchell B. Young for their memories of this.

29. Linn's description of the mess sergeant "Hoburna" (Sgt. James Koberna, #108180) as "enormously fat" must surely be an exaggeration. No "enormously fat" person is capable of covering 30-plus miles a day in heavy marching order.

30. "Squareheads" (a reference to the shape of their helmets) was doughboy slang for German soldiers.

31. Curtis and Long, *History*, pp. 9–10.

32. The Sibley stove, a small iron woodstove designed for use in tents, and shaped like an inverted funnel, was designed by Henry Hopkins Sibley, a Confederate general. The stove saw limited use during the Civil War and became widely used during the Indian Wars on the western frontier. It would continue in use by the military until World War II. See *Manual for the Quartermaster Corps, United States Army, 1916, Volume 2* (Washington, DC: Government Printing Office, 1917), Appendix 14–40, p. 288.

33. In military slang, a "dog robber" is an officer's orderly; also, one who will use any means necessary to obtain whatever an officer might request.

Chapter 4

1. Curtis and Long, *History*, p. 9.
2. Curtis and Long, *History*, p. 12.
3. "Sammy" is British slang for American soldier.
4. *The Graphic* is a lavishly illustrated weekly magazine published in London, begun in the 1860s until the 1930s. It is widely distributed in England and North America and frequently sent to soldiers at the front. Thanks to Brett Holman of the World War I Discussion List.
5. Curtis and Long, *History*, p. 12.

6. Lieutenant George C. Strott, Hospital Corps, USN (Ret.), *The Medical Department of the United States Navy with the Army and Marine Corps in France in World War I* (Washington, DC: U.S. Navy Department, 1947), p. 42.

7. McClellan, *The United States Marine Corps in the World War*, p. 39.

8. "Major Colin" is definitely Major Edward B. Cole, commander of the Sixth Machine Gun Battalion.

9. The French town "Flourette" is actually Venault-le-Châtel.

10. "Cpl. Burk" (Cpl. Stanley Zyglerski, #108208) appeared first in "A Ghost Among the French."

11. No mention of this incident is made in Curtis and Long, *History of the Sixth Machine Gun Battalion*, and "Burk" (Zyglarski) is not listed on the battalion's Roll of Honor, probably because his was not a combat death.

Sgt. Peter Wood, of 81st Company, makes a cursory note of this incident in his diary, stating only that a certain "Sgt. Massa of 23rd Company shot and killed a corporal of 77th Company. (Sleeper, David [ed], *Diary of Lt. Peter P. Wood, USMC, 6th Machine Gun Battalion, 1917–1919.* Bangor, Maine: David Sleeper, 2001).

The full story is recorded in the 77th Company May 1918 muster roll records, where it says of Cpl. Stanley P. Zyglerski that, on the 17th, he was "shot and fatally wounded (while in the execution of his office as Cpl of the guard and effecting the arrest of an enlisted man for creating a disturbance) by an enlisted man of the 23rd Co, 6 MGB, died in Field Hospital at Ravignay France at 12:00 noon, May 18, 1918, death in line of duty. Personal effects forwarded to Effects Depot A.E.F., place of burial not given by medical Authorities. Recommended for Character Excellent on decease. (Signed) A.B. Hale, Captain, M.C., Company Commander."

As for Cpl. Zyglerski's killer, the full story is found in the 23rd Company muster roll records for May 1918, where it says that Clarence L. Massey, #108529, on the 17th was "confined awaiting trial by G.C.M. for violation of the 92nd A.W., willful murder of Cpl. Stanley P. Zygloski, 108208, M.C., by shooting him in the chest with a service pistol caliber .45 on May 17, 1918."

Sgt. Massey's fate is recorded in the 23rd Company muster roll records for September 1918, where it states that on 11 August 1918, Sgt. Massey was "tried by General Court Martial. Found guilty.... To be reduced to ranks, to be dishonorably discharged the service, to forfeit all pay and allowances due or to become due, and to be confined at hard labor at such place as the reviewing authorities may direct for the term of his natural life. The sentence is applied and will be duly executed, U.S. Penitentiary at Fort Leavenworth, Kansas, is designated as the place of confinement to which place the prisoner will be sent under proper guard. Character given on discharge "Bad." Court published 7 Sept 18. (Signed) W.B. Croka, First Lieutenant, U.S.M.C., Commanding. Muster Rolls, 23rd Company, 6th Machine Gun Battalion, September 1918.

Chapter 5

1. Curtis and Long, *History*, pp. 12–13.

2. "Slack" is 77th Company trumpeter Leon Schack, #108209, from Newark, New Jersey. Schack re-enlisted in April 1917. Records of his prior service are missing. For most of the year he served with the Eastern and Central Recruiting divisions at the Marine Corps Rifle Range in Winthrop, Maryland. He was transferred to Quantico on August 3, joining the 77th Company. In late April 1918, while the company was in the trenches at Eix, just three or four weeks before the preceding event took place, Schack was brought up on court-martial charges for willfully disobeying the orders of a non-commissioned officer and sentenced to six months hard labor. He will be sent away on June 1. Five months later he will be hospitalized with illness. *Muster Rolls*, Leon Schack.

3. "Tilson" is the other trumpeter, Franz C. Wilson, #108210. He enlisted in January 1917 and spent most of that year at Winthrop, Maryland. During that time Wilson served 11th Company, First Regiment, Fixed Defense Force. In this company he would have been surrounded by veterans of both the Haiti and Santo Domingo campaigns, from whom he doubtless heard many a tropical tale of adventure. He himself never left the continental United States until

sailing for France in December. He served with 77th Company until July 1918, when he will be hospitalized with illness. He will not return to his company until shortly before the Armistice. He will again be hospitalized. *Muster Rolls*, Franz C. Wilson.

4. The farm would have been in or near the village of Beaugrenier.

5. Possibly Pvt. Harold L Moldestad, #108287, from St. Paul, Minnesota, who trained with Linn at Norfolk. During the terrible night march on Soissons, he will be picked up and held in detention. He will disappear from roll records until October 18, when he is court-martialed. His sentence is suspended due to "gallant conduct in the face of the enemy." Two weeks later Moldestad will be killed in the Meuse-Argone campaign while helping others of his company to charge and capture a battery of German artillery. He will be awarded posthumously the Silver Star Certificate. *Muster Rolls*, Harold L. Moldestad; Clark, *Decorated Marines*, p. 229.

6. The whole brigade received word on May 30 to pack up and be ready to move out the following morning. Curtis and Long, *History*, p. 12–13.

7. The muster roll records for the 77th Company show no record of anyone failing to report for duty on the 31st. *Muster Rolls*, 77th Company, Sixth Machine Gun Battalion, May 1918.

Chapter 6

1. Gray and Argyle, *Chronicle*, pp. 172–4; and Robert B. Asprey, *At Belleau Wood* (New York: G.P. Putnam's Sons, 1965), pp. 60–71.

2. In the pre-dawn hours of May 31, Linn, along with the entire Sixth Machine Gun Battalion (less the supply train), assembles at the junction of the Beaugrenier-Dieppe-Paris roads and begins loading onto French trucks driven by Indo-Chinese. Curtis and Long, *History*, p. 13. Linn is disappointed to learn that those Marines, including himself, who are responsible for the gun and ammunition carts and mules will not be leaving with the battalion, but are instead sent back to join the supply train in the village. It is still dark when Linn and his group return to their lofts for a little more sleep. The battalion will get underway about 9 A.M.

3. The "next morning" is still the 31st.

4. The supply train leaves Beaugrenier in two sections. Both Linn and Appenheimer are in the second. Linn says they leave around noon, Appenheimer records that they leave at 2 P.M. Appenheimer papers, diary entry for May 31; Curtis and Long, *History* p. 13.

5. The "quite a large city" is Chars. Curtis and Long, *History*, p.13.

6. According to battalion history, the first section of the Supply Train loads onto boxcars in Chars at 2 P.M. on the 31st. The second section loads onto boxcars at 4:30, according to *History*, but both Linn and Appenheimer record that it is nearly nightfall before they board. Curtis and Long, *History*, p. 13; Appenheimer papers, dairy entry May 31.

7. This was probably Gy. Sgt. Theodore Schuldt, #107953, Headquarters Detachment, who was in charge of all the battalion's horses and mules. (Among the personal papers of Cpl. Alpheus Appenheimer is a small typed personal order from the "Office of Battalion Quartermaster," dated 17 October 1918, directing Appenheimer to "take charge of the corral during the absence of Gy. Sgt. Schuldtt." The order is signed by Capt. Harvis.)

8. They unloaded in the town of Saint-Soupplets at daybreak, June 1. Curtis and Long, *History*, p. 13.

9. The evening of June 1. They detrained in Saint-Soupplets around noon and hiked until nightfall. Curtis and Long, *History*, p. 13.

10. The Château Marigny in Marigny-en-Orxois, close to Belleau Wood. Al Appenheimer noted in his diary for June 1: "Unload and leave at noon and hike till night and camp in a beautiful chateau court ... it's a beautiful place, lakes, fountains, deer, swans and ducks."

The chateau is now a hospital, bringing in wounded soldiers by the hundreds, very close to the front. I am indebted to Bill Graham and Charles Fair of the University of Kansas World War I Discussion List, as well as to historians Tom Gudmestad and Gilles Lagin, for information on the history of this chateau. Gilles Lagin, who lives near the chateau in Marigny, provided the World War I–era postcard of the chateau. Charles Fair provided the following description: "The chateau still exists today as a private property and is very attractive, with the style of turret that one imagines to be typical of a small French chateau. Apparently, the oldest part of the chateau was built during the 12th century, with 15th and 18th century additions. It was the chateau of Francois Gigot de La Peyronie, first surgeon to Louis XV, then after 1750, it was the property of Francois Poisson, the father of the Marquise de Pompadour, Louis XV's favorite."

11. Marigny-en-Orxois.

12. Pvt. Appenheimer also describes the chateau as a "hospital." In 1997, Bill Graham asked the then-mayor of Marigny-en-Orxois, M. Couillette, about the chateau and he confirmed that it was used as a hospital during the war. Appenheimer papers, dairy entry June 1; World War I Discussion List.

13. In fact, no one at this point considers the German advance stopped at all. The Germans have merely dug in, preparing to attack the following morning. No one in the Allied command seriously expects the green American troops to hold. As for the Germans, they assume they are facing exhausted French troops and fully expect to sweep them aside at first light. Curtis and Long, *History*, p. 13.

14. Curtis and Long, *History*, p. 27.

15. The attack of Berry's Third Battalion, Fifth Marines, including 77th Company, is most thoroughly covered in Asprey, *At Belleau Wood*, pp. 154–200; and Clark, *Devil Dogs*, pp. 101–129.

16. In these opening days of the Marines' assault, the Germans do very little in the way of retreating.

17. Accompanying the Marines of Berry's battalion was a war correspondent, Floyd Gibbons, who was shot in three places (among them his eye, which he lost), but who somehow survived and never lost consciousness. Like Linn, he later wrote a description of the moaning of the wounded men in the wheat during the evening of June 6, and the two accounts bear comparison: "Sometimes there were lulls in the firing. During these periods of comparative quiet, I could hear the occasional moan of other wounded on that field. Very few of them cried out and it seemed to me that those who did were unconscious when they did it. One man in particular had a long, low groan. I could not see him, yet I felt he was lying somewhere close to me. In the quiet intervals, his unconscious expression of pain reminded me of the sound I had once heard made by a calf which had been tied by a short rope to a tree. The animal had strayed round and round the tree until its entanglements in the rope had left it a helpless prisoner. The groan of the that unseen, unconscious wounded American who laid near me on the field that evening sounded exactly like the pitiful bawl of that calf." Floyd Gibbons, "And They Thought We Wouldn't Fight" (New York: George H. Doran Company, 1918), p. 320.

18. Curtis and Long, *History*, pp. 16–17.

19. The "continuously shifting line of graves" is a line of half dug shallow troughs scooped out by Marines under fire on the front lines. They move forward or back in response to the changing situation of the battlefield. Linn refers to them as graves because, all too often, that is precisely what they become.

Chapter 7

1. Curtis and Long, *History*, p. 25.

2. For more information about events leading up to the Battle of Soissons and the role of the Second Division AEF as part of General Mangin's Tenth Army, see especially Edward M. Coffman, *The War to End All Wars* (New York: Oxford University Press, 1968), pp. 234–48; Douglas V. Johnson and Rolfe L. Hillman, *Soissons 1918* (College Station: Texas A&M University Press, 1999), chapters 3 and 5; George B. Clark, *The Second Infantry Division in World War I: A History of the American Expeditionary Force Regulars, 1917–1919* (Jefferson, NC: McFarland, 2007), chapter 5; O.L. Spaulding and J.W. Wright, *The Second Division Expeditionary Force in France 1917–1919* (New York: Hillman, 1937), chapters 9 and 10; Stallings, *The Doughboys*, chapter 8.

3. Curtis and Long, *History*, pp. 25–6.

4. *Ibid.*, pp. 25–7.

5. *Ibid.*, pp. 26–7.

6. Linn's description of the long drive that ended at 3 P.M., of the 17th, being "dumped from the trucks," and making camp in a nearby forest, closely matches the battalion history: "The combat troops in camions with their machine guns, ammunition and machine gun equipment arrived at 3:00 P.M., at a point about 1-1/2 kilometers south of Taillefontaine, debussed and marched into the Bois de la Taillefontaine and halted." Curtis and Long, *History*, p. 26.

7. "At 10:30 P.M., the march was continued, carrying guns, ammunition, and machine gun equipment by hand through the dark forest under the most trying conditions. The rain was pouring in torrents, and this night in the forest was one of the blackest nights ever experienced. Exhausted men were carrying heavy guns and ammunition, unable to see where they were going, falling, stumbling against trees, against trucks, and every kind of obstacle." Curtis and Long, *History*, p. 26.

8. Linn was not alone in complaining about a terrible thirst. This complaint shows up in numerous accounts of that day. It also entered the medical record: "By mid-afternoon (of the 17th) the canteens, filled the night before, had been drained, and acute thirst was bothering the men.... There was no hope that either water or food would be available. Some men chewed on grass and some moistened their lips with mud." From the personal log of battalion surgeon Lt. George G. Strott, *Medical Department,* p. 63.

9. According to the battalion history, the men arrived at the northern edge of the Bois de Retz at 3 A.M. on the 18th, "where a halt was made owing to the exhausted condition of the men." They were permitted to sleep until 7 A.M., when they resumed marching to Verte Feuille Farm (Curtis and Long, *History*, p. 26). However, information regarding the location of the Sixth Machine Gun Battalion on July 18 is contradictory. (See the next piece, "A French Band at an Old Chateau," especially note 1).

10. *The History of the Sixth Machine Gun Battalion* states, "The battalion on July 18th continued its march, carrying all the guns, ammunition and machine gun equipment, arriving at the northern edge of Bois de Retz at 3:00 A.M., where a halt was made owing to the exhausted condition of the men." It goes on to say, "The march was resumed at 7:00 A.M., to Verte Feuille Farm; at this place the companies were assigned their combat missions. Battalion P.C. was established at Beaurepaire Farm." Curtis and Long, *History*, p. 26.

This would appear to be in error, because early on July 18, Verte Feuille Farm was still in German hands and would not be taken by the Marines until sometime later that morning. There is reason to believe that at least some elements of the Sixth Machine Gun Battalion, early on the 18th, were sent several miles to the west, away from the line, to Pierrefonds. A number of orders preserved in the records of the Second Division indicate that Pierrefonds was a destination of several Marine units early on the 18th, and General Harbord, on page 322 of his *Leaves from a War Diary*, notes, "The machine guns of the Marine Brigade had been dumped off near the old Chateau of Pierrefonds. The men had no transportation and no orders...." I have not been able to find conclusive evidence that the Sixth Machine Gun Battalion was in fact at Pierrefonds on the 18th, but Linn's story, "A French Band in an Old Chateau," almost certainly takes place there.

11. Curtis and Long, *History*, p. 27.

12. I can find no corroborating evidence that Linn and his fellow Marines (of the First Battalion, Sixth Regiment and his own 77th Company) came under "friendly" fire on the morning of the 19th during the attack on Tigny. Probably because they were caught in a crossfire on both flanks, Linn assumed the fire from one flank had to be American, but in fact the fire from both flanks came from German guns: 77s and 105s while Maxim machine guns fired on them from houses in the town, trapping the advancing Marines in a ferocious crossfire. Regarding the severity of the shellfire that morning, Linn is not exaggerating. The Marines attacking Tigny took the heaviest fire of all Marine units on that day and suffered the heaviest casualties. The Germans were firing on them at nearly point-blank range, so close that those not torn to pieces by bullets or shrapnel were knocked nearly senseless by the concussion. See Clark, *Devil Dogs*, pp. 248–250, and "Synopsis of the attack on Tigny by the 74th Company, 1st Battalion, 6th Regiment., July 22, 1918," *Records of the Second Division,* vol. 5.

13. The German army has a vehicle mounted quick-firing 88-mm gun at this time, the Krupp 8.8-cm KwFlak, which went into production in 1916. The Austro-Hungarian army also possesses an older 88-mm field gun, some of which reportedly show up on the Western Front.

Thanks to Rick Spence of World War I Discussion List. Apart from Linn's account, I have been unable to verify the use of German 88s at Soissons.

14. Linn is mistaken. The Marines failed to take Tigny at all. However, the commanding officer responsible for the attack on Tigny, Lt. Col. Harry Lee, sent a message (*Records of the Second Division*) to General Harbord at about 10 A.M. claiming Tigny had been captured (a claim which two hours later would be contradicted in a message to Sixth Regiment headquarters by the commander of the Third Battalion, Col. Sibley). The mistaken news of Tigny's capture may have briefly become a general rumor.

15. According to most sources, the Marines never made it into Tigny, but did manage to take up positions just outside the western outskirts of town (Clark, *Devil Dogs*, p. 250). The house where Linn and his comrades attempted to fill their canteens at a well, and where some of them were killed, must have been just on the perimeter of the town. Most descriptions of the fighting near Tigny on the 19th state that the Marines never got closer than about 300 yards west of town. However, one source (*2d Division Summary of Operations*, p. 31) states that several units *did* get closer, penetrating further to the east and northeast, until forced to withdraw. If Linn was among one of these forward units, it would suggest that his description of entering the outskirts of Tigny might in fact be accurate.

16. A sergeant of 77th Company, Daniel Morgan, leading the third platoon, also witnessed the explosion at the well which so nearly killed Linn on the 19th, on the outskirts of Tigny. He writes: "A high explosive shell hit a group of men at a pump while they were filling their canteens. I saw only one run out of the smoke; the others were killed or wounded. I passed on without any water." Morgan, *When the World Went Mad*, p. 47.

17. Some 24 hours earlier, the Red Cross had visited Marines of the First Battalion, Sixth Regiment on their march through the Forêt de Retz, distributing white "American" bread with molasses among the famished men, much to their delight. Warren R. Jackson, *His Time in Hell—A Texas Marine in France: The World War I Memoir of Warren R. Jackson*, ed. George B. Clark (Novato, CA: Presidio Press, 2001), p. 138.

18. Muster roll records for 77th Company, Sixth Machine Gun Battalion, confirm that Linn was wounded by shellfire on July 19, 1918. *Muster Rolls* 77th Company, July 1918.

19. "Sergeant Sike," as mentioned earlier, was almost certainly Sgt. Alfred G. Slyke, and was Linn's squad leader (his men referred to him as "Pop"). Linn consistently portrays him as just a regular guy who leads and looks after the men in his squad without making a point of his authority. Linn does not portray "Sgt. Sike" as being in any way out of the ordinary, but Sgt. Alfred Slyke was in fact a Marine of extraordinary physical courage and ability. He received a commendation for bravery and self-sacrifice for actions on the Verdun front where he continued to command his machine gun in action even though pinned under heavy timbers and debris (Clark, *Devil Dogs*, p. 50). At Blanc Mont, when Germans attacked his machine gun detachment at close range, cutting them off from their supply of ammunition, Slyke ran forward under heavy fire, secured the ammunition, then returned to his gun, opened fire and routed the enemy, an action for which he was awarded the Navy Cross. Stringer, *The Navy Book of Distinguished Service*. Slyke must have performed other feats of valor as well, but by war's end, in addition to the Navy Cross, he was awarded the Distinguished Service Cross, two Silver Star Citations and the French *Croix de Guerre*. So it is no surprise that during some of the heaviest fighting at Soissons, he was there to pull Linn to safety and attend to his wounds. He may well have saved Linn's life.

20. The only village close to Tigny was Parcy-Tigny, about one kilometer to the southwest, and this is the most likely location of the dressing station to which Linn walked (with someone helping him) after he was wounded. This village was under French control, which accords with Linn's description of French officers standing near a staff pennant.

21. The empty ammunition truck used to evacuate Linn and his wounded comrades would have been one of many commandeered by medical personnel from the divisional artillery train for the purpose of evacuating wounded from Vierzy and Tigny (Records, Derby). Lt. George Strott, USN, a battalion surgeon with the Second Division, described the evacuation in his journal, dated July 19: "Packed closely to conserve precious space on the hard floors of heavy trucks, load after load of critically injured men (were evacuated from the dressing stations). There were no litters to carry them and they had only improvised dressings. Passing through

poisonous gas and over shell-torn roads undergoing terrific bombardment, these trucks, with their groaning and screaming cargoes bouncing around, rushed to clear the area and reach possible safety many kilometers away. Suffering was extreme and many died en route" (Strott, *Medical Department*, p. 65).

22. The farmhouse which Linn describes as the place where he was dropped by the ammunition truck was most probably at Beaurepaire Ferme. "Collecting points," where the wounded were gathered for evacuation from front-line areas, had been set up at Maison Neuve Ferme, Verte Feuille Ferme, Beaurepaire Ferme, Vauxcastille and Vierzy (Richard Derby, *"Wade in Sanitary!" The Story of a Division Surgeon in France* (New York: G.P. Putnam's Sons, 1919, pp. 88–89). Vierzy lay the closest to Parcy-Tigny, but it was a sizeable town, not a farm, and in any case was still under shell-fire on the 19th. There was a great effort to evacuate all the wounded from its environs, so it is most unlikely that any wounded would have been brought in from outside. Beaurepaire Ferme, about a kilometer west of Vierzy, was the next closest dressing station, and received a flood of wounded from Vierzy and Tigny on the 18th and 19th, when Linn would have arrived there. Lt. Strott described this farm in his journal, dated July 18: "An entire Hun medical unit was taken with a good supply of dressings — a welcome event, as our supplies were running low. Our station advanced and took over this German position which was located at Beaurepaire Ferme. The surrounding buildings afforded good shelter for wounded who were pouring in and congesting the station. Returning ammunition trucks were loaded with slightly wounded and sent to field hospitals in the rear..." (Strott, *Medical Department*, p. 63). General Harbord's description, recorded in his diary, gets to the nitty-gritty: "Beaurepaire Ferme ... was an advanced dressing station and a very distressing scene. The congestion on the one country road prevented ambulances from getting to the front, and men had lain there in the yard of farm buildings all day (the 18th), and were to continue to lie there twelve or fourteen hours longer. Water was unobtainable, the buildings were in ruins from shell fire, and the Boche still dropped an occasional bomb from his air planes as they circled over..." (Harbord, *Leaves from a War Diary* [New York: Dodd, Mead, 1931], p. 327). Also present at Beaurepaire Ferme on the 18th, when the flood of wounded from Vierzy was still in its early stages, was a lieutenant from the 15th Field Artillery, Robert Winthrop Kean, who noted that there were completely inadequate medical provisions, no ambulances and only one doctor, who was overworked to the point of uselessness. Kean observed that many men were dying from lack of attention Robert Winthrop Kean, *Dear Marraine, 1917–1919* [n.p.: Robert Winthrop Kean, 1969], p. 150).

23. The night of July 19-20.

24. From Beaurepaire Ferme, Linn was evacuated to Field Hospital 23, located in a blacksmith's shop at Taillefontaine (located about 12 kilometers to the west). Regarding this hospital, on July 20 (the same day that Linn was there), Second Division surgeon Lt. Col. Richard Derby wrote: "With conditions such as have been described at the Front, there was no great amelioration in the hospitals farther back. As soon as the evacuation from the Front began they became choked with wounded. They had neither sufficient equipment nor personnel to handle the large numbers. The same scenes were being enacted in these hospitals on the twentieth as had occurred in the battalion stations during the two preceding days. Large numbers of wounded lay about, many of them in the open, waiting the arrival of hospital trains to take them back to Paris. The French had failed to make suitable provisions to meet this emergency themselves, and had refused to allow us to do so." *Muster Roll Records, Addenda Roll AEF*, July 1919, p. 341.

25. Linn's memory may be off the mark here. According to the journal of Lt. Strott, the storm — a fierce one — did not hit until 11 P.M. (2200) that night. Strott, *Medical Department*, p. 65.

26. According to the *Muster Roll Records, Addenda Roll AEF*, July 1919, p. 341, Linn was evacuated from Field Hospital 23 in Taillefontaine to Field Hospital 1 at Sery-Magneval on July 24. (Derby, *"Wade in Sanitary!"* p. 89). Sery-Magneval lies about 17 kilometers southwest of Taillefontaine. From FH#1 in Sery, he was then evacuated to the Red Cross hospital at Beauvais, some 75 kilometers further west, and finally to Base Hospital #27 in Angers, some 375 kilometers to the southwest. From Sery on, Linn almost certainly would have been transported via Red Cross hospital train. According to Linn's *Addenda Roll* record, the entire journey of some 475 kilometers, from Taillefontaine to Angers, took place on the 24th. However, during these few days following the Battle of Soissons, the congestion of hospital trains packed with wounded

soldiers attempting to move away from the battle zone to base hospitals in the rear was severe and it is probable that Linn was on board his train for several days before reaching Angers.

Chapter 8

1. Stallings, *The Doughboys*, pp. 184–5.
2. The "Carrel-Dakin technique" was an antiseptic wound irrigation procedure developed by Alexis Carrel, a 1912 Nobel Prize winner who served as a major in the French army during the war, and Henry Dakin, a chemist. The technique was credited with saving hundreds of thousands of wounded limbs during the First World War from otherwise certain amputation. Jack E. McCallum, *Military Medicine: From Ancient Times to the 21st Century* (Santa Barbara: ABC-CLIO, 2008), pp. 59–61.

Chapter 9

1. Strott, *Medical Department*, p. 76.
2. Curtis and Long, *History*, p. 33–4.
3. Sgt. Alfred G. Slyke. See "A Ghost Among the French," Chapter 2, note 18.
4. Major E.B. Cole, commander of the Sixth Machine Gun Battalion, was mortally wounded on June 10 during the fighting at Belleau Wood. It seems unlikely that Linn would only now be learning of it.
5. Major L.W.T. Waller assumed command of the battalion on June 20.
6. Officers Training Corps.
7. "The Sam Browne Belt" is a wide leather belt supported by a strap over the right shoulder, used for the carrying of sword or pistol and usually worn only by officers.
8. The "incendiary grenade" Linn describes was probably a "smoke grenade" which employed white phosphorus. It produced an effective smoke-screen but was also used to clear dugouts by scattering bits of white-hot phosphorus which ignited spontaneously upon contact with the air and would burn right through the human body. They were an especially horrific weapon. Anthony Saunders, *Weapons of the Trench War 1914–1918* (Gloucestershire: Alan Sutton, 1999), pp. 105–6. I am indebted to members of the University of Kansas World War I Discussion List, especially Geoffrey Miller and Edward Rudnicki, for a detailed discussion of these weapons.
9. Curtis and Long, *History*, pp. 34–5. Wood, *op. cit.* Diary, p. 23; Appenheimer papers, diary entry for September 3 through 11.

Chapter 10

1. Gray and Argyle, *Chronicle, Volume 2*, p. 214.
2. Clark, *Devil Dogs*, pp. 272–3.
3. The night of September 11-12.
4. The Marine Brigade was actually in the second wave, behind the Third Brigade.
5. Linn and 77th Company were probably still in the Bois des Hayes, between the villages of Noviant-aux-Pres and St. Jean, some three miles south of their objective, the village of Limey. The entire battalion had arrived here on the 8th. Curtis and Long, *History*, pp. 34–5.
6. The movements of 77th Company on the 11th must be surmised from fragmentary records. Sometime after dark, 77th Company began moving north out of the Bois des Hayes towards Limey in heavy rain. The time of their departure and their route are unknown. Curtis and Long, *History*, pp. 36–7; "Operation Report, Company 'C,' 6th M.G. Bn, September 12th–September 15th, inclusive." *Records of the Second Division*, Sept. 12–15, 1918.
7. Records of 77th Company fail to indicate where precisely they were positioned when the massive barrage commenced at 1 A.M. on September 12, but, like the other companies of the battalion, they would have been somewhere in the vicinity of Limey.
8. "The artillery bombardment of the enemy's territory started at 0100 (Sept. 12) as sched-

uled. For 4 hours the long-range guns pounded the enemy's back areas while the lighter guns did terrific damage to front line and support positions. The fire was furnished entirely by American artillery and it was of such intensity that the noise-hardened citizens of Toul got out of bed to watch the fire flashes on the north horizon. During this 4-hour bombardment, while a heavy rain continued to fall, the troops slumped in the mud of the trenches around Limey and obtained a little sleep." Strott, *Medical Department*, p. 86.

9. At about 4 A.M., the four companies of the Sixth Machine Gun Battalion began moving from their various positions around Limey to their assigned barrage position northeast of Limey. "Operation Report, Company 'C,'" *Records of the Second Division.*

10. The assigned barrage position of 77th Company was at coordinates 366.53-234.45. Beginning at 5 A.M., the four companies of the battalion laid down a heavy machine gun barrage on enemy positions. Linn apparently did not take part in this barrage, but remained idle for the next three and a half hours. Curtis and Long, *History*, pp. 36–7.

11. "(77th Company) ... remained in position till 8:30 A.M. the 12 (of September). Joined 3rd Battalion, 5th Marines as they passed through in support of the 9th Infantry, assigned 1st Platoon under command of 2Lt. Galtowski to operate with 16th Company, 5th Marines, the 3rd Platoon under command of 2Lt. Buchanan to the 20th Co. 5th Marines...." "Operation Report, Company 'C,'" *Records of the Second Division.* Pvt. Linn was a member either of First Platoon or Third Platoon.

12. These were light French tanks: Char Renault FT 17s. Linn refers to them as "whippets," which is technically incorrect, as the whippet was a British tank substantially different from the Renault, but in 1918 the term "whippet" was widely used to refer to any light Allied tank. B.T. White, *Tanks and Other Armored Fighting Vehicles, 1900–1918* (New York: Macmillan, 1970), pp. 166–7.

13. "As the Infantry advance passed through the M.G. Barrage position, the companies of the 6th Machine Gun Battalion joined the infantry battalions to which assigned.... The Company of light tanks, however, experienced some difficulty in advancing to the attack to positions assigned owing to terrain. Through the entire advance these tanks did not seem to be able to operate properly owing to the speed of the Infantry. They were continually out of position and the Battalion Commanders practically disregarded them." "Operations Report of the 4th Brigade, Marines," September 12–15, 1918. Headquarters, Fourth Brigade, Marines, AEF, 17 September 1918. *Records of the Second Division.*

14. What it was precisely that nearly killed Pvt. Linn at this point in the attack was recorded in the 77th Company "Operation Report": "During [the] advance, 2Lt. Joeryer and six enlisted men [were] wounded by [a] grenade mine in wire entanglements, and one gun [was] so damaged that it was put out of action.... The six enlisted men wounded by this explosion were Cpl Edwin L. Ellison, Pvt Steven H. Keating, Pvt Louis C. Linn, Cpl Neil J. O'Hearn, Pvt. William M. Olive, and Cpl. James Shaw. Apart from this one incident, 77th Company suffered no casualties on this date." "Operation Report, Company 'C.'" *Records of the Second Division.*

As to what the "grenade mine" might have been, this must remain a matter of conjecture. In 1918 land mines had not yet been developed. On Linn's roster roll record, the weapon which wounded him and the other six Marines is described as a "concealed grenade" (*Muster Roll Records*, "Attached to Company 'C,' 6th Machine Gun Battalion, AEF," p. 1162) — in other words, a "booby-trap," probably set off by some sort of tripwire. Most of the German hand grenades used a friction igniter, which was easily adapted to a tripwire setup. I am obliged to Edward Rudnicki of the University of Kansas World War I Discussion List for this information.

Chapter 11

1. Derby, "*Wade In Sanitary!*" p. 110.
2. *Ibid.*, p. 110.
3. *Ibid.*, p. 119.
4. The succession of hospitals to which Linn was taken are identified in the *Muster Roll Records, Addenda Roll AEF*, July 1919, p. 341.
5. That Linn arrived by train is an indication that he had finally landed at a base hospital,

and according to his muster roll record the first base hospital where he stayed for more than a day following the Battle of Saint-Mihiel was Base Hospital #66 in Neufchâteau. He remained here from September 14 to the 23rd, which was probably just long enough to recover from his surgery before being transferred on the 23rd to Base Hospital #202 in Orleans. *Muster Roll Records, Addenda Roll AEF,* July 1919, p. 341.

    6. The "ATS injection" is an anti-tetanus serum used to prevent infection of battlefield wounds. It is produced from the blood of infected horses. Thanks to Naill Ferguson of the World War I Discussion List.

Chapter 12

    1. Lt. Edgar Allan Poe, Jr., was with 74th Company, First Battalion, Sixth Marines.

Chapter 13

    1. During all of December 1918 Pvt. Linn was in Orleans, in Base Hospital #202 until the 21st, and in a casual company barracks thereafter, until the end of February.

    2. Either of the two egregious offenses described in this section — dereliction of duty and going AWOL — would have been sufficient to land Linn in a general court martial. However, nothing in Linn's records refers to either offense, nor do they make any mention of a court martial proceeding. On the other hand, there are no existing records at all for Pvt. Linn for the period December 1918 to January 1919. Not even Linn's Service Record Book has information for these months, stating simply that "no data exists for that period." But if Linn had been brought up on charges for either offense, the court proceedings would have been reflected in later records, which do exist, and had he faced court martial charges he would certainly not have received his honorable discharge. So what actually happened? Either Linn invented these offenses to enliven his memoir, or to make a point, or these events in fact did occur and he was lucky enough — somehow — to have gotten away with them.

Epilogue

    1. According to Pvt. Linn's War Service Record, he embarked on the USS *Tiger* at Le Havre on February 6, 1919, arrived at Hampton Roads, Virginia, at 3 A.M. on February 28, and disembarked at Newport News, Virginia, at 9:30 A.M. on March 1. However, Linn's muster roll records record him as being in St. Aignan until March 8. The muster roll records are evidently in error, as the *Tiger* is recorded as having left Le Havre on February 7. The *Tiger* was a single-screw, steam freighter built in 1917 and initially operated as a merchant ship until chartered by the War Department on 12 November 1917. It was then fitted out for the Army Transportation Service and carried supplies to France for the AEF through late 1918. In late December of 1918 the *Tiger* was transferred to the Navy Department, assigned to the Naval Overseas Transportation Service and refitted for naval service. She took on a cargo of food and supplies and sailed from Hampton Roads on January 9, 1919, bound for France. She reached Le Havre on the 24th. After unloading her cargo and undergoing repairs, the *Tiger* steamed from Le Havre on February 7 (with Pvt. Linn on board) and proceeded, via Norfolk, to New York City, where she arrived on March 3. Soon after, the *Tiger* would be converted to a troop transport and spend the remainder of the war carrying American troops home from France. James L. Mooney, *Dictionary of Naval Fighting Ships,* Vol. VII (Annapolis: Naval Historical Center, 1981).

    2. Pvt. Linn joined St. Aignan Casual Company #994 on February 1, 1919, and was transferred to Casual Company #203 at Quantico, Virginia, on March 3.

    3. If true, both events (court martial and fine) should have appeared in Linn's muster roll records, but no mention is made of either event in his records for March, April, May or June 1919, when he was honorably discharged.

Bibliography

Appenheimer, Alpheus. Unpublished diary, service papers and letters covering his service with Headquarters Detachment, Sixth Machine Gun Battalion, Fourth Brigade, U.S. Marine Corps, in France and Germany from July 1917 to June 1919. Used by permission of his son, Clay Appenheimer.

Asprey, Robert B. *At Belleau Wood.* New York: G.P. Putnam's Sons, 1965.

Brannen, Carl Andrew. *Over There: A Marine in the Great War.* Preface and Annotation by Rolfe L. Hillman, Jr., and Peter F. Owen. Afterward by J.P. Brannen. College Station: Texas A&M University Press, 1996.

Clark, George B. *Decorated Marines of the Fourth Brigade in World War I.* Jefferson, NC: McFarland, 2007.

_____. *Devil Dogs: Fighting Marines of World War I.* Novato, CA: Presidio Press, 1999.

_____. *Legendary Marines of the Old Corps.* Pike, NH: The Brass Hat, 2002.

_____. *The Second Infantry Division in World War I: A History of the American Expeditionary Force Regulars, 1917–1919.* Jefferson, NC: McFarland, 2007.

Cockfield, Jamie H. *With Snow on Their Boots: The Tragic Odyssey of the Russian Expeditionary Force in France During World War I.* New York: St. Martin's Press, 1998.

Curtis, T.J., Captain, USMC, and Captain L.R. Long, USMC. *History of the Sixth Machine Gun Battalion, Fourth Brigade, U.S. Marines, Second Division, and Its Participation in the Great War.* Neuwied-on-the-Rhine, Germany, 1919.

Cushing, Harvey Williams. *From a Surgeon's Journal, 1915–1918.* Boston: Little, Brown, 1936.

Derby, Richard. *"Wade in Sanitary!" The Story of a Division Surgeon in France.* New York: G.P. Putnam's Sons, 1919.

Gernand, Bradley E., and Michelle A. Krowl. *Quantico, Semper Progredi, Always Forward.* Virginia Beach: Donning Company, 2004.

Gibbons, Floyd. *"And They Thought We Wouldn't Fight."* New York: George H. Doran, 1918.

Gleaves, Albert. *A History of the Transport Service: Adventures and Experiences of United States Transports and Cruisers in the World War.* New York: George H. Doran, 1921.

Gray, Randal, with Christopher Argyle. *Chronicle of the First World War, 1917–1919.* Two vols. New York: Facts on File, 1991.

Harbord, James G., Major General. *The American Army in France, 1917–1919.* Boston: Little, Brown, 1936.

_____. *Leaves from a War Diary.* New York: Dodd, Mead, 1931.

Helgason, Gudmundur. "U-boat Losses, 1914–1918." uboat.net.

Henry, Mark R. *U.S. Marine Corps in World War I, 1917–1918.* Men-at-Arms Series, #327. Illustrated by Darko Pavlovic. Oxford: Osprey, 1999.

Horne, Alistair. *The Price of Glory, Verdun 1916.* New York: Mcmillan, 1962.

Jackson, Warren R. *His Time in Hell—A Texas Marine in France: The World War I Memoir of Warren R. Jackson.* Edited by George B. Clark. Novato, CA: Presidio Press, 2001.

Jaffin, Jonathan H., Major. *Medical Support for the American Expeditionary Forces in France During the First World War.* A Thesis presented to the Faculty of the U.S. Army Command and General Staff College, Fort Leavenworth, Kansas, 1990.

Johnson, Douglas V., II, and Rolfe L. Hillman, Jr. *Soissons 1918.* College Station: Texas A&M University Press, 1999.

Kean, Robert Winthrop. *Dear Marraine, 1917–1919.* Robert Winthrop Kean, 1969.

Lane, Herschel V. Unpublished diary, covering his service with 77th Company, Sixth Machine Gun Battalion, Fourth Brigade, U.S. Marine Corps in France from May 1917 to September 1918. Used by permission of his granddaughter, Laura Hall.

Linn, Louis Carlisle. *Service Record Book.* U.S. Government. Covering dates June 8, 1917, to June 9, 1919.

Lynch, Charles, Frank W. Weed, and Loy McAfee, eds. *The Medical Department of the United States Army in the World War.* 15 vols. Washington, DC: Government Printing Office, 1923.

Mackin, Elton E. *Suddenly We Didn't Want to Die: Memoirs of a World War I Marine.* Introduction and Annotation by George B. Clark. Forward by LtGen Victor H. Krulak, USMC (Ret.). Novato, CA: Presidio Press, 1993.

Manual for the Quartermaster Corps, United States Army, 1916. 2 vols. Washington, DC: Government Printing Office, 1917.

Mayo, Katherine. *"That Damn Y": A Record of Overseas Service.* Boston and New York: Houghton Mifflin, 1920.

McCallum, Jack E. *Military Medicine: From Ancient Times to the 21st Century.* Santa Barbara: ABC-CLIO, 2008.

McClellan, Edwin N., Major, USMC. *The United States Marine Corps in the World War.* Washington, DC: Government Printing Office, 1920.

Mooney, James L. *Dictionary of Naval Fighting Ships,* Nine vols. Annapolis: Naval Historical Center, 1959–1991.

Morgan, Daniel. *When the World Went Mad: A Thrilling Story of the Late War, Told in the Language of the Trenches* (Christopher Publishing House, 1931). Rpt. *Memoirs of a Sergeant in the 77th Co., 6th Machine Gun Battalion.* Pike, NH: The Brass Hat 1993.

Muster Rolls of the U.S. Marine Corps, 1893–1940. National Archives Microfilm Publication T977, 460 rolls. Records of the U.S. Marine Corps, Record Group 127; National Archives, Washington, D.C.

Owen, Peter F. *To the Limit of Endurance: A Battalion of Marines in the Great War.* College Station: Texas A&M University Press, 2007.

Saunders, Anthony. *Weapons of the Trench War 1914–1918.* Gloucestershire: Alan Sutton, 1999.

Schmalenbach, Paul. *German Raiders.* Annapolis: Naval Institute Press, 1977.

Spaulding, O.L., and J.W. Wright. *The Second Division American Expeditionary Force in France, 1917–1919.* New York: The Hillman Press, 1937.

Stallings, Laurence. *The Doughboys.* New York: Harper and Row, 1963.

Strott, Lt. George G., USN. *The Medical Department of the United States Navy with the Army and Marine Corps in France in World War I: Its Functions and Employment.* Washington, DC: Bureau of Medicine and Surgery, U.S. Navy Department, 1947.

Sumner, Captain Allen Melancthon. Unpublished letters written during his service in France with, and later as the commander of, 81st Company, Sixth Machine Gun Battalion, from April 1917 to July 1918, when he was killed in action at Soissons. Used by permission of Richard F. Hinton.

Taft, William Howard. *Service with Fighting Men: An Account of the Work of the American Young Men's Christian Associations in the World War.* 2 vols. New York: Association Press, 1922.

Thomas, Shipley. *The History of the A.E.F.* New York: George H. Doran, 1920.

Toland, John. *No Man's Land: 1918—The Last Year of the Great War.* New York: Doubleday, 1980.

U.S. Army. *Records of the Second Division (Regular).* 9 vols. Washington, DC: The Army War College, 1927.

Waller, Littleton W.T., Jr., Major. *Final Report of the 6th Machine Gun Battalion. Marine Corps Gazette,* March 1920. Later reprinted as a booklet (Pike, NH: The Brass Hat, n.d.).

Where the Marines Fought in France. Chicago: Park and Antrim, n.d.

Wilgus, William J. *Transporting the A.E.F. in Western Europe, 1917–1919*. New York: Columbia University Press, 1931.

White, B.T. *Tanks and Other Armored Fighting Vehicles, 1900–1918*. New York: Macmillan, 1970.

Wood, Lt. Peter P., USMC. *Diary of Lt. Peter P. Wood, USMC, 6th Machine Gun Battalion, 1917–1919*. Bangor, ME: David Sleeper, 2001.

Index